THE DIRECTOR'S VISION

A CONCISE GUIDE TO THE ART
OF 250 GREAT FILMMAKERS

ABOUT THE AUTHOR

Geoff Andrew is Film Editor of London's *Time Out* magazine, programmer of London's National Film Theatre and one of Britain's leading film critics. Prior to becoming a full-time writer, he managed and programmed London's Electric Cinema. His other books include *Hollywood Gangsters*; *The Film Handbook*; *The Films of Nicholas Ray*; *Krzysztof Kieslowski's Three Colours Trilogy* and *Stranger Than Paradise – Maverick Filmmakers in Recent American Cinema*.

ACKNOWLEDGEMENTS

While this book represents only my own opinions, as ever it is partly the product of many discussions held over the years with friends and colleagues. For their encouragement, advice, understanding and patience in various capacities, I should therefore like to offer my thanks to the following:

To my colleagues at *Time Out*, particularly Tom Charity, Wally Hammond, Derek Adams, Nick Bradshaw, Dominic Wells, Patricia Callaghan, and Tony Elliott; to John Woodward and Adrian Wootton of the British Film Institute, and Jim Hamilton and Hilary Smith of the National Film Theatre; to Andrew Goodfellow and Kate Ward at Prion, for all their help in seeing this book to fruition; to the Kobal Collection, the Ronald Grant Archive and Joel Finler for the extensive use of their picture libraries; and to my parents and, especially, Ane Roteta for sympathy, support and tolerance of the reclusive habits writing a book inevitably fosters.

· More specifically, for help and advice with materials and resources, I should like to thank: Tony Rayns, David Thompson, Im Hyun-Ock, David Sin, Gilbert Adair, Keith Griffiths, Jayne Pilling, Adrian Turner, Jonathan Romney, Heather Stewart, Carolyn Andrews, Paul Morrissey, Emma Pycroft, Charlotte Tudor, Simon Field, Juliette Jansen, Barry Edson, Jean-Noël Félix, Michael Haneke and, for his powers of persuasion, Eric Fellner. Last but certainly not least, I should like to thank Ethan and Joel Coen for their profoundly insightful corrective comments on a director's art and responsibilities.

Finally, I should like to dedicate this book to my friends and my parents, and above all to Ane.

THE DIRECTOR'S VISION

A CONCISE GUIDE TO THE ART
OF 250 GRE

Geof

with a
Ethan a

North American edition published in 1999
by A Cappella Books, an imprint of
Chicago Review Press, Incorporated
814 N. Franklin Street
Chicago, Illinois 60610

ISBN 1-55652-366-1

Jacket design by Jamie Keenan

Printed by Kyodo, Singapore

Foreword

The Film Director as Practising Artist
by Ethan and Joel Coen

'But what exactly does a film director *do*?' is something that a person standing in a bookstore, cracking this particular book and considering whether to buy it, might wonder. The person might be aware in a general way that the film director coordinates the making of the movie and sees the bigger picture that the actors and the crew members with their more specialised responsibilities do not. But in a concrete way, how does the director work? Some insight here from two people who practise the craft might enhance the value of this book. The layman who knows no more than that the director is the man who yells 'Action!' might be interested to learn that the director also:

—yells 'Cut!' It is not always easy to know when to do this. In general it should be done when the actors have lapsed into silence and the crew becomes restive and begins to cast furtive looks in your direction. It is a breach of protocol for the camera crew to stop rolling or for the actors to break character until they hear your call; therefore, if your mind wanders during the take and does not register its natural conclusion, the professional actor, thinking that perhaps you are holding for a very long dissolve, will shuffle through the papers on his desk (if it is an office set, say), or continue to scan the horizon for wagon trains (if it is a Western exterior). Cueing your 'cut!' off a performer can be tricky, however. Many actors have an obsessive fascination with their characters' 'inner truth', and in performance this preoccupation usually manifests itself in the taking of long pauses between lines, during which, presumably, the actor is depicting the character's 'feelings'. Should you yell 'Cut!' during one of these pauses, mistaking silent interpolation for completion, the actor will give you the startled look of a slobbering dog who has just discovered that his chain is much shorter than expected. You can hide your mistake by explaining that you 'only needed that one bit – we'll get the rest in coverage.' ('Coverage' consists of the other angles from which the scene will be shot.) It is important never to admit to mistakes or inattention, lest you lose credibility and prestige.

This brings us to the second responsibility of the director, which is to:

—consult with the actors. After each take, director and actor discuss what might be done differently. From the director's side there is an art to this; comments like, 'Could we try it a little less fakey?' or 'You call that acting?' or 'Why did you keep making that stupid face?' must be edited. There is a sanctioned director-actor vocabulary consisting of by and large fruity terms such as 'vulnerability', 'passion', 'woundedness', 'woundingness', 'hesitancy', 'yearning', and the like. But the use of this language on a film set can also be tricky. If you are saying to the leading lady, for instance, 'When Robert murmurs, "I always felt that the tender moments between us were built upon a lie," perhaps you react with a hollow sort of mirth to cover what might be the character's deeper but unacknowledgable conviction that—' and the assistant director at that moment calls 'Lunch!', you will be confronted with a difficult choice. You can instantly whip about and sprint for the catering truck, leaving the actress to goggle at your retreating back, but this will entail a loss of credibility and prestige. If, on the other hand, you pretend to be more interested in the discussions at hand than you are in eating, and you pursue it to some natural break at which you may turn and walk in a more dignified manner towards the catering truck, then, odds are, you will find your-self near the end of a very long line. And cutting in line (or 'queue-barging' as it is known in the Scottish Highlands and Hebrides) is greatly frowned upon. (We have a friend who was arrested in Scotland for queue-barging, breaking into a line that had formed, no doubt, for some kind of oaten porridge. One pictures the police flinging him into a holding cell already crowded with queue-bargers who bestir themselves to look at the new arrival, many with porridge drying on their chins, their attitudes variously chastened and defiant.)

For ourselves, we have frequently solved this problem by making the leading lady of our films our respective wife (Joel's) and sister-in-law (Ethan's), to wit, Frances McDormand, whose alacrity in joining the stampede for the chuckwagon forestalls any embarrassment others might feel in doing likewise. But reflection along these lines breeds respect for some of the directors of great longevity – Bergman, Jean Renoir, Vincente Minnelli – who must have found the race to lunch increasingly dispiriting as the years conspired to drag them ever nearer the back of the herd; and those directors blind in one eye (more than you might think – John Ford, Raoul Walsh, André de Toth) who, lacking stereo vision, cannot have found it easy to gauge the distance to the catering truck and pace themselves accordingly.

Most of these directors, at any rate, are discussed in this book. We apologise that our outline of the director's duties seems to have stalled after a paltry two points, but we have been thrown badly off our game by the earlier reference to porridge. It is perhaps unwise to mention porridge in any serious essay as it interrupts the thematic flow, snagging the consciousness of the reader so that he cannot but continue to think about it at an almost subliminal level, the porridge now a hippo, as it were, submerged to its eyeballs in the purling current of the ongoing prose. Porridge is one of those intrinsically ostentatious notions, like sex or submerged hippos for that matter, that, once introduced, cannot be counted on to quietly withdraw. Then too, for Americans it is always disconcerting to mention a 'queue', because the word can't help but look wrong, causing the reader to stumble and check his footing, so to speak, and making his eye hesitant and mistrustful for as long as the memory of the word lingers. There is no letter that, placed before the string u-e-u-e, would make it look like a proper word, and even if there were such a letter, it would certainly not be 'q'. 'B', perhaps, could be plausibly put there to make the French word for sludge, say, or some emolient to be slathered upon a scaly patch of skin. But 'queue' seems very unlikely.

What a shame that such a shambles of a prolegomenon should deface an otherwise creditable book. Be assured, if you are still standing in the bookstore weighing its purchase, that these remarks do not presage prolixity and confusion in the book itself. If you are indeed looking for a concise guide to the work of 250 (are we counted as one or two?) great film-makers, then *The Director's Vision* is your only man.

Ethan Coen
Joel Coen
1999

Introduction

When planning a visit to the cinema, we often ask, 'Which picture shall we go and see?' Films have long been referred to as 'moving pictures' (and finally as 'movies') or 'motion pictures'. The names evoke the essence of the medium; though it has been accompanied by sound since the latter half of the 1920s, even as we proceed further into its second century of existence, we still think of film as a primarily visual form of art or entertainment. Of course, dialogue, music and sound effects are now fundamental to our appreciation and understanding of most movies; but ever since the Lumière Brothers, Edison and others conducted their first experiments towards the end of the nineteenth century, it has been moving imagery that has distinguished the cinema from the other art forms – literature, theatre, painting, photography – which were its antecedents and ancestors.

However, though pictures are crucial to cinematic meaning, and the basis of all good storytelling in the medium, very little writing on film pays adequate attention to visual style; often, cinema is treated as if it were literature, with illustrations. Yet any film-maker worthy of the name spends an enormous amount of time, thought and energy ensuring that the images shot and assembled for his or her movie will best convey its mood and meaning. A film bereft of its visual elements would merely be a kind of radio-play; even in the 'talkies', spectacle (in the broadest sense of the word) is such an integral part of the cinema-going experience that it is impossible to imagine deriving a full understanding of (or pleasure from), say, *Citizen Kane* without the vast, brooding rooms of the palatial Xanadu; *The Godfather* without the sumptuous wedding-party sequence; *Titanic* without the sight of the ship up-ending before it plunges into the cold, dark waters; or Tom getting flattened out of shape once again as he continues his eternal pursuit of Jerry. Images, then, are the *sine qua non* of the cinema, and not surprisingly, many of the finest film-makers have developed, consciously or otherwise, their own distinctive visual styles.

That, then, is the subject of this book: how 250 film-makers have used certain grammatical elements of cinematic storytelling – composition, lighting, camera-movement, colour and cutting – to express, for want of a better, more appropriate word, their 'vision'. Of course, even if we are considering their respective styles simply in visual terms, stills inevitably tell only half the story: they are pictures, but they are not moving. In my analyses of each still, therefore, I have tried to contextualise the image not only with regard to the film as a whole (and indeed to the director's overall output), but also, very often, in terms of what happens just before or after the moment captured therein. Perhaps the only way to fully appreciate a film's visual style is to see it on screen from start to finish; nevertheless, this book at least allows for a prolonged scrutiny of any given image's details, which on screen often pass before our eyes so quickly that we may not even notice their existence, let alone grasp their import.

A few words about my selection of images, films and directors. Inevitably, given the enormous amount of footage shot over the years, any choice is to some extent arbitrary and open to argument or criticism. First, I have attempted to select a still or frame (from the surprisingly and regrettably limited number available) that I felt was somehow representative of the film-maker in question, which is not the same as saying it is the most visually beautiful image (let alone the most familiar) from his or her finest or most famous film. Second, with regard to the selection of the directors themselves, I have generally adhered to the principle that he or she should have a recognisably distinctive visual style. This does not, then, mean that I would argue that the film-makers included here are the 250 best in cinema history (though many, of course, would figure in such a pantheon). Clearly, to take an extreme example, most directors have displayed infinitely more talent than Edward D Wood; yet his films are not only immediately recognisable as his own (at least to those sad individuals among us who have born witness to his economically and imaginatively impoverished 'vision'), but endearingly representative of a style of film-making worlds away from the polished studio artifice that marks most of the classic Hollywood movies featured herein. Similarly, some may wonder why successful, important or fine film-makers like, say, John McTiernan, Robert Rossen or Bertrand Tavernier are not included; the simple answer is that I do not feel that their respective strengths lie primarily in a consistent or recognisable visual style.

Finally, I have attempted to suggest the range and diversity of cinema by selecting film-makers from all over the world, from the very earliest years of the medium to the present day. (In this last respect, I have included – perhaps rashly – a few directors yet to prove themselves with a substantial body of work, but who I suspect may become artistically important and influential in the future.) For obvious reasons, the Hollywood mainstream is well represented, with the great masters of European art-cinema lagging not too far behind; but it seemed essential to recognise recent exciting developments elsewhere, particularly in Asia, Africa and the US 'indie' scene. I have also included a number of documentarists, animators and 'underground' film-makers; while these fields of film-making, usually ignored by books focused on commercial fiction features, are big and fascinating enough to warrant separate books of their own, I felt it would be negligent to ignore them entirely, and decided to include a number of important figures whose work may have had some influence on and relevance to feature film-making.

These, then, were the criteria for selecting the images for this book. Inevitably, you will disagree with some of the omissions, and be surprised at some of those included (not to mention my conclusions about them). Hopefully, however, the selection, the analyses, and the way the images are juxtaposed will lead not only to much fond remembrance of individual films and film-makers (in this respect, too, many of the pictures are 'moving'), but to a reappraisal of the crucial importance of the image in cinema history. As the old saying goes, every picture tells a story.

Geoff Andrew

ROBERT ALDRICH

Like the titular exclamation mark, the rugged pugilist's profile and taut muscularity of Jack Palance – along with Burt Lancaster a classic Aldrich actor – typify the brute, even deranged frenzy of the director's anarchic, resolutely masculine world. *Attack!* is concerned less with the war between Americans and Germans than with idealistic lieutenant Palance's slide into embittered psychosis as he struggles to function in a platoon disastrously led by a cowardly officer tolerated only because of family connections. The film is a devastating critique of institutional corruption and privilege; accordingly, Aldrich's film depicts violent tensions and conflict with claustrophobic images of entrapment, outrage and hysteria, coldly lit and jarringly spliced together. Typically, he was at his best with westerns (*Apache*, *Ulzana's Raid*), thrillers (*Kiss Me Deadly*, *Twilight's Last Gleaming*) and war films, though a weakness for lip-smacking sensationalism occasionally produced crass heroics and facile ironies; his films about women (*Whatever Happened to Baby Jane?*, *The Killing of Sister George*) were grotesque, lurid melodramas, with the exception of *All the Marbles*, an unexpectedly wry, tender look at women's wrestling, of all things. Ironically, his artistry deteriorated as commercial success in the 60s brought increased independence, but his finest work remains powerful for its visual and narrative energy, its dynamic blend of visceral action and psychological neurosis, and its sense of a world inexorably descending into insanity.

Robert Aldrich b. 1918 USA, d. 1983 USA. **Attack!** USA 1956/ w Jack Palance, Eddie Albert, Lee Marvin, Robert Strauss, Richaed Jaeckel. **Films include** *Apache*, 1954; *Kiss Me Deadly*, 1955; *Whatever Happened to Baby Jane?*, 1962; *The Dirty Dozen*, 1967; *Ulzana's Raid*, 1972; *Twilight's Last Gleaming*, 1977; *All the Marbles*, 1981. **See also** FULLER, PECKINPAH, NICHOLAS RAY, SCORSESE, SIEGEL

You can almost hear, over the oddly distant murmur of Manhattan's streets, Woody's whining, angst-ridden confusion as he strolls in deep, self-obsessed conversation with Mia Farrow, here playing an ex-wife whose current husband is equally confused by his romantic infatuation with her sister. Allen's world – almost invariably that of well-off, intellectually gifted New Yorkers – is defined by guilty neuroses about sex, artistic frustration, a chaotic and unjust universe, divided loyalties and, above all, the transience of happiness and love. Where other comics often focus on physical misfortune, Allen, proceeding from his early slapdash genre parody centred on a Chaplinesque 'little man' to bitter-sweet studies of fragile relationships, has made his subject the adult anxieties of the contemporary American mind; both in comedy (thematically) and drama (stylistically) he reveals a special reverence for Bergman. That said, he has yet to develop a consistent visual style. Too often, he simply films conversations, breaking away from a comically exaggerated form of 'naturalism' only occasionally to include movie-parody gags, although in more recent work he has dabbled with jump-cuts, hand-held camera, and other less 'polished' stylistic devices; moreover, the former stand-up comedian and gag-writer still resorts too readily to one-liners. However, despite its erratic quality (the more overtly serious dramas are pretentious and dramatically wooden), Allen's witty, insightful, ambitious body of work – a seemingly inexhaustible series of often self-referential variations on a theme – is as distinctive and distinguished as any in modern American film.

Allen Stewart Konigsberg b. 1935 USA. **Hannah and Her Sisters** USA 1986/ w Michael Caine, Barbara Hershey, Woody Allen, Mia Farrow, Dianne Wiest, Max Von Sydow. **Films include** *Love and Death*, 1975; *Annie Hall*, 1977; *Manhattan*, 1979; *Zelig*, 1983; *Broadway Danny Rose*, 1984; *The Purple Rose of Cairo*, 1985; *Crimes and Misdemeanors*, 1989; *Husbands and Wives*, 1992; *Deconstructing Harry*, 1997; *Celebrity*, 1999. **See also** BERGMAN, BROOKS, CHAPLIN, FELLINI, KEATON, STILLMAN

PEDRO ALMODÓVAR

Julieta Serrano, deranged for years since her husband left, holds hostage Carmen Maura, recently made pregnant and abandoned by the same philanderer: frustrated desire threatens both women's lives and sanity. The theatricality of the moment, typifying the openly gay Almodóvar's sympathy for women, is just one ingredient in his hallucinatory gazpacho of cinematic styles, the recipe for which includes Feydeauesque farce, Mexican melodrama, Hitchcockian suspense, cartoonish comedy and campy kitsch, most evident in the garish decor and overheated acting. Luridly improbable plotting (here involving terrorism, garbled phone messages and inevitable infidelity) may evoke Buñuel's surrealist legacy, but Almodóvar's vision of Spain is determinedly post-Franco: more concerned with the heady pursuit of pleasure than politics, and gleefully amoral – rather than genuinely shocking – in its celebration of all forms of sexual preference (his earliest films were mostly bawdy sex comedies). The accent on extravagant design and excessive behaviour has frequently resulted in madly incoherent narratives, insubstantial characterisation and a preoccupation with style for style's sake; recently, however, in *The Flower of My Secret, Live Flesh* and *All About My Mother*, Spain's most fashionable director has toned down his more self-conscious stylistic mannerisms to concentrate on an emotionally affecting, psychologically astute contemplation of lives damaged by disappointment, destiny and, as ever, obsessive desire.

Pedro Almodóvar b. 1951 Spain. **Women on the Verge of a Nervous Breakdown** Spain 1988/ w Carmen Maura, Fernando Guillen, Julieta Serrano, Antonio Banderas, Rossy de Palma. **Films include** *Labyrinth of Passion,* 1982; *What Have I Done to Deserve This?*, 1984; *Matador,* 1986; *Law of Desire,* 1987; *High Heels,* 1991; *The Flower of My Secret,* 1996; *Live Flesh,* 1997; *All About My Mother,* 1999. **See also** Buñuel, Cocteau, Fassbinder, Godard, Hitchcock, Sirk, Tashlin, Warhol, Wilder

Though purists complained that Altman's Philip Marlowe (Elliott Gould) had little to do with Raymond Chandler's private-eye hero, the idea of transposing him, values almost intact, to the spaced-out, self-obsessed, well-off LA of the early 70s, was inspired: a slobby shamus bent on doing his job, he is a bemused, helpless anachronism whose sense of honour serves to illuminate both the social and moral changes undergone by America and the romantic fictions favoured by main-stream Hollywood. Altman's best work, mostly ironic parodies/deconstructions of traditional genres, depicts loners and losers dreaming of survival and success in a society devoted to wealth, fame, power; the poignant tragi-comic tone, derived from their confusion, failure and absurd optimism, is accentuated by his use of a restlessly prowling shallow-focus camera and garrulous overlapping dialogue – techniques which, along with a seemingly incidental, free-wheeling narrative style, demote the protagonist from 'hero' to just another component in the chaotic whirl of babbling humanity. Hence, Altman is usually happier with large casts than small; while elegantly shot and acted, the intimate theatrical adaptations he was reduced to making in the 80s (he's always been an outsider in Hollywood) lack the social, historical and philosophical import of *McCabe and Mrs Miller*, *Nashville*, the made-for-TV *Tanner '88*, *The Player* and *Short Cuts* – movies which confirm him, however erratic his output, as one of the greatest – and most stylististically innovative – film-makers of the modern era.

Robert Altman b. 1925 USA. **The Long Goodbye** USA 1973/ w Elliott Gould, Nina Van Pallandt, Sterling Hayden, Henry Gibson, Mark Rydell. **Films include** *M*A*S*H*, 1970; *McCabe and Mrs Miller*, 1971; *Thieves Like Us*, 1974; *Nashville*, 1975; *3 Women*, 1977; *Popeye*, 1980; *Secret Honor*, 1984; *Tanner '88*, 1988; *The Player*, 1992; *Short Cuts*, 1993; *Cookie's Fortune*, 1999. **See also** HAWKS, RENOIR, RIVETTE, RUDOLPH

The shabby grey setting – a working-class bedroom in England's industrial north – may betoken Anderson's involvement in the realist Free Cinema movement of the early 60s, but the vehement passions on display, between boorish rugby player Richard Harris and Rachel Roberts, the widowed landlady reluctant to continue their affair, do not: the former film critic, documentarist and frequent theatre director was at least as interested in inner, emotional lives as in socio-political realities. Indeed, in its tough, unsentimental study of Harris's tormented inarticulacy, his tenderness undermined by violent eruptions of repressed emotions, and in its poetic use of giant slow-motion scenes of muddy rugby games played by seemingly primeval beings, the film anticipated the critique of masculine pride, insecurity and brutality in Scorsese's *Raging Bull*. For Anderson was not only fascinated and disturbed by the way authority, tradition and conformism in British life subdued natural impulses, but alert to the lyrical dramatic potential of desire and fantasy: hence the celebration of rebellion against public school regimentation in *If...* . Sadly, his distaste for the limitations of realism (Ford and Vigo were his heroes) and his anti-establishment sympathies eventually led to the facile allegories, broad caricatures and splenetic satire of *O Lucky Man!* and *Brittania Hospital*, but the earlier movies remain affecting, persuasive indictments of bourgeois society's attempts to restrain the human spirit.

Lindsay Anderson b. 1923 India, d. 1994 France. **This Sporting Life** GB 1963/ w Richard Harris, Rachel Roberts, Alan Badel, Colin Blakely, William Hartnell. **Films include** *If...*, 1968; *O Lucky Man!*, 1973; *Brittania Hospital*, 1982. **See also** FORD, FORMAN, JENNINGS, VIGO

THEO ANGELOPOULOS

A small boy and his pubescent sister, seeking a father they've been given to believe is working in Germany, land up lost on the bleak shore of modern Thessaloniki, and find brief respite from their arduous wanderings in the protective friendship of Orestes, member of an itinerant theatrical troupe whose plays about Greek history no longer meet with enthusiasm. Angelopoulos' elegant, epic meditations on the crisis of personal and political identity in the Balkans tell of futile odysseys, both through a frequently grey, rainy, unglamorously industrialised Greece and through time itself: myth, rumour and history hang heavily over his characters as they seek somewhere to call 'home'. Giorgos Arvanitis' stately camerawork perfectly embodies the director's unique vision. Often accompanied by little dialogue and by the poignant music of Eleni Karaindrou, the long, gliding travelling shots track characters, at a discreetly respectful distance, as they wander from tableau to tableau and, more remarkably, from year to year: a single take may embrace moments, decades, even centuries apart (invoking time as a continuum, Angelopoulos eschews ordinary flashbacks). The result is a mesmerisingly poetic visual and narrative style which erases conventional borders of space and time, yet paradoxically locates protagonists in a clearly defined social, political and historical context. A master of cinema, Angelopoulos – who paid homage to his forebears in *Ulysses' Gaze*, about a film-maker who, searching for the first footage shot in the Balkans, ends up in war-torn Sarajevo – has refined and expanded its language.

Theo Angelopoulos b. 1936 Greece. **Landscape in the Mist** Greece/France/Italy 1989/ w Michalis Zeke, Tania Palaiologou, Stratos Tzortzoglou, Eva Kotamanidou. **Films include** *Days of '36*, 1972; *The Travelling Players*, 1975; *Alexander the Great*, 1980; *Voyage to Cythera*, 1983; *The Beekeeper*, 1986; *Ulysses' Gaze*, 1995; *Eternity and a Day*, 1998. **See also** ANTONIONI, JANCSO, MIZOGUCHI, MURNAU, RENOIR, TAVIANI BROTHERS, WELLES

A lonely homosexual (Anger), brutally beaten by sailors, is cradled in the arms of a dream lover. Part masochistic wish-fulfilment fantasy, part cinepoem (with sexual ecstasy represented by exploding phallic fireworks), Anger's film was a characteristically self-mythologising landmark of the 'underground' cinema. Erotic or violent ritual, exotic spectacle, and a fascination with the occult (notably the 'magick' of Aleister Crowley) are recurrent elements in the films by the former child-actor: reference points ranged from private remembrance (starry, orgiastic Hollywood costume parties in *Puce Moment* and *Inauguration of the Pleasure Dome*); popular culture (rock 'n' roll, Hollywood movies and fetishistic homoerotic iconography in *Kustom Kar Kommandos* and *Scorpio Rising*); and fairy tale (a dwarf lost in the labyrinthine gardens of Tivoli in *Eaux d'Artifice*); to ancient myth (*Invocation of My Demon Brother* and *Lucifer Rising*). Accordingly, Anger's imagery embraced lyricism and psychedelia, the camp and the diabolical, Romanticism and mysticism, the sacred and profane. Here and in his masterpiece *Scorpio Rising*, which brilliantly intercuts images of Christ (from DeMille's *King of Kings*) and Hitler with shots of gay bikers to mount a profoundly ironic study of hero-worship and the death wish in Western culture, the effect is often startlingly original, resonant and almost hypnotically beautiful. Sadly, various misadventures have resulted in much of Anger's work remaining unfinished or even lost, and he is now perhaps better known as the author of two gleefully scurrillous accounts of starry scandal entitled *Hollywood Bablyon*.

Kenneth Anger b. 1930 USA. **Fireworks** USA 1947/ w Kenneth Anger. **Films include** *Puce Moment*, 1949; *Rabbit's Moon*, 1950; *Eaux d'Artifice*, 1953; *Inauguration of the Pleasure Dome*, 1954; *Kustom Kar Kommandos, Scorpio Rising*, 1964; *Lucifer Rising*, 1967-80; *Invocation of My Demon Brother*, 1969. **See also** COCTEAU, EISENSTEIN, HAYNES, JARMAN, WARHOL

MICHELANGELO ANTONIONI

The reporter (Jack Nicholson), in North Africa to cover political unrest, sits in anguish contemplating a desert that has defeated his jeep's technology and which, he senses, is as barren as his efforts to deliver 'truth' to his TV public; soon, despondency will lead him to exchange identities with a gun-runner he finds dead in a hotel room, and he will attempt to start afresh – in vain, given that both his wife and the gun-runner's contacts will be looking for him. A promising thriller premise, but Antonioni, typically, shows scant interest in suspense: the 'mystery', for him, lies in the reporter's mental/ emotional state, and in how it is affected/reflected by the environment through which he passes aimlessly. The long, slow travelling shots, austere but elegant, of figures in a landscape, and the de-dramatised narrative have long been the director's main tools in exploring bourgeois ennui, isolation and lassitude in a world where communication and the search for love and self-identity are futile; in *L'Avventura*, arguably the first truly modern art-movie, he had shown even less interest in the reasons for a woman's sudden disappearance than the friends who begin a perfunctory affair while half-heartedly searching for her. At times, his cool, detached observations tend towards abstraction, reducing humans to objects; but in his best work, as in *The Passenger*, whose stunning, slowly advancing final seven-minute shot shows life in a Spanish village continuing while the reporter is killed off-screen, his bold, masterly style transcends pictorial mannerisms to achieve a metaphys-ical resonance and rigour.

Michelangelo Antonioni b. 1912, Italy. **The Passenger (Professione: Reporter)** Italy/Spain/France 1975/ w Jack Nicholson, Maria Schneider, Jenny Runacre, Ian Hendry. **Films include** *Cronaca di un Amore*, 1950; *Il Grido*, 1957; *L'Avventura*, 1960; *L'Eclisse*, 1962; *Blow Up*, 1966; *Zabriskie Point*, 1969; *Identification of a Woman*, 1982; *Beyond the Clouds*, 1995. **See also** ANGELOPOULOS, BERGMAN, JANCSO, ROSSELLINI, TARKOVSKY, WENDERS

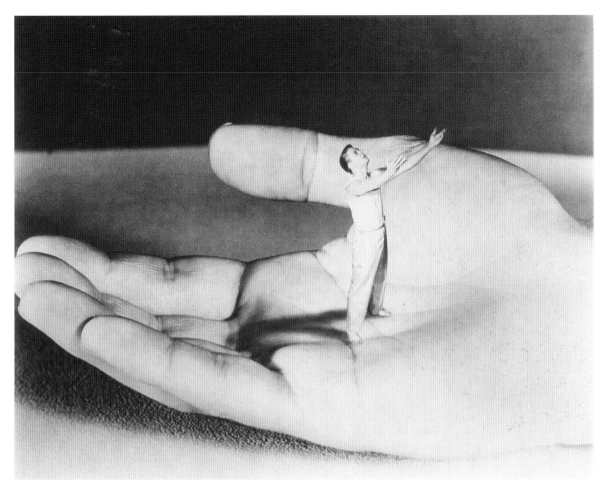

While sci-fi B-movies of the 50s are rightly seen as expressions of American Cold War paranoia, Jack Arnold regularly side-stepped the pitfalls of the monster/commie equation through a quasi-allegorical sense of civilisation's thin veneer being eroded by repressed, primeval forces of nature (most notably the sexually suggestive Amazon amphibian in *Creature from the Black Lagoon*, a precursor to *Jaws*). But Arnold's pulp poetry reached its zenith with the parable-like tale – scripted by Richard Matheson from his own story – of a man who finds himself getting irreversibly smaller after he is enveloped by a strange radiocative mist while on a boating holiday. As his hero shrinks, Arnold has a field day using props and special effects to milk suspense from his life-threatening encounters with cats, spiders and other inhabitants of the home he once considered his castle; but the film's prime virtue is in its concise, intelligent exploration of the way this Everyman's relationship with his wife (he experiences feelings of humiliation and impotence), his environment and, finally, himself steadily change, unexpectedly culminating not in his restoration to normal size but in the becalmed, pantheistic realisation that every living thing, however small or seemingly insignificant, has its place and purpose in the cosmos. Arnold, who later moved on to more mundane fare, certainly remains a minor Hollywood talent, but here his imaginative, dreamlike imagery displays a sure grasp of subconscious fears and, rarer still, of philosophical ideas.

Jack Arnold b. 1916 USA, d. 1992 USA. **The Incredible Shrinking Man** USA 1957/ w Grant Williams, Randy Stuart, April Kent, Paul Langton. **Films include** *It Came from Outer Space*, 1953; *Creature from the Black Lagoon*, 1954; *Revenge of the Creature*; *Tarantula*, 1955.
See also BAVA, CORMAN, CRONENBERG, DANTE, SPIELBERG, WOOD

DOROTHY ARZNER

Sassy showgirl Lucille Ball looks on sceptically as comparatively sophisticated would-be ballerina Maureen O'Hara opens her heart to a friend. The iconography of Arzner's backstage comedy-drama highlights conventional good-girl/bad-girl stereotypes – if she was the only woman director to work regularly during Hollywood's 'Golden Age', she seldom moved outside of traditional genres like comedy and melodrama – but her stories often stressed the plight of women. *Dance, Girl, Dance*, about the rivalries and friendships among a group of women trying to make a living by working at a burlesque hall, contrasts (and finally reconciles) Ball's hard-nosed pragmatism with O'Hara's almost virginal idealism while examining the notion of dance as erotic spectacle performed by women for men: its climax comes when O'Hara, at the end of her rope, turns on and shames a leering male audience. Arzner's best work explores the economic, sexual and social options available to women living and working in patriarchal society: *Merrily We Go to Hell* charts the courtship of a wealthy heiress by a failed alcoholic playwright; in *Christopher Strong*, a champion aviatrix chooses career and suicide rather than bear an illegitimate child to a feckless married lover; *The Bride Wore Red* has a gold-digger impersonate a society woman to trap a millionaire. If there was little that was stylistically radical or even genuinely 'feminist' in Arzner's films, her preference for strong-willed, independent heroines and witty dialogue, often at the expense of patriarchal customs, gave her work an unusual, interesting satirical edge.

Dorothy Arzner b. 1900 USA, d. 1979 USA. **Dance, Girl, Dance** USA 1940/ w Maureen O'Hara, Lucille Ball, Louis Hayward, Ralph Bellamy, Virginia Field, Maria Ouspenskaya. **Films include** *Get Your Man*, 1927; *The Wild Party*, 1929; *Working Girls*, 1931; *Merrily We Go to Hell*, 1932; *Christopher Strong*, 1933; *Craig's Wife*, 1936; *The Bride Wore Red*, 1937. **See also** BIGELOW, LUBITSCH, LUPINO, WELLMAN

©1949 Turner Entertainment Co.

A sophisticated city wolf, aroused by the sight of Red, literally comes apart with desire. First at Warners, then at MGM, Avery established himself as one of the most idiosyncratic, influential animation directors, with frantic shorts comprising relentlessly inventive series of visual and verbal gags. Adept at parodying topical genres (as in the gangster spoof *Thugs with Dirty Mugs*), travelogues, documentaries, and fairy tales (including several variations on *Red Riding Hood*), he favoured an anarchically exaggerated style centred on violent action and absurd representations of sexual excitement: crazed by lust, the wolf's eyes stand out on stalks, his heart leaps from his chest, and his limbs are temporarily but suggestively riven by paroxysms of uncontrollable desire curable only by a hefty swipe from a mallet. Avery's humour was gleefully irreverent: *Of Fox and Hounds* guys Steinbeck's *Of Mice and Men*, while *Red Hot Riding Hood* opens with a false-start in which wolf, Red and her granny refuse, straight to camera, to perform in another hokey retelling of the story, so that the rural cottage becomes a penthouse, Red a torch-singing burlesque dancer, the wolf lechery incarnate. While Avery's backgrounds might be comparatively 'realistic', even soft, his characters were brash, emphatically modern (anachronistic details wittily punctuate his 'period' films), prone to sudden fragmentation and transformation, and often fantastically grotesque – a far cry from Disney's cloying cuteness; not that there was time to ponder their amorality, since speed, in terms of action and narrative, was of the essence in Avery's irrepressibly wild, dark comedies.

Fred B Avery b. 1907 USA, d. 1980 USA. **Little Rural Riding Hood** USA 1949. **Films include** *Ham-Ateur Night*, 1938; *Thugs with Dirty Mugs*, 1939; *Porky's Preview, Of Fox and Hounds* 1941; *Red Hot Riding Hood*, 1943; *Screwball Squirel*, 1944; *Swingshift Cinderella*, 1945; *North West Hounded Police*, 1946; *King-Size Canary*, 1947; *Bad Luck Blackie*, 1949. **See also** DISNEY, FLEISCHER, HANNA AND BARBERA, JONES, PARK

MARIO BAVA

Italian B-movies have never been particularly noted for subtlety or originality, but Bava's extraordinary debut has both. Hugely influential on later horror films (Bava even 'discovered' horror queen Barbara Steele as a British starlet), the film, based on a Gogol story about the revenge taken by a resurrected vampire two centuries after medieval villagers executed her as a witch, is notable for its ornate imagery, the camera gliding through dank, dusty corridors and crypts and misty moonlit glades to alight on one exquisitely lit chiaroscuro composition after another. But Bava's special brand of spectral beauty (he was a cinematographer before becoming a director) was also often cruel and sadistic: the (in)famous opening sequence shows Steele tortured by having a spiked mask hammered into her face, and her scarred, once-lovely face in its resurrected form provides not only chilling suspense but also a perverse erotic frisson. Never again did Bava quite fulfil the promise of his first film as he ranged through sub-Hitchcockian thrillers, spaghetti westerns, slasher movies and further horror fare, though films like *Black Sabbath*, *Blood and Black Lace*, *Kill Baby Kill* and *Danger: Diabolik* were sufficiently distinguished by his visual flair (often in lavish, even lurid colour) that their frequently formulaic stories, not to mention the iniquities of insensitive dubbing, re-editing and cutting perpetrated by distributors abroad, could be ignored in the knowledge that here, at the very least, was the work of a great pictorial stylist.

Mario Bava b. 1914 Italy, d. 1980 Italy **Black Sunday (La Maschera del Demonio)** Italy 1960/ w Barbara Steele, John Richardson, Ivo Garrani, Andrea Cecchi. **Films include** *Black Sabbath*, 1963; *Blood and Black Lace*, 1964; *Kill Baby Kill*, 1966; *Danger: Diabolik*, 1968. **See also** ARNOLD, CORMAN, FRANJU, LEONE, ROMERO, VISCONTI, WHALE

A brief, idyllic moment of untroubled love, fondly remembered: sensuality and bitter-sweet nostalgia form the core of Becker's romance about the love – natural, easy and wholly mutual – between Simone Signoret, hitherto caught up in the 'apache' underworld of 1890s Paris, and honest artisan Serge Reggiani, driven by pride, passion and the desire for a peaceful life to go up against a crime boss, with inevitably tragic results. Set in the world immortalised by the Impressionists, the film is appropriately full of luminous imagery, though it offers far more than mere pictorial elegance: a friend and disciple of Renoir, Becker was adept at evoking the everyday lives of ordinary people, alert to delicate emotional nuances, and endowed with a strong sense of time, place and social milieu. If his work is now underrated, that is perhaps because he placed greater emphasis on characters and relationships than on narrative complexity: *Edouard et Caroline*, one of several comedies set in contemporary Paris, was virtually plotless, while even his later, tougher, more laconic movies about criminals – *Touchez pas au Grisbi* and the prison-escape drama *Le Trou* – were more concerned with questions of camaraderie, loyalty and betrayal than with eventful action. Deftly balancing dispassionate observation with a sympathetic interest in individual motivation, Becker's unassertive but often lyrical style evinces a quiet, unforced humanism that to this day seems somehow typical of the classic French cinema at its most engaging.

Jacques Becker b. 1906 France, d. 1960 France. **Casque d'Or** France 1952/ w Simone Signoret, Serge Reggiani, Claude Dauphin, Raymond Bussières, Gaston Modot. **Films include** *Goupi-Mains-Rouges*, 1943; *Antoine et Antoinette*, 1946; *Rendez-vous de Juillet,* 1949; *Edouard et Caroline*, 1951; *Touchez pas au Grisbi*, 1953; *Le Trou*, 1959. **See also** BRESSON, CARNÉ, MELVILLE, RENOIR, ROHMER, TRUFFAUT

INGMAR BERGMAN

An actress (Liv Ullmann), recuperating from a break-down that has left her speechless at the horrors of the modern world, is unable to look at the talkative nurse (Bibi Andersson) tending her at a remote cottage; their communication seems entirely one-sided, but eventually, in a strange, inexplicable symbiosis, the pair will be seen briefly to merge, their shared humanity acknowledged as a healing force. With *Persona*, Bergman, whose early work had mostly concerned destructive relationships and religious doubt, made his most intense, intimate, complex study of the fraught connection between inner and outer lives; its cool, austere, psychologically and philosophically astute account of suffering, solitude and the sterility of contemporary existence was given deeper resonance by innovative formal devices (non-narrative shots frequently evoking the film's own genesis) related to the theme of the inadequacy of art's response to 'real' life. At once forthright (Sven Nykvist's stark camera-work is vividly precise) and metaphorical, the film may lack the warmth of the likewise remarkable *Wild Strawberries* or the dark wit of *The Face*, but stylistically and thematically it paved the way for such rich, challenging work as *Hour of the Wolf, Shame, A Passion, Cries and Whispers* and *Face to Face* – a consistently bleak but brilliantly sustained contemplation of souls in anguish. No other film-maker has revealed so much about the human condition by examining faces in extreme, lucid close-up; few have made as many outright masterpieces.

Ingmar Bergman b. 1918 Sweden. **Persona** Sweden 1966/ w Liv Ullmann, Bibi Andersson, Margaretha Krook, Gunnar Bjornstrand, Jorgen Lindstrom. **Films include** *Summer with Monika*, 1952; *Smiles of a Summer Night*, 1955; *The Seventh Seal, Wild Strawberries*, 1957; *The Face*, 1958; *The Silence*, 1963; *Hour of the Wolf, Shame*, 1968; *A Passion*, 1970; *Cries and Whispers*, 1972; *Face to Face*, 1975; *Fanny and Alexander*, 1982. **See also** Allen, Antonioni, Dreyer, Kieslowski, Sjöström, Tarkovsky

No matter that this shot was cut from the 'By a Waterfall' scene in *Footlight Parade*, nor that the film is credited to Lloyd Bacon (for some years Berkeley was 'dance director'): the kaleidoscopic aquacade of semi-naked chorines in their exotic, erotic splendour is typical of his unique vision, which regularly brought a climax to flabbily plotted 30s backstage musicals. He seldom integrated his sumptuous, surreal routines into the plot, or indeed directed dance. More to his taste was a cinematically audacious display, by means of a single camera swooping over, round or through the parted legs of hundreds of eagerly smiling girls or statically observing them from above as they writhed in sexually suggestive floral formation, of semi-abstract symmetrical patterns expanding and contracting among odd props

and tumescent fountains. Both an escapist response to the Depression and a gleeful flouting of the Hays Code, his orgiastic fantasies abandoned the proscenium arch and the perspective of the stalls to reveal impossibly dreamlike, lascivious worlds of luminous nubile flesh, ripe with visual (and often, through the songs, verbal) innuendo: though his best work was for Warners in the 30s (where he teamed with top cameraman Sol Polito), even later at MGM he surrounded Carmen Miranda and her kitschy tutti-frutti hat with 60 girls sporting giant bananas for *The Gang's All Here*. Not that he was wholly flippant and perverse: in *Gold Diggers of 1933*, he memorably staged a sombre, expressionist file of jobless war veterans for the song 'Remember My Forgotten Man'.

William Berkeley Enos b. 1895 USA, d. 1976 USA. **Footlight Parade** USA 1933/ w James Cagney, Joan Blondell, Ruby Keeler, Dick Powell. **Films include** *42nd Street*, 1933; *Gold Diggers of 1933*, 1933; *Dames*, 1934; *For Me and My Gal*, 1942; *The Gang's All Here*, 1943; *Take Me Out to the Ball Game*, 1949; *Million Dollar Mermaid*, 1952. **See also** ANGER, DONEN, MCLAREN, MINNELLI

BERNARDO BERTOLUCCI

Into a gaudily lifeless Parisian dance-hall, populated by couples whose stiff movements make a mockery of tango's erotic communion, stumble a drunken Marlon Brando and Maria Schneider, involved in their own animalistic sexual rebellion. He, angered by his wife's suicide, wants anonymous carnality; she, a 'bourgeoise', is torn between his passion and the prospect of marrying an obsessive film-maker. Though famed for its raw depiction of their savage liaisons in an empty apartment, the film typifies Bertolucci's work in its focus on the conflict between conformism and rebellion, on destructive, damaged, even Oedipal relationships and on tensions between past, present and future. At the same time, the ballroom scene displays his tendency to flamboyant stylistic flourishes. Usually working with cameraman Vittorio Storaro, he uses lavish set design, lush colour and fluid camera movements to construct a visual sheen so seductive it may seem mere rhetoric; indeed, in later work like *The Sheltering Sky* and *Little Buddha*, and even *The Last Emperor*, visual exoticism dominates at the expense of dramatic substance, whereas in his more modest films – notably *The Conformist, The Spider's Stratagem*, and *Besieged*– cinematic bravura and political and psychological insights are more keenly balanced. And while there can remain niggling flaws, such as the fact that Brando's hugely impressive soul-baring performance leaves Schneider's character virtually unexplored, there is no denying the immense ambition, skill and enthusiasm Bertolucci brings to his virtuoso film-making.

Bernardo Bertolucci b. 1940 Italy. **Last Tango in Paris** Italy/France 1972/ w Marlon Brando, Maria Schneider, Jean-Pierre Léaud, Darling Legitimus. **Films include** *Before the Revolution*, 1964; *The Spider's Stratagem*, 1969; *The Conformist*, 1970; *1900 (Novecento)*, 1976; *La Luna*, 1979; *The Last Emperor*, 1987; *Stealing Beauty*, 1995; *Besieged*, 1998. **See also** COPPOLA, GODARD, OPHÜLS, PASOLINI, SCORSESE, VIGO, WELLES

LUC BESSON

A punk, junkie sociopath (Anne Parillaud) is imprisoned, drugged and given a new identity by government agents after being caught in a drug-store robbery; cleaned up and trained as a professional undercover assassin, she will undergo a crisis of identity, torn between her old and new lives. Whether dealing with apocalyptic sci-fi fantasy (*The Last Battle*, *The Fifth Element*), urban crime (*Subway*, *Nikita*) or his own passion for the mysterious beauty of the sea (*The Big Blue*), Besson's films are marked by an emphasis on bright, brash, punk-chic design, redolent of comic-strip and advertising. The narratives, too, tend towards simple, fairy-tale plotting (though the visually and conceptually grandiose *The Fifth Element* was often incomprehensible and incoherent), two-dimensional characterisation, and an adolescent, clumsily romantic emotionalism: the heroines, especially, for all their feistiness, are like damsels in distress awaiting rescue by a tough but devoted square-jawed hero. As with the older Jean-Jacques Beineix, it's easy to accuse Besson of an insubstantial, flashy concern with style for style's sake and implausibility – how many junkies remain as arrestingly attractive as his Nikita? – and he undeniably remains a minor (albeit commercially very successful) talent. There is, however, a real energy to his taut, pacy, bravura action sequences, while the childlike innocence of his stories (shorn of their occasional pretensions to existential weight), coupled with a flair for startling fantastic imagery, can often result in engagingly inventive hokum.

Luc Besson b. 1959 France. **Nikita** France 1990/ w Anne Parillaud, Tcheky Karyo, Jean-Hugues Anglade, Jean Reno, Roland Blanche.
Films include *The Last Battle*, 1983; *Subway*, 1985; *The Big Blue*, 1988; *Leon*, 1994; *The Fifth Element*, 1997. **See also** BIGELOW, BURTON, CAMERON, CARAX, JEUNET AND CARO

KATHRYN BIGELOW

In a millennial, *noir*-tinted Los Angeles on the verge of social, political and moral breakdown, a tough, determined, sleekly clad single mother (Angela Bassett) exerts control through a display of hi-tech firepower. Kathryn Bigelow's robust films inhabit the traditionally male preserve of the violent action movie, which she simultaneously celebrates and subverts with strong female characters who are ready participants in, rather than victims of, physical conflict. Often, like the work of former husband James Cameron, her films fall prey to sensationalist excess (*Strange Days*, a futuristic fable in which Ralph Fiennes' seedy hero sells and tunes in to recordings of other people's experiences taken directly from their brains, includes an unpleasant, leering scene of rape and murder) and simplistic sociological fantasy.

All the same, her lean, taut imagery (she was formerly an art student, and her dynamic style was already to be found in the biker-movie *The Loveless*) and an almost fetishistic fascination with weaponry and costume mark her out as an idiosyncratic if erratic talent. In comparatively controlled work like *Blue Steel*, about a rookie female cop recklessly and obsessively involved with a psychotic killer, characterisation and action are dramatically balanced; elsewhere, as in the bizarre *Point Break*, in which an undercover cop is seduced by the surfing philosophy of the bank-robbers he is investigating, the undeniable expertise of the action set-pieces is undermined by overall incoherence and pretentiousness. Too often, still, style dominates at the expense of substance.

Kathryn Bigelow b. 1952 USA. **Strange Days** USA 1995/ w Ralph Fiennes, Angela Bassett, Juliette Lewis, Tom Sizemore, Michael Wincott, Vincent D'Onofrio. **Films include** *The Loveless*, 1981; *Near Dark*, 1987; *Blue Steel*, 1990; *Point-Break*, 1991. **See also** BESSON, CAMERON, HILL, SCOTT, STONE

Though the situation – at least in the context of a movie – may be subversive and shocking, the air of melancholy in this ménage-à-trois between Miou-Miou and best friends Patrick Dewaere and Gerard Depardieu is immediately evident. While Blier's films are all marked by an apparent desire to shock conventional bourgeois notions of morality – here, he 'celebrates' the self-centred, impulsive delinquency of its two young heroes – he is finally, at the same time, something of a romantic. In film after film, whether involved in taboo-breaking sexual obsession, anti-social crime or even murder, his protagonists are driven to perverse or extreme behaviour by frustration, despair, confusion and a rather forlorn hope of finding happiness in a restrictively conformist society: in *Préparez Vos Mouchoirs*, Depardieu tries to cheer up his sexually troubled wife by introducing her to a stranger (she ends up preferring a schoolboy); in *Trop Belle Pour Toi!*, when he cheats on his elegant, beautiful wife with a frumpy secretary, he is uncomprehendingly vilified for poor taste rather than deceit or infidelity. Notwithstanding their politically incorrect thrust (and it may be argued that there is a misogynistic side to their cynicism), Blier's black comedies are often surprisingly tender, such is his identification with the hapless protagonists; inner lives explain seemingly illogical acts as the narratives, cooly shot in a low-key naturalistic style, slip between undifferentiated reality and fantasy. Hence, Blier may be seen as a surrealist, albeit less rigorous than Buñuel; in recent years, however, his sly inventiveness seems to have deserted him.

Bertrand Blier b. 1939 France. **Les Valseuses (Going Places)** France 1974/ w Gérard Depardieu, Patrick Dewaere, Miou-Miou, Jeanne Moreau, Isabelle Huppert. **Films include** *Préparez Vos Mouchoirs*, 1977; *Buffet Froid*, 1979; *Beau-Père*, 1981; *La Femme de Mon Pote*, 1983; *Notre Histoire*, 1984; *Tenue de Soirée*, 1986; *Trop Belle Pour Toi!*, 1989; *Merci la Vie*, 1991; *Mon Homme*, 1996. **See also** BUÑUEL, MEYER, PIALAT

BUDD BOETTICHER

An amiably scheming bounty hunter, a righteous loner doomed to wander the desert in search of a wife taken years earlier by Comanches, and a woman he's just rescued from the same tribe watch as marauding Indians retreat. The perilous situation, the arid, hostile landscape and deftly drawn characters typify the compelling B-westerns Boetticher made in the late 50s with Randolph Scott, writer Burt Kennedy and producer Harry Joe Brown. With locations, sets and props constrained by low budgets, he relied on his wits. The result was an imaginative series of variations on the theme of a lone, stoic, often vengeful hero, psychologically trapped in a painful past, playing a game of bravery, bluff and counter-bluff with treacherous outlaws determined to make off with his woman or fortune. The latter, however, are destined to fail (or die) in their efforts to find the money to start a new life, he to return to his solitary nomadic existence. Boetticher told his stark, ritualistic stories with laconic dialogue and a minimum of visual fuss, refusing to romanticise his antagonists and using the rocky, parched landscape to lend a mythic, timeless dimension to their conflict. Sometimes, as in *Buchanan Rides Alone*, gentle absurdist humour lightened the deadly rivalry, but here and in *The Tall T* and *Ride Lonesome* the ironies were darker, producing accounts of obsessive ambition and doomed quests as visually and psychologically bleak as in his similarly masterful gangster saga *The Rise and Fall of Legs Diamond*. Elsewhere, his work, for all its solid craftmanship, was less distinctive.

Oscar 'Budd' Boetticher b. 1916 USA. **Comanche Station** 1960 USA/ w Randolph Scott, Claude Akins, Nancy Gates, Skip Homeier, Richard Rust. **Films include** *The Bullfighter and the Lady*, 1951; *Horizons West*, 1952; *The Killer Is Loose, Seven Men from Now*, 1956; *The Tall T, Decision at Sundown*, 1957; *Buchanan Rides Alone*, 1958; *Ride Lonesome*, 1959; *The Rise and Fall of Legs Diamond*, 1960; *A Time for Dying*, 1969. **See also** EASTWOOD, HILL, LEONE, ANTHONY MANN, PECKINPAH

A lone gangster (Lee Marvin) stares with deadened eyes from the shadows of a San Francisco club of the late 60s. He's clearly out of place, out of time and equally clearly has a mission. Shot and left for dead by partners who stole his share of a heist, he wants to know who betrayed him, he wants his money and he wants revenge. A familiar thriller story, but Boorman's modernist *film noir* is anything but conventional. Structured as a dying man's dream of rectifying a fatal mistake and emerging somehow intact, it succeeds as a viscerally brutal thriller, as a tale of an old-fashioned independent up against a faceless criminal Organisation and as a study of the twisted nexus of time, memory and desire. As Marvin's fantasy quest brings him back from the dead to settle scores, Boorman deploys ellipses, repetition and flashbacks to explore his confusion, obsessive hatred and need to make sense of events; at the same time, the cold, sharp images of contemporary California (used-car lots, psychedelic out clubs, concrete-and-glass apartment blocks, sewer drains) imply that the ubiquitous Organisation may be modern corporate America. Boorman repeatedly depicts the conflict between individual and society, civilisation and nature, with erratic results; a taste for myth and allegory, as in *Zardoz* and *The Emerald Forest*, may result in woolly whimsy or obviousness, but with material closer to home (*Excalibur, Hope and Glory*) and, more particularly, action fare (*Deliverance, The General*), his ambition, eye for landscape, cool sense of irony, and unpretentious stylistic assurance serve him well.

John Boorman b. 1933 England. **Point Blank** USA 1967/ w Lee Marvin, Angie Dickinson, Keenan Wynn, John Vernon, Carroll O'Connor. **Films include** *Leo the Last,* 1969, *Deliverance,* 1972; *Excalibur,* 1981; *Hope and Glory,* 1987; *The General,* 1998. **See also** MICHAEL MANN, RESNAIS, ROEG, SCORSESE

WALERIAN BOROWCZYK

The frame is divided, its two-dimensional flatness and cramped borders confining the characters; the woman (the director's wife Ligia Branice) looks locked in erotic reverie, the man engrossed in (possibly malevolent) voyeurism; his antiquated binoculars, a focus of our attention through a clear patch in the grimy glass, seem invested with a cruel power of their own. Making his first live-action feature – a dark tale of destructive passions set in a bizarre, primitive prison colony, with the ruler's wife subject to intense scrutiny as she embarks on a clandestine affair with a young officer – former animator Borowczyk remained true to the style, spirit and substance of his earlier work. The perspective, kept head-on, is foreshortened, the compositions fragmented and restrictive, the emphasis on paraphernalia and gestures almost grotesquely fetishistic; a world of familiar objects and actions is made strange by design and the camera's cool, detached gaze. Borowczyk's films depict the fragility of love and the cruelty of possessive desire; his next, *Blanche*, was a similarly exquisite account of court intrigue and deadly jealousy subverting notions of chivalry in a thirteenth-century French chateau. Thereafter, his taste for perverse eroticism led him steadily down the path towards tittilating pornography, though his surrealist's eye for arcane ornaments and equipment and his fascination with *amour fou* continued spasmodically to invest works like *The Blood of Doctor Jekyll* with a dark, unsettling poetry. His decline into material unworthy of his talents is sad indeed.

Walerian Borowczyk b. 1923 Poland. **Goto, Island of Love** 1968 France/ w Ligia Branice, Pierre Brasseur, Jean-Pierre Andreani, Guy Saint-Jean, Ginette Leclerc. **Films include** *Renaissance*, 1963; *Rosalie*, 1966; *Blanche*, 1972; *Immoral Tales*, 1974; *The Story of Sin*, 1975; *The Beast*, 1975; *The Blood of Doctor Jekyll*, 1981. **See also** BUÑUEL, GILLIAM, LYNCH, SVANKMAJER, QUAY BROTHERS

In the Paris gutters, a street-cleaner (Charles Farrell) tries to comfort a destitute girl (Janet Gaynor): the start of a rapturous love which, when the couple are separated by the Great War, will transcend time, space and death itself. Borzage, whose film won the first Oscars for Best Director and Best Actress, is neglected now, but his work from the mid-20s to World War Two confirms him as one of cinema's true Romantics. Time and again, lovers survive and even triumph over poverty, despair, oppression and war through the sheer force of their feelings for and faith in each other; here, when Farrell is sent to the trenches, they vow to think of and so commune with each other at the same time every day – when he is wounded and apparently dies in a priest's arms, Gaynor is so distraught that, miraculously,

he returns, blind but alive, keeping his promise at the moment war ends. Rationally, of course, this climax is nonsense, but Borzage's commitment to the emotional veracity of his material, to the regenerative power of his lovers' inner lives, somehow transcends melodramatic cliché so that their union achieves an almost divine dimension. Crucial to his films' incandescent romanticism were his fluid use of the camera, floating through unoccupied spaces to suggest mysterious invisible forces existing beyond the material realm, and a focus on luminous faces; his attention to actresses, especially Gaynor and Margaret Sullavan (who shone in *Little Man What Now?*, *Three Comrades*, and *The Mortal Storm*), made unusually palpable the strength of their undying love.

Frank Borzage b. 1893 USA, d. 1962 USA. **7th Heaven** USA 1927/ w Janet Gaynor, Charles Farrell, Ben Bard, David Butler, Albert Gran, Marie Mosquini. **Films include** *Street Angel*, 1928; *A Farewell to Arms*, 1932; *Little Man What Now?*, 1934; *Three Comrades*, 1938; *The Mortal Storm*, 1940; *Strange Cargo*, 1940; *Moonrise*, 1948. **See also** CARAX, GRIFFITH, MURNAU, NICHOLAS RAY, SIRK

JOÃO BOTELHO

In Elso Roque's exquisitely crisp, painterly monochrome images, the ornate elegance of a bourgeois Lisbon mansion overwhelms and oppresses a young bride, pushed into a loveless marriage in which she is just another possession, as forcefully as the forbidding gaze of her wealthy husband; visibly trapped by his devotion to materialism, she has subdued all emotion. Botelho's transposition of Dickens' *Hard Times* to a modern but oddly timeless Lisbon is a model of imaginative adaptation: lucid, precise, respectful yet an original in itself. Like his other works, it is imbued with a peculiarly Portuguese melancholy, coupled with an absurdist wit that reveals itself in highly stylised compositions and gestures reminiscent of silent melodrama; as if aware of their status as social 'types', characters are made to assume positions in static, sometimes almost theatrical tableaux that speak of submission and dominance, helplessness and power, innocence and experience. Here the detached, deeply ironic tone is quasi-Brechtian; in later work, such as *Here on Earth* and *Three Palm Trees*, Botelho's formalism was still more radical, with mysterious, wayward narratives notable for their diversity of mood and for moments indicative of his love for a more abstract form of visual poetry. As with compatriots Manoel de Oliveira and João Cesar Monteiro, Botelho is too idiosyncratic to attract mainstream audiences; his experimentalism, however, is intelligent, assured and tantalising, and deserves wider exposure than it has hitherto received.

João Botelho b. 1949 Portugal. **Hard Times** Portugal/GB 1988/ w Luis Estrela, Julia Britton, Ruy Furtado, Isabel de Castro, Inéz Medeiros. **Films include** *The Other One*, 1981; *A Portuguese Goodbye*, 1985; *Here On Earth*, 1993; *Three Palm Trees*, 1994; *Trafico*, 1998. **See also** BRESSON, FASSBINDER, GODARD, JARMUSCH, KAURISMÄKI, OZU, RUIZ

A hand withdraws minutely away from another; a girl, now involved with a delinquent, reveals her change of feelings for a childhood sweetheart and so seals her fate.Bresson's austere, elliptical narrative style assembles static, discrete shots of such moments, his camera focused on essentials – objects, hands, purposefully inexpressive faces (usually of non-professional actors) – not to depict naturalistic behaviour but to convey the mystery of inner lives: the soul of the matter. With drama, dialogue, music pared down to create a kind of 'pure' cinema, lacking incidental detail or superfluous spectacle, Bresson is less interested in pictorial beauty or psychological realism than in the achievement of grace and redemption in a world marked by hardship, cruelty, solitude. Here, the girl is just one owner of an ass, Balthazar, who, as he passes from human to human, is both witness and victim to pride, avarice, envy, brutality, neglect – and, occasionally, love; he accepts his suffering like a saint and dies, shot while hauling smugglers' contraband, in a sheep-filled meadow – the Catholic film-maker's most wondrously moving ending and the ultimate proof of the value of his uniquely ascetic methods. In film after film (though he was never prolific), he finds spiritual transcendence, through death and communion, in a resolutely unglamorous France peopled by closed-off, often unsympathetic characters: a prisoner of the Gestapo, a pickpocket, a moody 14-year-old peasant girl who kills herself, an axe-murderer. The uncompromising gravity of his vision is demanding, his humanity and genius undeniable.

Robert Bresson b. 1907 France. **Au Hasard, Balthazar** France 1966/ w Anne Wiazemsky, François Lafarge, Philippe Asselin, Nathalie Joyaut. **Films include** *Les Anges du Péché*, 1943; *Diary of a Country Priest*, 1950; *A Man Escaped*, 1956; *Pickpocket*, 1966; *Mouchette*, 1966; *Lancelot du Lac*, 1974; *The Devil, Probably*, 1977; *L'Argent*, 1983. **See also** BERGMAN, BOTELHO, DREYER, DAVIES, HANEKE, KAURISMÄKI, SCHRADER, SCORSESE, TARKOVSKY

MEL BROOKS

A kindly blind hermit (Gene Hackman) ladles broth into the lap of Frankenstein's monster (Peter Boyle). The moment is archetypally Brooksian: broad, brash, defiantly vulgar genre spoof. Actually, *Young Frankenstein*, with its meticulously designed sets and its atmospheric black and white photography signalling the writer-director's knowledgeable affection for Whale's original films, was far more controlled than most of his work, even though it lacked the sophistication of Whale's own semi-parodic *Bride of Frankenstein*. Nevertheless, it still had more than its fair share of hamminess (with Gene Wilder mugging as relentlessly as does Brooks in many of his other comic assaults on popular genres), deliberate bad taste, and woefully predictable gags. Brooks' narratives are ragbag, uneven affairs, invariably and all too unimaginatively predicated on the ludicrous absurdity of filmic conventions; slapstick, innuendo and cartoon stereotypes hold sway, and only *The Producers*, with two down-and-out would-be impresarios mounting what they believe is a sure-fire flop (the gloriously awful musical 'Springtime for Hitler') as a financial scam, successfully steers away from lame-brain parody. But while his unashamedly lowbrow, pitifully unsubversive and frequently off-target spoofs have declined in popularity, they have been influential: themselves not so very far removed from the antics of Abbott and Costello, they are recognisably ancestors to, among others, the (far funnier) *Airplane!* and *Naked Gun* films and the dumbed-down, gross-out comedies of the Farrelly Brothers.

Mel Brooks b. 1927 USA. **Young Frankenstein** USA 1974/ w Gene Wilder, Peter Boyle, Marty Feldman, Teri Garr, Cloris Leachman, Madeline Kahn, Gene Hackman. **Films include** *The Producers*, 1968; *Blazing Saddles*, 1974; *Silent Movie*, 1976; *High Anxiety*, 1977; *Spaceballs*, 1987; *Robin Hood: Men in Tights*, 1993. **See also** ALLEN, MEYER, SENNETT, WHALE

Banned for many years, Browning's dark masterpiece offers a cast unimaginable in today's cinema: Siamese twins, cretins, pinheads, a bearded lady, dwarfs and a 'human torso'. More importantly, and also almost inconceivable, is the fact that, though he had made his name with macabre horror films (not only *Dracula* but many starring Lon Chaney, doyen of masochistic, grotesque roles), Browning, himself a veteran of carnival life, portrayed his authentic 'freaks' with great, unsentimental sympathy, celebrating their wit, courage and camaraderie. Miraculously, he avoids the pitfalls of voyeurism, introducing them in lyrical longshot as they relax in a woodland glade; gradually moving closer to forestall shock and allow us to get to know them better, he insists on their humanity, observing them cope with the trials and tribulations of everyday life, and subverting traditional equations of goodness and physical health and beauty. Indeed, it's the film's 'normal' circus folk who tend to moral deformity and whose callous, conniving attitude to their unfortunate colleagues finally meets with rough, savagely ironic justice. Cruel twists of fate were common in Browning's universe: in *The Unknown*, believing that his beloved Joan Crawford cannot bear to be touched by men, circus knife-thrower Chaney has his arms amputated, only to discover she loves another, while Bela Lugosi's *Dracula* elicits our sympathy as effectively as our fear. A minor talent, perhaps, but Browning's darkly imaginative eccentricity remains peculiarly fascinating and rewarding.

Tod Browning b. 1882 USA, d. 1962 USA. **Freaks** 1932 USA/ w Harry Earles, Olga Baclanova, Wallace Ford, Lelia Hyams, Daisy Earles.
Films include *The Unholy Three*, 1925; *The Unknown, London After Midnight*, 1927; *Dracula*, 1931; *Freaks*, 1932; *The Devil Doll*, 1936.
See also BAVA, CRONENBERG, GILLIAM, JEUNET AND CARO, LYNCH, WHALE

LUIS BUÑUEL

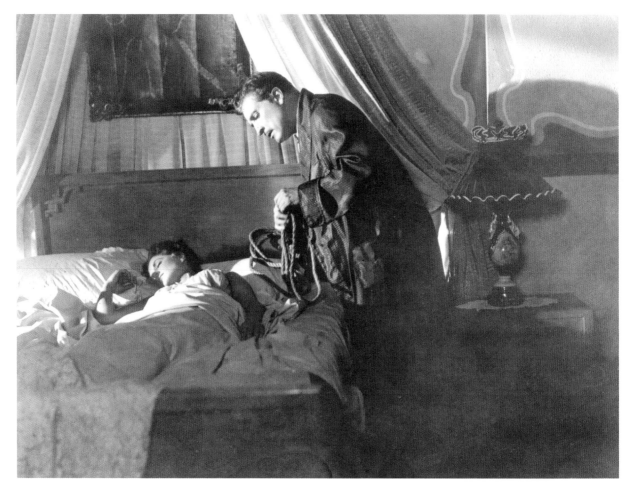

A well-off, church-going husband creeps up on his sleeping wife with rope, scissors, needle and thread: one of the most sinister displays of male jealousy in cinema history, but staged, shot and played without a hint of sensationalist hysteria. For the surrealist Buñuel, humanity – especially the bourgoisie – is wont to such cruel irrationality; it's typical of his awareness of hypocrisy that the man's paranoia about his wife's fidelity is rooted not in her acts but in the projection of his own impotent, repressed lust on to others (among other things, he is a foot fetishist). After the more savagely explicit, blatantly dreamlike surrealism of his two films with Dali (*Un Chien Andalou*, *L'Age d'Or*), Buñuel adopted a stealthier form of attack, using a reticent camera to observe and study the perverse by-ways of human behaviour, and making scant distinction between reality and fantasy, desire and act: in *The Exterminating Angel* guests remain unable to leave a party only because of their own sheep-like lassitude; inexplicably, meanwhile, a bear stalks the salon. Little escaped his imaginative eye. Though the Church and bourgeoisie were his prime targets, beggars might be thieves and rapists, blind men paedophiles, virginal cripples harridans, and housewives afternoon whores; all were calmly and coolly examined as if insects under the microscope, with the fascinated, bemused Buñuel never hammering home a moral sermon, but merely revealing, in a strange spirit of sympathy, the fundamental comedy of the human condition. He was, in short, one of cinema's greatest, most unassertive masters.

Luis Buñuel b. 1900 Spain, d. 1983 Mexico. **El** Mexico 1952/ w Arturo de Córdova, Delia Garcés, Luis Beristáin, Jose Pidal.
Films include *Un Chien Andalou*, 1928; *L'Age d'Or*, 1930; *Las Hurdes*, 1932; *Los Olvidados*, 1950; *Nazarin*, 1958; *Viridiana*, 1961; *The Exterminating Angel*, 1962; *Belle de Jour*, 1966; *The Discreet Charm of the Bourgeoisie*, 1972; *That Obscure Object of Desire*, 1977.
See also ALMODÓVAR, BLIER, BOROWCZYK, LYNCH, RENOIR, SVANKMAJER, VIGO

A strangely beautiful boy (Johnny Depp) stands among the surreal topiary he has cut with the scissorhands he was left with when his creator died before completing his work; though his solitude ends when an Avon Lady discovers him and takes him back to pastel suburbia, the world has little time for those who are different. Former animator Burton's weird fairytale is, characteristically, a visually inventive and sumptuous feast, the childlike naiveté of the world depicted considerably darkened by an adult awareness of humanity's harsh cruelty; even his two *Batman* films were more concerned with psychological neurosis and social breakdown than previous incarnations. But the imaginative designs (often echoing German expressionism) and quirky conceptualisations of his films are often betrayed by narrative incoherence and a reluctance or inability properly to confront the thematic implications of his nightmarish scenarios; despite a maverick sensibility, he perhaps remains too much the Hollywood entertainer to delve deeply into his unsettling preoccupations. Only when blessed with and constrained by material based on real lives, in *Ed Wood* – the tragi-comic story of an eternally optimistic but talentless no-budget film-maker and his relationship with penniless, drug-addict has-been Bela Lugosi – did he find the self-discipline to restrain his flights of fancy and mount a study of obsessive ambition and loyal friendship that was quirky, funny and unusually moving. As a fantasist, he shows great promise; with maturity, he may yet make something more emotionally profound.

Tim Burton b. 1958 USA. **Edward Scissorhands** USA 1990/ w Johnny Depp, Winona Ryder, Dianne Wiest, Anthony Michael Hall, Kathy Baker. **Films include** *Beetlejuice*, 1988; *Batman*, 1989; *Batman Returns*, 1992; *Ed Wood*, 1994; *Mars Attacks!*, 1996. **See also** BROWNING, GILLIAM, LYNCH, SVANKMAJER, WHALE, WOOD

JAMES CAMERON

The set is spectacular and ornately authentic, the lighting and colours glossily decorative, the action – a young, glamorous, romantic couple struggling against all odds for survival – as old and formulaic as in a silent serial. For all the extravagant expenditure, the mostly superb effects work, and the needless claims to historical accuracy, Cameron's recreation of the tragic sinking of the world's most famous ocean-liner is dramatically archaic and primitive. Lauded for his expertise with exciting action set-pieces since making the ingenious cult hit *The Terminator*, he had never successfully shown much interest in his stories' emotional or psychological aspects; *Titanic*'s relentless focus on a crudely drawn ill-starred couple (upper-crust Kate Winslet and salt-of-the-earth impoverished artist Leonardo DiCaprio), trying to save their lives and love from the schemes of stereotypical rich villains and an incovenient iceberg, is hackneyed, cartoon-thin and frankly something of an insult to those who perished in the real disaster. Overblown and clumsily scripted, the doomed romance wrecks the narrative's momentum, though once the ship starts going down, Cameron, clearly happier with chaos, carnage and high-tech, displays the grasp of rapid cutting, epic-scale terror and visual bravura that defines the most memorable scenes in his earlier work. Sadly, as he aims, ambitiously but all-too-conspicuously, for the mythic, he equates more with better: good business sense in the era of the 'event movie', maybe, but grandiose, simplistic and artistically limiting.

James Cameron b. 1954 USA. **Titanic** USA 1997/ w Leonardo DiCaprio, Kate Winslet, Billy Zane, David Warner, Frances Fisher. **Films include** *The Terminator*, 1984; *Aliens*, 1986; *The Abyss*, 1989; *Terminator 2: Judgment Day*, 1991; *True Lies*, 1994. **See also** BIGELOW, CARPENTER, CORMAN, DE MILLE, GRIFFITH, SPIELBERG

JANE CAMPION

A dark, brooding Scotswoman sits unbowed amid her few belongings, set down, improbably, on a bleak New Zealand shore; wilfully mute since she was six (her daughter 'translates'), she's there to wed a stranger, whose refusal to transport her beloved piano to their home in the wilderness drives her to make a sexual bargain with a local settler to retrieve it... a deal resulting in violence and love. Campion's unusually unsentimental and erotic romance, often shot from unfamiliar, unsettling angles, uses wild landscapes to parallel the harsh, banked-down emotions of its uncommunicative, barely fathomable characters, trapped in their private dreams and needs. The elliptical narrative respects their mystery but allows visual epiphanies to shed light on the passing moments of peace, pain (emotional and physical abuse regularly punctuate Campion's tales) and passion that make up a life. Mostly, her protagonists are clumsy, confused but intelligent and deeply determined women – unsurprisingly, her portrait of Henry James' Isabel Archer was insightful and imaginative – but there is no feminist orthodoxy on view: Campion understands that humanity is too unpredictable, strange and complicated for simplification, so that in *Sweetie*, *An Angel at My Table* and her masterly short *A Girl's Own Story*, tragedy often jostles with comedy, fear with desire, the surreal with the banal. Defying categorisation, Campion's work is sharp, instinctive and confidently original; a restless talent, she encourages and allows us to look at the world, and ourselves, afresh.

Jane Campion b. 1954 New Zealand. **The Piano** Australia 1993/ w Holly Hunter, Harvey Keitel, Sam Neill, Anna Paquin, Kerry Walker. **Films include** *A Girl's Own Story*, 1983; *Two Friends*, 1986; *Sweetie*, 1989; *An Angel at My Table*, 1990; *The Portrait of a Lady*, 1996; *Holy Smoke*, 1999. **See also** BUÑUEL, LUHRMANN, LUPINO, SIRK, WEIR, WELLES

FRANK CAPRA

Tuba-playing poet Longfellow Deeds may be outnumbered by the rich cynics bent on discrediting him as crazy for planning to donate an inherited fortune to the poor, but since this is Capra-corn and Deeds is played by shy, sexy, laconically common-sensical Gary Cooper, it's a given that the Everyman hick will win in the end, on behalf of all America's 'ordinary folk'. Capra's early films were pacy, polished comedies and adventures, but with Mr Deeds he found his mission: to preach the true American Way in sentimental populist comedies whose Utopian moral uplift sprang from a lone folksy hero overcoming corrupt city sophisticates, politicians and lawyers by means of simple traditional values. Seen as a New Deal liberal, Capra was in fact advocating demagoguery; as his films became more

heavy-handedly finger-wagging, so they became more complacent, reactionary and less amusing: *Mr Smith Goes to Washington* ends with James Stewart – another Capra favourite – filibustering with grandly inarticulate patriotic sentiments to defeat the Senate's few rotten apples. Again with Stewart (and, like most of Capra's work, featuring fine performances), *It's a Wonderful Life* is more tolerable in that its vision of smalltown life is tempered by a real, troubled sense of life's compromises, but even then the cosy optimism is restored by a cute Christmas angel. However much Capra may have wanted to pay tribute to his adopted country, his best-known work now seems wordy visually and morally trite, plodding, dated and, politically, disturbingly out of touch with reality.

Frank Capra b. 1897 Sicily, d. 1991 USA. **Mr Deeds Goes to Town** USA 1936/ w Gary Cooper, Jean Arthur, George Bancroft, Lionel Stander, Douglas Dumbrille. **Films include** *The Strong Man*, 1927; *The Miracle Woman*, 1931; *The Bitter Tea of General Yen*, 1933; *It Happened One Night*, 1934; *Lost Horizon*, 1937; *Mr Smith Goes to Washington*, 1939; *It's a Wonderful Life*, 1946. **See also** CHAPLIN, CLAIR, GRIFFITH, SPIELBERG

Two unlikely lovers – a middle-class art student fearful of losing her sight (Juliette Binoche) and a down-and-out fire-eater (Denis Lavant) – who live among the other homeless on Paris's oldest bridge see their heady mutual enthralment reflected in France's bicentennial celebrations. Though Carax, an avowed fan of Godard, is regarded with some justification as an heir to the French New Wave, his sumptuously romantic imagery is in fact more evocative of silent cinema: even in this modern fairy tale about the despairing and dispossessed, his extravagantly poetic use of lighting, colour and camera movement speaks more eloquently of his protagonists' passions than does his occasionally portentous dialogue. Though his stories – usually about moody, disenchanted young people consumed by solitude, brought together by chance and redeemed by love – are slight and sometimes implausible, his eye for startling, even surreal compositions and his dynamic sense of movement (in this film, for example, water-skiing on the Seine by night) ensures that his work is frequently exhilarating. Most notably, he recreates Paris as a dreamlike city of the mind: in the rapturous, black and white *Boy Meets Girl*, it was transformed into a purgatory populated by troubled loners and lost souls. At times, Carax's ambitious perfectionism smacks of pretentiousness, a *folie de grandeur* (the Pont Neuf, the Seine and the buildings on its banks were recreated at great expense in southern France), but even if his taste for grand metaphors sometimes seems naive, one cannot deny his virtuosity or his profound love of cinema.

Léos Carax b. 1962 France. **Les Amants du Pont Neuf** France 1991/ w Juliette Binoche, Denis Lavant, Klaus-Michael Gruber, Daniel Buain, Edith Scob. **Films include** *Boy Meets Girl*, 1984; *Mauvais Sang (The Night Is Young)*, 1986; *Pola X*, 1999. **See also** FEUILLADE, FRANJU, GODARD, TRUFFAUT, VIGO

Standing in the grey shadows of a Le Havre bedroom, army deserter Jean Gabin surveys Michèle Morgan, with whom he has recently and passionately fallen in love. Their respite is brief; Gabin needs a passport to go abroad, and is in troubled negotiations with a fixer who has his own malevolent designs on Morgan, his ward. Though it has often been characterised as 'poetic realism', the best of Carné's work, mostly from scripts by the writer Jacques Prévert and made between 1935 and 1945, is simply poetic; its melancholy fatalism and romantic fascination with doomed affairs and low-life crime was incarnated on screen in streets shrouded in swirling mists, smoky bars, seedy hotel rooms, and beautiful, compliant, supportive women in trench coats and berets. (The air of gloomy pessimism has often

been attributed to the coming war.) Here as ever, however, the sturdily handsome Gabin dominated as the decent but disenchanted working-class man, holed up away from the authorities until he's driven by desperation, love and honour to a violence that will inevitably rebound. Perhaps Carné needed his talented collaborators (production designer Alexandre Trauner and composer Maurice Jaubert were also regulars), for after the war his work went into severe decline. He and Prévert, however, certainly deserve a place in film history not only for their taut thrillers (*Le Jour se Lève* is another fine example), but for the delicious surreal comedy *Drôle de Drame* and their masterpiece, the epic theatrical romance *Les Enfants du Paradis*.

Marcel Carné b. 1909 France, d. 1996 France. **Le Quai des Brumes** France 1938/ w Jean Gabin, Michèle Morgan, Michel Simon, Pierre Brasseur, Robert Le Vigan. **Films include** *Drôle de Drame*, 1937; *Hotel du Nord*, 1938; *Le Jour se Lève*, 1939; *Les Visiteurs du Soir*, 1942; *Les Enfants du Paradis*, 1945; *Thérèse Raquin*, 1953. **See also** BECKER, RENOIR, MELVILLE

Ghosts from a shipwreck emerge from the fog to exact revenge on a small north Californian resort which neglected their plight 100 years earlier and now smugly celebrates its centenary. Carpenter's films – mostly cheap(-ish) and cheerful reworkings of sci-fi, horror and thriller situations familiar from 40s and 50s B-movies – are full of hokum, yet at their best they are gripping, witty and mythic. From the opening of *The Fog*, with an old salt entrancing children with a chilling tale, it's clear we're to be spun a preposterous yarn; but it's hard to resist the appeal of a tale in which rights are wronged and a handful of determined individuals fend off death by pooling their skills. The group-under-siege theme – also featured in *Dark Star* and *Assault on Precinct 13* – was lifted from Carpenter's beloved Hawks (he later

remade *The Thing*), the coastal community menaced by an implacable force evoked Hitchcock's *The Birds*, while the grotesque avengers might have stumbled in from a Jack Arnold monster movie. Though Carpenter's stories gleefully eschewed originality, he displayed his expertise in creating suspense by cutting back and forth between various endangered individuals and groups and by his canny, much-copied use of the wide screen, with the threat to victims suddenly appearing from the side of the frame or emerging from a murky background. The technique may not be sophisticated, but in taut thrillers like *Halloween* and *The Fog* it was so effective that, sadly, he has since relied largely on more of the same.

John Carpenter b. 1948 USA. **The Fog** USA 1979/ w Adrienne Barbeau, Jamie Lee Curtis, Tom Atkins, Janet Leigh, Hal Holbrook, John Houseman, Nancy Loomis. **Films include** *Dark Star*, 1974; *Assault on Precinct 13*, 1976; *Halloween*, 1978; *Escape from New York*, 1981; *The Thing*, 1982; *Starman*, 1984; *They Live*, 1988; *In the Mouth of Madness*, 1994. **See also** ARNOLD, CORMAN, CRONENBERG, FISHER, HAWKS, HITCHCOCK

JOHN CASSAVETES

Both the graininess of the 16mm black-and-white footage and the impression of a moment of time snatched from a longer story (Gena Rowlands' prostitute carousing drunkenly with John Marley during the breakdown of his 14-year-old marriage to Lynn Carlin) suggest the documentary-like immediacy of Cassavetes' distinctive visual and narrative style. Though widely believed to be improvised, his work (mostly about crises in relationships, emotional instability and the tensions that arise between men and women in their search for love) was in fact carefully scripted and rehearsed; the aura of naturalism derived from his preference for mere observation of behaviour over conventional tightly-structured plotting and from a deceptively casual visual style (involving lengthy takes, hand-held camera and erratic focus) which was entirely at the service of the intense, close-up study of chaotically confused, barely articulate characters. Made on low budgets (financed partly by his own performances in Hollywood movies), often with a group of actors that included his wife Rowlands and friends Peter Falk, Ben Gazzara and Seymour Cassel, films like *Shadows*, *Husbands* and *A Woman Under the Influence* had little in common with mainstream cinema; their rambling narratives, technical rawness and honest depiction of middle-class life made him a true, very influential independent. But his finest achievement remains the superb, edgy performances he elicited – acting was both a tool for exploring the human condition and a metaphor for it: the conflation of form and content assures his status as one of film's greatest talents.

John Cassavetes b. 1929 USA, d. 1989 USA. **Faces** USA 1968/ w John Marley, Gena Rowlands, Lynn Carlin, Fred Draper, Seymour Cassel, Val Avery. **Films include** *Shadows*, 1961; *Husbands*, 1970; *Minnie and Moskowitz*, 1971; *A Woman Under the Influence*, 1974; *The Killing of a Chinese Bookie*, 1976; *Opening Night*, 1978; *Gloria*, 1980; *Love Streams*, 1983. **See also** ALTMAN, LOACH, PENNEBAKER, RENOIR, RIVETTE, SCORCESE

CLAUDE CHABROL

Serge wallows in drunken, self-piteous remembrance of his dead, Down's Syndrome child; in seconds, bitter despair will make him drive off the boys playing soccer in the village square. Chabrol's feature début, widely regarded as the first film of the *nouvelle vague*, concerns a convalescing student returning home to find his childhood friend sunk into alcoholism; as he strives, with mixed success, to sort out Serge's sordid family life (adultery, rape, abuse), the pair become embroiled in a love-hate relationship in which they 'exchange' misdemeanours, guilt and, finally, redemption. Profoundly influenced by Hitchcock, Chabrol repeatedly centres his tales of guilt, recrimination, violence and murder on 'doubles': ego- and id-like characters trapped in complex psychological or ethical power struggles. Whether depicting the bourgeoisie or, as here, an economically and culturally impoverished working-class, his gaze is detached, even cynical in its observation of humanity's capacity for cruelty and crime. Here, what first looks like a bleak portrait of village life soon reveals itself as a carefully shot and structured allegory about sin and salvation: despite the realist veneer, symbolic touches – the would-be saviour's final, possibly fatal trek through the snow to find Serge is intercut with the latter's wife in the throes of painful but redemptive childbirth – lift the film into the realm of poetic melodrama. Chabrol's cool intellectualism has produced variable results, but in his best films, like *Les Bonnes Femmes*, *La Femme Infidèle*, *Le Boucher* and *Violette Nozière*, his visually precise, expressive compositions offer subtle psychological insights.

Claude Chabrol b. 1930 France. **Le Beau Serge** France 1958/ w Gérard Blain, Jean-Claude Brialy, Bernardette Lafont, Michèle Meritz, Jeanne Perez, Claude Cerval. **Films include** *Les Cousins, Les Bonnes Femmes,* 1959; *Les Biches, La Femme Infidèle,* 1968; *Le Boucher,* 1970; *Ten Days' Wonder,* 1971; *Nada,* 1974; *Violette Nozière,* 1978; *Poulet au Vinaigre,* 1985; *Une Affaire des Femmes,* 1988; *Enfer,* 1994; *Rien Ne Va Plus,* 1997. **See also** BUÑUEL, CLOUZOT, GODARD, HITCHCOCK, LANG, LOSEY, ROHMER, RIVETTE, TRUFFAUT

YOUSSEF CHAHINE

In twelfth-century Andalucia, Islamic fundamentalists praise God and swear opposition to both Christians and free-thinking Muslims – notably Averroës, philosopher and adviser to the Caliph – who enjoy song, dance and debate. Chahine's hymn to tolerance is a typically sensual blend of epic adventure, robust satire, political parable and (making inventive use of a popular Egyptian tradition) musical extravaganza: the dynamic gypsy dance sequences are a physical expression of spiritual freedom and joy, characteristic of Chahine's transformation of moral and metaphysical ideas into concrete actions, and his portrayal of political struggle and conflict in terms of individual experience. Raised in cosmopolitan Alexandria, and trained as an actor in California's Pasadena Playhouse, Chahine is a devotee not only of liberty and earthly love but of a wide range of cinematic styles and genres; whether working in epic historical allegory (*Saladin, Adieu Bonaparte*), *noir*-tinted melodrama (*Cairo Station*), rural neo-realism (*The Land*), or the enthralling mix of arty, autobiographical introspection, comedy, tragedy and historical reconstruction that was his 'Alexandria Trilogy', he makes remarkably versatile, expressively precise use of lighting, colour, camera-movement, editing and symbolism to bring his often anti-authoritarian fables to vibrant life. Few other film-makers so successfully combine populist drama with intelligent political, social and ethical analysis, and *Destiny*'s exhilararating blend of sensual poetry and ideological commitment deservedly won him a special lifetime achievement award at the 50th Cannes Festival.

Youssef Chahine b. 1926 Egypt. **Destiny (Al Massir)** Egypt/France 1997/ w Nour El Cherif, Laila Eloui, Mahmoud Hémeida, Safia El Emary, Khaled El Nabaoui. **Films include** *Son of the Nile*, 1951; *Cairo Station*, 1958; *Saladin*, 1963; *The Land*, 1969; *The Choice*, 1970; *The Sparrow,* 1973; *Alexandria Why?*, 1978; *Adieu Bonaparte*, 1984; *An Egyptian Story*, 1982; *The Sixth Day*, 1987; *Alexandria Again and Always*, 1989; *The Other*, 1999. **See also** DONEN, FELLINI, MINNELLI, NICHOLAS RAY, SIRK, WELLES

CHARLES CHAPLIN

Though Charlie is neither in tramp costume (this was his final appearance in that role) nor soliciting audience sympathies with an ingratiating smile to the camera, the scene is archetypically Chaplin: the eternal underdog menaced by belligerent bullies and authority-figures in a hostile Depression-era world of inhuman technology, hardship and despair. The mix of simplistic socio-political comment and slapstick mime served him well, making him the best-known, best-loved entertainer the world has ever known, though more recently the maudlin sentimentality, aura of self-pity, and childishly spiteful attitude to the rich and powerful – almost everyone, in fact, excepting kids and waifish women – have fallen from favour. Nor was he an especially sophisticated or inventive film-maker: the camera merely recorded his pratfalls and pranks. Nonetheless, his dark, sad, beautiful eyes, simpering expressions, fastidious manners and balletic grace, coupled with a lyrical depiction of poverty (inspired by childhood memories), made him an iconic identification-figure for filmgoers raised on vaudeville and Victorian melodrama; only in 1940 did he abandon the formula to make a proper talkie, the anti-Hitler satire *The Great Dictator*. Save for the misogynist black comedy *Monsieur Verdoux* and the dire *A Countess from Hong Kong*, his later work was marred by sermonising: *Limelight* and *A King in New York* reek of personal resentment at a no longer appreciative world. All the same, he remains an extraordinary twentieth-century phenomenon, however dated his films may now seem.

Charles Chaplin b. 1889 England, d. 1977 Switzerland. **Modern Times** USA 1936/ w Chaplin, Paulette Goddard, Henry Bergman, Chester Conklin, Tiny Sanford. **Films include** *The Kid*, 1921; *The Pilgrim*, 1923; *The Gold Rush*, 1925; *City Lights*, 1931; *The Great Dictator*, 1940; *Monsieur Verdoux*, 1947; *Limelight*, 1952; *A King in New York*, 1957. **See also** ALLEN, CAPRA, CLAIR, GRIFFITH, KEATON, SENNETT, TATI

CHEN KAIGE

Two colleagues in the Peking Opera: one a male star, the other a specialist in female concubine roles who, reflecting their stage relationship, has come to harbour a passion for his friend which manifests itself in jealous tantrums at the former's marriage to a prostitute. Notwithstanding the homosexuality, the story is the stuff of traditional melodrama, and Chen's mise-en-scène is suitably operatic – the lavish sets and costumes and sumptuous colour photography provide a parallel to the heightened emotions. The disciplinarian cruelties suffered by the pair at the opera academy, their rise to fame and the subsequent acts of loyalty and betrayal traverse 50 turbulent years of Chinese history: the rule of the warlords, the Japanese occupation, the Communist victory, and the wretched iniquities of the Cultural Revolution; though here Chen is more concerned with the dramatic potential of the historical backdrop, in earlier films like *Yellow Earth*, *The Big Parade* and *King of the Children*, his subject – treated obliquely with an allusive, elliptical narrative style, in order to avoid censorship – had been the effect of political realities on individual lives. (Like others of his age, during the Cultural Revolution he was sent to toil in a remote rural community). Nevertheless, ever since first attracting attention as a leading light of the Film Academy's 'Fifth Generation', he has consistently shown himself to be an imaginative and intelligent stylist; even as he has moved from political parable to more conventional accounts of human desire and despair, his work has remained notable for its visual bravura.

Chen Kaige b. 1952 China. **Farewell My Concubine** Hong Kong/China 1993/ w Leslie Cheung, Zhang Fengyi, Gong Li, Lu Qi, Ying Da, Ge You. **Films include** *Yellow Earth,* 1984; *The Big Parade,* 1986; *King of the Children,* 1987; *Life on a String,* 1991; *Temptress Moon,* 1996. *The Emperor and the Assassin,* 1999. **See also** BERTOLUCCI, HU, KUROSAWA, SCORSESE, SCHRADER, SIRK, ZHANG

Far from home, in a South-East Asian river, prisoners of war – friends from a Pennsylvanian steel-town – try to escape the Vietcong; fear and determination show in their haunted faces, while the violence they've suffered is suggested by scars and bruises, the difficulty of their task by the uninvitingly murky water. Cimino's epic, emotionally draining tale of working-class men fighting for their country in a war that shook America's faith in itself is a troubled, troubling tribute to homegrown heroism: honest about despair, doubt and muted hope, touching in its depiction of loyalty and camaraderie (first evoked in a long, authentically detailed party sequence), but racist and overstated as it portrays the Vietcong primarily as sadists forcing their captives to play Russian roulette. Strong characterisation (already impressive in Cimino's earlier *Thunderbolt and Lightfoot*); a symphonic sense of scale blending the intimate and epic, personal and political; and conspicuously serious ambition manifest in the emphasis on grim 'realism', distinguished this, his finest film. Sadly, only the last two qualities recurred in the western *Heaven's Gate*, an extravagant, incoherent *folie de grandeur* of sporadically arresting set-pieces; its budget, out of control, contributed to the downfall of United Artists. Thereafter, excess in terms of dramatic tone and overall style has become Cimino's trademark in occasional films of increasingly negligible worth. But *The Deer Hunter* remains not only a considerable war film but a fascinating monument to an era when America entertained doubts about its place in the world, and Hollywood, briefly, confidently made truly adult movies.

Michael Cimino b. 1943 USA. **The Deer Hunter** USA 1978/ w Robert De Niro, Christopher Walken, Jon Savage, John Cazale, Meryl Streep, George Dzundza. **Films include** *Thunderbolt and Lightfoot*, 1974; *Heaven's Gate*, 1980; *The Year of the Dragon*, 1985; *The Sicilian*, 1987; *Desperate Hours*, 1990; *The Sunchaser*, 1996. **See also** CAMERON, COPPOLA, FORD, LEAN, LEONE, SPIELBERG, VISCONTI

SOULEYMANE CISSÉ

A small boy unearths two egg-like orbs in the sand: both he and they symbolise rebirth, a new era for Africa in which new and ancient knowledge will together define the future. This luminescent image comes at the very end of Cissé's fable in which a shaman pursues his newly adult son (the infant's father) across a timeless, elemental landscape, angry at the challenge posed to his own status by his offspring's knowledge of magic and his appropriation of powerful fetishes. Cissé has repeatedly depicted the conflict between old and new, using mythical, dreamlike symbols within an otherwise realistic milieu: though *Finye*'s central characters are modern-day students, its clash between traditional rural and Westernised urban values allows him to abandon, here and there, the scenes of drug-taking, demonstrations and examinations for others in which images of nature – the sea, a ram, a massive tree – dominate. In *Yeelen*, such imagery was even more pervasive, evoking arcane ritual and elemental forces: the sun beats down on the parched earth, visions are seen in water, flames and smoke abound, and magical power is embodied in oxen, an elephant and a lion, until father and son finally confront each other in a battle that culminates in thunderous sound and blinding light. Cissé's compositions are unfussy, usually framing just one or two characters in an otherwise empty landscape; magic is evoked through sound, golden light or the simplest of special effects: a dog walking backwards, a face superimposed on water in a pestle. The result is poetic, strikingly effective, and wholly attuned to an African cultural tradition.

Souleymane Cissé (Solomani Sise) b. 1940 Mali. **Yeelen (The Light)** Mali 1987/ w Issiaka Kane, Aoua Sangare, Niamanto Sanogo, Balla Moussa Keita, Youssouf Tenin Cissé. **Films include** *Five Days of a Life*, 1972; *Den Muso*, 1975; *Baara*, 1978; *Finye (The Wind)*, 1982; *Waati*, 1995. **See also** CHAHINE, SEMBENE, OUÉDRAOGO

RENÉ CLAIR

Which other city's roofs could it possibly be? Yet the lively, romantic, vibrantly 'ordinary' Parisians clustered on the streets and balconies are actually on a magnificent Lazare Meerson studio set, one of the technical triumphs of Clair's first sound film. Indeed, the movies for which he is best known (which also include *Le Quatorze Juillet*, *Le Million* and *A Nous la Liberté*, and which were made between a light-hearted, engaging flirtation with Dadaist fantasy in *Entr'Acte* and a stint making rather more anonymous movies in England and America), are memorable less for their slight stories – here, about best friends, one wrongfully sent to jail, involved with the same girl – or their gently madcap satire than for their look and sound. Georges Perinal's fluid camera follows the characters' almost balletic progress around

Leerson's detailed but charmingly artificial recreations of the city of light and love, while dialogue is regularly replaced, as in an operetta, by music and song. Style, in the end, tended to swamp substance in Clair's meticulously self-contained world, so that very often the films, while charming and polished, now seem shallow and dated. His films abroad, too, were basically elegant fluff, but those made in France after the War tended to be darker dramas in the 'poetic realism' mould; sadly, while *Les Grandes Manœuvres* is an affecting tragi-comic romance, many were as remote from reality as his earlier comedies, contributing to the steep, seemingly irreversible decline of Clair's once high reputation.

René Clair (Chomette) b. 1898 France, d. 1981 France. **Sous les Toits de Paris** (**Under the Roofs of Paris**) France 1930/ w Albert Préjean, Pola Illéry, Edmond Greville, Gaston Modot. **Films include** *Paris Qui Dort*, 1923; *The Italian Straw Hat*, 1927; *Le Million, A Nous la Liberté,* 1931; *Le Quatorze Juillet*, 1932; *I Married a Witch*, 1942; *Les Belles de Nuit*, 1952, *Les Grandes Manœuvres,* 1955. **See also** CARNÉ, CHAPLIN, JEUNET AND CARO, RENOIR

The old man (Charles Vanel), his leg agonisingly broken by the truckload of explosives his friend (Yves Montand) has driven over it lest the vehicle remain stuck in a pool of crude oil where the former had fallen, is pulled to safety. Look closely: Montand's face shows no remorse, sympathy or shame, but hatred and disgust at the way the accident has delayed their drive over treacherous South American mountain roads on a life-threatening assignment that might provide the money for a return to France. Clouzot's misanthropic movies are populated by characters who exhibit only the basest instincts; in his supremely suspenseful road-thriller, dirt, sweat and grime match their moral decay, while the sun's harsh glare mirrors Clouzot's own relentless gaze, illuminating vice and desperation in every nook and cranny of the human soul. Devoid of sentimentality, his sour pessimism portrays people as predators and prey bent on self-preservation; though everyone, as in Renoir, has his reasons, the motivation is at best primevally instinctive, at worst malicious. In *Le Corbeau*, a small town's inhabitants, petrified by a plague of poison-pen letters, turn on each other; *Quai des Orfèvres* – a relatively light-hearted murder mystery – features pornographers, whores and adulterers; *Les Diaboliques* depicts deadly intrigue among a sadistic boarding school headmaster, his wife and mistress; fittingly, each film features seedy, sordid locations and gloomily precise camerawork. An unappealing vision, for sure, but Clouzot's dramatic expertise and undeniable conviction are perversely, chillingly persuasive.

Henri-Georges Clouzot b. 1907 France, d. 1977 France. **The Wages of Fear** France 1953/ w Yves Montand, Charles Vanel, Peter Van Eyck, Folco Lulli, Vera Clouzot. **Films include** *L'Assassin Habite au 21*, 1942; *Le Corbeau*, 1943; *Quai des Orfèvres*, 1947; *Les Diaboliques*, 1955; *La Verité*, 1960; *La Prisonnière*, 1968. **See also** ALDRICH, CARNÉ, CHABROL, FULLER, HITCHCOCK, PECKINPAH

JEAN COCTEAU

As the poet Orphée is led by Heurtebise – an emissary of Death – through his bedroom mirror into the dark, devastated Zone, in a quest both to bring back his recently departed wife and to meet his own Death in the form of a beautiful Princess with whom he has fallen in love, we are struck by the charmingly simple yet inventive amateurism of Cocteau's appropriation of myth. The writer, painter and film-maker may have been a self-preoccupied aesthete given to flowery pronouncements about the predicament of the artist but in his best work (*La Belle et la Bête*, *Orphée*) the personal symbolism that made *Le Sang d'un Poète* and *Le Testament d'Orphée* seem slight and inaccessible to all but his aficionados was imaginatively and fruitfully applied to stories with a more universal appeal. Partly, their success derives

from Cocteau's childlike delight in his medium's magical potential: slow motion, reverse projection, mirrors and mercury-vats were among the basic but effective techniques used to depict Orphée's journey between Life and Death. Equally engaging, however, was the way he created mythic characters and locations from the world we know: leather-clad bikers as Death's executioners, obscure messages from the afterlife announced on a car radio, bombed ruins as the Zone. As ever, Cocteau's romantic ideas about art, love and mortality were fey, shallow and self-celebratory, but his often extraordinarily dreamlike images and fundamentally playful, almost home-movie approach to narrative and style not only linked him with the avant-garde but in many ways anticipated the French New Wave.

Jean Cocteau b. 1889 France, d. 1963 France. **Orphée** France 1950/ w Jean Marais, Maria Casarès, François Périer, Marie Déa, Edouard Dermithe, Juliette Greco. **Films include** *Le Sang d'un Poète*, 1930; *La Belle et la Bête*,1945; *L'Aigle à Deux Têtes*, 1947; *Les Parents Terribles*, 1948; *Le Testament d'Orphée*, 1960. **See also** ANGER, BRESSON, BUÑUEL, GODARD, MELVILLE, TRUFFAUT

Two kidnappers laugh as their terrified captive stumbles blindly into the snow in a vain attempt to escape: the image is funny yet horrific, surreal yet all too credible. The collision of comedy and violent crime, of bizarre grotesquerie and everyday banality, typically intensifies the unsettling mood of the Coens' superbly imaginative abduction drama. Theirs is an America of the mind, in which petty jealousies and greed lead to an out-of-control spiral of full-blown Gothic carnage; here, a timid man's plans to make money by arranging a bogus kidnapping of his wife results in mass murder. The Coens have been accused of concentrating excessively on style, yet the dynamic, startling images, the tortuous, even enigmatic narratives and the heightened colour of their dialogue create an almost expressionist world of nightmarish passions in which few of the characters are aware of the true consequences of their or anyone else's actions. It is a world at one remove both from reality and, thanks to the Coens' skewed comic sensibility, from traditional crime genres; and while the cruel ironies and precision plotting of *Blood Simple*, *Miller's Crossing* and *Barton Fink* were charged with manipulative coldness, more recently *The Hudsucker Proxy*, *Fargo* and *The Big Lebowski* have confirmed the brothers' affection for unexceptional, well-meaning people acting honorably, even heroically amidst corruption. Behind the dazzling pastiche lies an awareness of human solitude, overcome only by trust, friendship and love – an awareness that makes the Coens' brilliant comedies intellectually *and* emotionally satisfying.

Joel Coen b. 1954 USA **Ethan Coen** b. 1957 USA. **Fargo** USA 1995/ w Frances McDormand, William H Macy, Steve Buscemi, Peter Stormare, Harve Presnell, Kristin Rudrud. **Films include** *Blood Simple*, 1984; *Raising Arizona*, 1987; *Miller's Crossing*, 1990; *Barton Fink*, 1991; *The Hudsucker Proxy*, 1994; *The Big Lebowski*, 1998. **See also** KUBRICK, LUHRMANN, POLANSKI, STURGES, WELLES, WILDER

FRANCIS FORD COPPOLA

A wedding ceremony. The church. Guns. Italy. Family. As Michael Corleone (Al Pacino), son of the *capo* of a leading American Mafia family, marries his Sicilian bride, the themes of Coppola's epic crime trilogy are gathered together in an ironically loaded shot. Like the Corleone clan, Michael leads a double life: devotion to the American way, with its free enterprise, social respectability and loyalty to the family (including an American wife), goes hand in hand with an older adherence to tribal violence and the faith that God will absolve sin. If it's hard to discern any consistent style in Coppola's varied and variable movies, beyond a frequent preference for lavish spectacle evident in the *Godfather* films, *Apocalypse Now*, *One from the Heart* and *Bram Stoker's Dracula*, he repeatedly returns to the theme of an individual's uneasy relationship both with himself and with the society in which he lives: questions of responsibility, loyalty, ambition and failure recur in films as diverse as *The Rain People*, *The Conversation*, *Rumble Fish*, *Tucker* and *The Rainmaker*. Coppola restlessly veers between commercial and personal projects, social criticism and a celebration of ritual tradition; as an artist he is as divided a personality as many of his creations. That's why, perhaps, his finest work is ironic and ambivalent: the cross-cutting between baptism and bloody murder in *The Godfather*, the conflict between professionalism and ethics in *The Conversation*, the idea that war can be horrific and exciting in *Apocalypse Now*. Sadly, his recent work is a pale shadow of those audacious, ambitious movies.

Francis Ford Coppola b. 1939 USA. **The Godfather** USA 1972/ w Marlon Brando, Al Pacino, James Caan, Robert Duvall, John Cazale, Diane Keaton, Sterling Hayden. **Films include** *The Rain People*, 1969; *The Conversation, The Godfather Part II*, 1974; *Apocalypse Now*, 1979; *One from the Heart*, 1982; *Rumble Fish*, 1983; *Tucker*, 1988; *The Godfather Part III*, 1990; *Bram Stoker's Dracula*, 1992; *The Rainmaker*, 1998. **See also** BERTOLUCCI, CIMINO, CORMAN, LEAN, LUCAS, SCORSESE, SPIELBERG

Nerdy, none-too-bright Walter (Dick Miller) surveys one of the gruesome 'sculptures' – a cat he accidentally stabbed and poured plaster over while extricating it from behind a wall in his seedy apartment – which have made him the darling of the arty poseurs at the Greenwich Village bar where he waits tables. This cheap, cheerfully macabre scene is typical of Corman's B-movie wizardry: though production values are distinctly tacky (the film was shot in five days), a darkly witty script, tongue-in-cheek acting and no-nonsense direction made for a minor masterpiece of horror-comedy. (Indeed, the deft satirising of the Beat poets, including a thinly disguised Ginsberg caricature, lent real, topical bite.) Though, for most of his prolific directing career, Corman churned out sci-fi, horror, westerns and teen melodramas for the drive-in crowd, inventive pragmatism and absurdist irony ensured that they were not only entertaining and to-the-point (virtually every film displayed its requisite quota of sexual intrigue, fast-paced action and violence), but surprisingly intelligent: highpoints include the hilariously bitchy *Sorority Girl*, the taut gangster sagas *Machine Gun Kelly* and *The St Valentine's Day Massacre*, a visually elegant series of Edgar Allen Poe adaptations (some genuinely unsettling, others fond pastiche), and the metaphysical fable *The Man with the X-Ray Eyes*. As a producer, he is hugely influential in having hired and encouraged countless now famous talents including Coppola, Dante, Demme, Sayles, Scorsese and Jack Nicholson; hence, he may be seen as a progenitor of the 'movie brats' and the current indie scene.

Roger Corman b. 1926 USA. **A Bucket of Blood** USA 1959/ w Dick Miller, Anthony Carbone, Barboura Morris, Julian Burtin, Ed Nelson. **Films include** *Sorority Girl*, 1957; *Machine Gun Kelly*, 1958; *The Little Shop of Horrors*, 1960; *The Pit and the Pendulum*, 1961; *The Man with the X-Ray Eyes*, 1963; *The Tomb of Ligeia*, 1964; *The Wild Angels*, 1966; *The St Valentine's Day Massacre, The Trip*, 1967. **See also** CARPENTER, DWAN, LEWIS, MEYER, ULMER, WOOD

The father and wife of a man who has 'disappeared' during a military coup in a South American country (unnamed, but clearly meant to suggest Chile in 1973) conduct a desperate search among piles of corpses. At their best, Costa-Gavras' muck-raking melodramas about conspiracy and corruption blend the personal and the political to dynamic, moving effect. With thinly disguised stories based on real-life events (an assassination sanctioned and covered up by the Greek colonels in *Z*, Stalinist show-trials in *The Confession*, CIA involvement in Uruguayan torture methods in *State of Siege*), he opted for polemics rather than objectivity to explore the abuse of power: casting stars as heroes, depicting governmental figures as boorish, shifty and self-serving, and structuring his stories as mysteries and thrillers, he aimed to bring political cinema to the masses. The result is often contrived, even stridently simplistic, but with its rapid editing, gritty, almost documentary-style camerawork, and impressive crowd scenes showing chaotic or violent action, his finest work has an urgency and immediacy at times reminiscent of newsreel footage. Nor can one deny his readiness to face controversy: in *Missing*, his first American film, the canny use of the dead man's conservative father as an audience surrogate, slowly coming to recognise America's self-interested involvement in the coup, provoked a denial of any such allegations from the country's Secretary of State. More recently, however, Costa-Gavras' taste for emotionally manipulative melodrama has come to the fore, so that his later movies seem hackneyed, obvious and overwrought.

Costa-Gavras (Konstantinos Gavras) b. 1933 Greece. **Missing** USA 1981/ w Jack Lemmon, Sissy Spacek, John Shea, Melanie Mayron, Charles Cioffi, Richard Bradford. **Films include** *The Sleeping Car Murders*, 1965; *Z*, 1969; *The Confession*, 1970; *State of Siege*, 1973; *Hannah K*, 1983; *Betrayed*, 1988; *The Music Box*, 1989; *Mad City*, 1998. **See also** EISENSTEIN, GÜNEY, PONTECORVO, ROSI, SAYLES, STONE

DAVID CRONENBERG

An exploded television, hitherto both agent and receptacle of the hallunicatory sadistic and erotic fantasies of a TV executive keen to give his public unprecedentedly sensational programmes, spews forth seemingly human entrails and gore. Cronenberg's often shockingly innovative horror and sci-fi movies explore the outer limits of human experience, focusing on the way technology and obsession might transform our psychology and anatomy. Here, as James Woods becomes almost psychotically fascinated by a masochistic lover and by transgressive imagery, not only does he 'imagine' (the film makes no distinction between reality and fantasy) the woman and himself as participants in cruelly erotic broadcasts, but his hand turns into a gun and his stomach develops a vagina-like fissure into which videocassettes are inserted to programme his increasingly violent behaviour. Cronenberg's work is seldom very coherent, let alone plausible, in hypothesising about human evolution, but the best is imbued with a cool, nightmarish logic, based on the premise that as technology develops, new diseases, desires, even a new flesh, will arise. *Shivers* and *Rabid* concern epidemics of deadly promiscuity, *Scanners* the risks of telepathic experimentation; *The Fly* is a dark fable about AIDS, *Dead Ringers* a metaphorical study of a precariously symbiotic relationship betweeen identical twins, and *Crash* (his most lucid, controlled film) considers the social, sexual and psychological side-effects of our fetishistic obsession with the car. Cerebral, visceral and subversive, his work remains in the vanguard of modern horror.

David Cronenberg b. 1943 Canada. **Videodrome** Canada 1982/ w James Woods, Deborah Harry, Sonja Smits, Peter Dvorsky, Les Carlson, Jack Creley. **Films include** *Shivers*, 1975; *Rabid*, 1976; *Scanners*, 1980; *The Fly*, 1986; *Dead Ringers*, 1988; *Naked Lunch*, 1991; *Crash*, 1996; *eXistenZ*, 1999. **See also** ARNOLD, BAVA, BROWNING, CARPENTER, FISHER, ROMERO

Would you trust Cary Grant? Neither former wife Katharine Hepburn (about to remarry, this time to a more stolidly reliable man) nor reporter Jimmy Stewart, covering the society wedding but falling for Hepburn himself, appear to do so, and they're right: not only because Philip Barry's stage original has the Grant character manipulate all around him in a devious scheme to win back his ex, but because this is a Cukor movie. Sometimes dismissed as an expert adaptor of theatrical and literary material, Cukor in fact made theatricality – or, more precisely, performance and pretence – his abiding theme. Not only did a number of his films deal explicitly with the relationship between life and the art of 'acting' (*What Price Hollywood?*, *Sylvia Scarlett*, *A Double Life*, *Adam's Rib*, *A Star Is Born*), but his char- acters are seldom what they seem: here, both Hepburn's 'ice-queen' facade and Stewart's anti-bourgeois hatred are discovered to be as unreal as Hepburn's upper-class complacency in *Holiday*, a Fascist's heroic reputation in *Keeper of the Flame*, Charles Boyer's love in *Gaslight*, or Judy Holliday's dumbness in *Born Yesterday*. Stylistically, the films are defined by their unshowy sophistication, with the discreetly fluid camera focused firmly on the dazzling performances; he was particularly adept with and sympathetic to actresses, and made numerous films with women centre-stage (*The Women*, especially, is a superb ensemble piece, and a marvellous example of his interest in role-playing, deceit and delusion). Fittingly, the secret of Cukor's eminently civilised artistry lies in its deceptive ease.

George Cukor b. 1899 USA, d. 1983 USA. **The Philadelphia Story** USA 1940/ w Katharine Hepburn, Cary Grant, James Stewart, Ruth Hussey, Roland Young, Virginia Weidler. **Films include** *What Price Hollywood?*, 1932; *David Copperfield*, 1934; *Sylvia Scarlett*, 1936; *Holiday*, 1938; *The Women*, 1939; *Keeper of the Flame*, 1942; *Gaslight*, 1944; *Adam's Rib*, 1949; *Born Yesterday*, 1950; *A Star Is Born*, 1954; *Les Girls*, 1957; *My Fair Lady*, 1964. **See also** CASSAVETES, HAWKS, KAZAN, RENOIR, RIVETTE, WELLES

MICHAEL CURTIZ

The moment is pure Hollywood melodrama: waitress-turned-wealthy restaurateur Mildred (Joan Crawford, an icon of female strength, determination and suffering), who for years slaved to give her daughter a better life, finds the ungrateful girl *in flagrante* with her own heel of a second husband. Both the expert lighting and the film's narrative structure (a long flashback revealing how decent, self-sacrificing Mildred came to be arrested for murder) are typically *noir*, but the Hungarian-born Curtiz was always a *dilettante* stylist specialising in glossy escapism (just look at those outfits and the size of the room!); this particular example – a cleaned-up version of James M Cain's novel – was as much perversely reassuring 'woman's weepie' as dark crime drama. Given Curtiz's versatility and somewhat anonymous romanticism, it would have been as representative to show a still from such hack works (in the best sense of the term) as *The Mystery of the Wax Museum, The Adventures of Robin Hood, Angels with Dirty Faces, The Sea Wolf, Yankee Doodle Dandy* or *Casablanca*; neither a common theme nor a consistent style exists to confirm him as an *auteur*, yet his solid craftsmanship and an ability to elicit, if not the best, then the 'starriest' performances from his actors made him a superior purveyor of polished hokum. Crawford, Cagney, Bogart and other Warners actors (memorably Errol Flynn) flourished, at least at the box-office, in his uncomplicatedly heroic world, and later, when age rendered their glamour more problematic, Curtiz's output declined into dull biopics and the bland *White Christmas*.

Michael Curtiz (Mihaly Kertesz) b. 1888 Hungary, d. 1962 USA. **Mildred Pierce** USA 1945/ w Joan Crawford, Zachary Scott, Jack Carson, Ann Blyth, Eve Arden, Bruce Bennett. **Films include** *The Mystery of the Wax Museum*, 1933; *Captain Blood,* 1935; *The Adventures of Robin Hood, Angels with Dirty Faces*, 1938; *Dodge City*, 1939; *The Sea Wolf*, 1941; *Yankee Doodle Dandy*, 1942; *Casablanca*, 1943; *White Christmas*, 1954. **See also** ARZNER, DIETERLE, DWAN, HUSTON, SCOTT, WELLMAN

At a smalltown screening of Disney's *Snow White*, boozy, brawling, gleefully malicious killer-monsters – the offspring, ironically, of a coy, cute furry creature given as a Christmas present to a young boy – loudly voice derision and disgust at the wholesome sentimentality before them. Starting like a rosy suburban fantasy by Spielberg (who produced *Gremlins*), Dante's darkly comic sci-fi saga soon turns into an inferno of manic, gratuitous destruction, with the titular anti-heroes trashing the American Dream to the point of nightmare. Dante – the id to Spielberg's ego – is one of contemporary Hollywood's most engagingly erratic and anarchic filmmakers, who mercifully has never outgrown his love for the surreal cartoon chaos of Chuck Jones, the portentous but tacky sci-fi paranoia of the 50s, and the ironic,

imaginative B-movie sensibility of Corman, who gave Dante his start as a director. Though he himself now works to blockbuster budgets, Dante's work is notable less for its (superior) special effects than for his abiding affection for the cruel visual gag, the in-joke allusion to film-buff lore, and the sheer absurdity of Hollywood fantasy; the almost invariable result is ramshackle plotting, hit-and-miss humour, and some of the most inspired, energetic, even subversive moments in the modern mainstream. *Piranha* and *The Howling*, both scripted by John Sayles, intelligently parodied *Jaws* and werewolf movies, while *The 'burbs*, *Matinee* and *Small Soldiers* even manage to poke fun, in passing, at America's conformism and militarist ethos. His wily irreverence, however unfocused, is cherishable.

Joe Dante b. 1946 USA. **Gremlins** USA 1984/ w Zack Galligan, Hoyt Axton, Phoebe Cates, Frances Lee McCain, Polly Holliday, Dick Miller, Judge Reinhold. **Films include** *Piranha*, 1978; *The Howling*, 1980; *Explorers*, 1985; *The 'burbs*, 1988; *Gremlins 2: The New Batch*, 1990; *Matinee*, 1993; *Small Soldiers*, 1998. **See also** ARNOLD, CORMAN, DEMME, JONES, SAYLES, SPIELBERG

Prison inmates serve rough justice on an informer in their midst, forcing him into a steam press with blow-torches. This uncommonly stark, unsentimental display of violence in a 40s Hollywood film is characteristic of Dassin's work at its most controlled: social conscience drama meets low-key 'realism' in a prison drama less notable for its rather hackneyed humanist back-stories, outlining how desperately misguided actions (mostly to do with gratifying their loved ones) landed the various ordinary Joes in jail, than for its allegorical depiction of the institution as a Fascistic hell (the sadistic head guard even listens to Wagner). For a brief period in the late 40s, Dassin was at the forefront of Hollywood's efforts to produce its own (inevitably melodramatic) brand of neo-realism: location shooting, gritty grey camerawork, and a focus on working-class heroes were favoured in purportedly 'tell-it-like-it-is' tales of determinedly unglamorous lives such as *The Naked City*, *Thieves' Highway* and *Night and the City*, a seedily atmospheric, London-set *film noir* which stands alongside *Brute Force* as Dassin's finest movie. Thereafter, blacklisted as a communist, he worked in Europe, and following the stylish but shallow *Rififi*, collaborated with his Greek actress wife Melina Mercouri on a series of increasingly absurd, pretentious dramas, including *Never on Sunday*, *Topkapi* and – both risible updates of Greek tragedy – *Phaedra* and *A Dream of Passion*. The highpoint of his career was short-lived; the constraints of Hollywood's studio system seem to have reined in his flair for hysterical nonsense.

Jules Dassin b. 1911 USA. **Brute Force** USA 1947/ w Burt Lancaster, Hume Cronyn, Charles Bickford, Howard Duff, Sam Levene, Whit Bissell. **Films include** *The Naked City*, 1948; *Thieves' Highway*, 1949; *Night and the City*, 1950; *Rififi*, 1956; *Never on Sunday*, 1960; *Phaedra*, 1962; *Topkapi*, 1964; *A Dream of Passion*, 1978. **See also** ANDERSON, CIMINO, COSTA-GAVRAS, KAZAN, LOSEY

TERENCE DAVIES

A darkly beautiful tableau of family unity, crystallised forever as a memory; the parents are praying, probably, out of religious conviction, the children out of habitual duty and, perhaps, in the hope that the Virgin will deliver them from the cruel tyranny of their father. In charting the rituals of a painful childhood and early adulthood, Davies' autobiographical reminiscences are assembled not along traditional chronological lines but according to a deeper, personal, associative logic of emotional resonance. Slow dissolves, changes in lighting and elegantly gliding camera movements lead us through time and space as if in a dream; music and song, rather than dialogue, evoke a spirit of working-class solidarity and familial community; physical action erupting in a previously static composition makes

palpable man's capacity for anger and violence in a world defined by oppressive constraint. Davies is one of the most original, audacious talents of British cinema, eschewing both conventional 'realism' and generic fantasy in his quest for emotional truth; his narrative style and content may be subjective, but his material – loneliness and love, fear and desire, hope and despair, death – is universal. Few film-makers have matched his ability (or readiness) to confront pain or, indeed, to evoke the exquisite poignancy of transient joy; in the likewise autobiographical *The Long Day Closes*, quiet pleasure may be found in the play of light on a carpet, a radio show, the verbal sparring of neighbours or clouds passing over the moon. In short, Davies is a visionary, and one of the cinema's true poets.

Terence Davies b. 1945 England. **Distant Voices, Still Lives** GB 1986-88/ w Pete Postlethwaite, Freda Dowie, Angela Walsh, Dean Williams, Lorraine Ashbourne. **Films include** *The Terence Davies Trilogy (Children, Madonna and Child, Death and Transfiguration)*, 1976-83; *The Long Day Closes*, 1992; *The Neon Bible*, 1995. **See also** ANGELOPOULOS, BERGMAN, BRESSON, DEMY, ERICE, HOU, MALICK

Forget the fact that he made, in his early years, some relatively sophisticated marital comedies and, later, decent if unremarkable westerns; think of DeMille, and the epic springs to mind. Forget, too, that *The Sign of the Cross*, about Christians persecuted in Nero's Rome, is typically full of banal pieties about tolerance, faith and evil (a prologue was added in 1944, crassly forging a parallel between Imperial Rome and that of Mussolini). Most immediately striking about DeMille's historical extravaganzas is not the pretension to spiritual probity but the gleeful depiction of the corruption and lascivious decadence they purport to condemn: here, with Roman prefect Fredric March clutching a scantily clad woman histrionically on the brink of ecstasy, our eyes are drawn, inevitably, not to the Christian maid in disapprovingly virginal white, but to the bare flesh of the bejewelled, woozily orgiastic extras, to the palpably exotic physicality of the tableau. One of cinema's great showmen, DeMille clearly regarded history as bunk, an opportunity for indulging in the alluring spectacle of erotic abandon even as he appealed to his audience's puritan instincts by bemoaning moral bankruptcy; this film is still more famous for its scene of Poppaea (Claudette Colbert) bathing in asses' milk, while even *The King of Kings*, a life of Christ, kicks off with an orgy at Mary Magdalen's place. Excess, behavioural and visual, is the keynote to his best-known work; the lurid pageantry is often absurdly watchable, but the historical and moral simplifications, coupled with wooden acting, frequently make for dramatic tedium.

Cecil Blount DeMille b. 1881 USA, d. 1959 USA. **The Sign of the Cross** USA 1932/ w Fredric March, Elissa Landi, Charles Laughton, Claudette Colbert, Ian Keith, Vivian Tobin. **Films include** *Joan the Woman*, 1917; *Male and Female*, 1919; *The King of Kings*, 1927; *Madam Satan*, 1931; *The Plainsman*, 1936; *Cleopatra*, 1934; *Union Pacific*, 1939; *Reap the Wild Wind*, 1942; *Samson and Delilah*, 1949; *The Ten Commandments*, 1956. **See also** ANGER, GRIFFITH, LEAN, LUCAS, MEYER, SPIELBERG, VISCONTI, WARHOL

Housewife Mary Steenburgen gets her moment of fame, displaying her none too remarkable tapdancing skills in a faintly ludicrous costume on a TV talent-contest show. A funny moment, but in Demme's sympathetic hands, the scene is unusually free of patronising condescension or cruelty: in his finest work, his genuine affection and respect for 'ordinary' people and their aspirations is immediately evident, so that the audience really roots for Steenburgen's milkman husband (Paul Le Mat) – left a fortune by reclusive millionaire Howard Hughes but denied it by unbelieving lawyers – however absurd or mundane his dreams of fame, wealth and success. Graduating from exploitation pictures made for Corman, Demme hit his stride with a series of gentle, populist comedies about working-class life (*Handle with*

Care, *Swing Shift*), quirky celebrations of eccentricity, community and friendship in which the humour derived from character rather than one-liners or pratfalls; even in the darker *Something Wild* and *Married to the Mob*, suspense was balanced by an acknowledgement that psychotics and Mafia wives have recognisably human emotions and by an amused interest in kitschy costume and decor. While his more recent features – *The Silence of the Lambs*, *Philadelphia*, *Beloved* – may be more closely aligned to mainstream genres and more upfront in their 'progressive' treatment of serious issues (feminism and violence, AIDS and homophobia, slavery and racism), Demme's fundamental humanism, embodied in a subtly stylish, slightly old-fashioned, unassertive brand of direction, remains intact.

Jonathan Demme b. 1944 USA. **Melvin and Howard** USA 1980/ w Paul Le Mat, Mary Steenburgen, Jason Robards, Elizabeth Cheshire, Chip Taylor, Gloria Grahame. **Films include** *Caged Heat*, 1974; *Handle With Care (Citizens Band)*, 1977; *Swing Shift*, 1984; *Something Wild*, 1986; *Married to the Mob*, 1988; *The Silence of the Lambs*, 1990; *Philadelphia*, 1993; *Beloved*, 1998. **See also** BECKER, HAWKS, RENOIR, SAYLES, STILLMAN

JACQUES DEMY

A young girl (Catherine Deneuve) is comforted by her mother, who is unaware that her fainting fit is due to pregnancy. Normally, the story of an unmarried mother pushed into an unwanted marriage after her lover is sent to the Algerian War would be seen as the stuff of dour social realism or feverish melodrama, but in Demy's confident hands it became the basis for a ravishing, pastel-hued fairy-tale in which all the dialogue was sung to music by Michel Legrand. Using long fluid takes and careful colour-coding, Demy transformed the drab port of Cherbourg into a vibrant, enchanted dreamworld of poignant romance, just as he did with Nantes, Nice and Rochefort in *Lola*, *La Baie des Anges* and *The Young Ladies of Rochefort*. (For this last, even though he shot, as usual, on location, by way of tribute to the Hollywood musical he cast Gene Kelly and added dance.) Demy's fables focus on the transient joys, cruel disappointments and enduring memories of love; chance and coincidence dog the lives of his protagonists, whose pasts and futures are often mirrored by subsidiary characters. (Indeed, some of his films make passing reference to or include characters from earlier works.) Notwithstanding the air of romantic fantasy, the films eschew easy sentimentality: when at last the well-off adult Deneuve meets up again with her former sweetheart, working in an Esso garage and also married, while they're awkwardly aware of how fate cheated them, they both realise they are content with their respective lots. No other film-maker has depicted the banal realities of modern life so elegantly, imaginatively or tenderly.

Jacques Demy b. 1931 France, d. 1990 France. **The Umbrellas of Cherbourg** France 1964/ w Catherine Deneuve, Nino Castelnuovo, Anne Vernon, Marc Michel, Ellen Farner. **Films include** *Lola*, 1960; *La Baie des Anges*, 1962; *The Young Ladies of Rochefort*, 1967; *Model Shop*, 1969; *Peau d'Ane*, 1970; *The Pied Piper*, 1972; *Une Chambre en Ville*, 1982; *Parking*, 1985; *Trois Places pour le 26*, 1988. **See also** COCTEAU, DAVIES, DONEN, LUHRMANN, MINNELLI, OPHÜLS, VON STERNBERG, VIGO

The shot of a vicious hoodlum with a deadly weapon is instantly familiar from countless gangster movies; hardly surprising given not only that De Palma's film is a needlessly extenuated, updated remake of Hawks' gangster classic, but that the director has made an entire career of imitating earlier movies, most notably, with *Sisters, Obsession, Dressed to Kill, Blow Out, Body Double* and *Raising Cain*, those of his idol Hitchcock. Like Hitch, De Palma is famed for his elegant camera movements, shock cutting, use of lurid colour (especially red), and meticulously staged set-pieces of violent action – in short, technique – but unlike the master he lacks originality and ideas. *Scarface* replaces the original's subtlety and wit with swaggering, histrionic excess as it charts Pacino's rise from ruthless henchman to drug-demented gang boss: what sticks in the mind is not any intriguing development in the protagonist but piles of white cocaine, bloody carnage, torture by chainsaw. There is a cold, clinical misanthropy (and, indeed, misogyny) to much of De Palma's work, evident in his readiness to subordinate his thinly drawn characters to flashy visual effect. Though formally experimental early films like *Greetings, Hi Mom!, Phantom of the Paradise* and *Sisters* suggested he was a restless, erratic talent, after the success of the gruesome shocker *Carrie* his work soon declined into hollow mannerism. The concern with style for style's sake has produced some of the glossiest, most lazily hand-me-down nonsense to emerge from Hollywood in recent years, undermining his reputation as an 'important' film-maker.

Brian De Palma b. 1940 USA. **Scarface** USA 1983/ w Al Pacino, Steven Bauer, Michelle Pfeiffer, Mary Elizabeth Mastrantonio, Robert Loggia, Harris Yulin. **Films include** *Hi Mom!*, 1970; *Sisters*, 1972; *Phantom of the Paradise*, 1974; *Carrie*, 1976; *Dressed to Kill*, 1980; *Blow Out*, 1981; *The Untouchables*, 1987; *Casualties of War*, 1989; *Raising Cain*, 1992; *Carlito's Way*, 1993; *Snake Eyes*, 1998. See also Cameron, Godard, Hitchcock, Spielberg, Stone, Tarantino

VITTORIO DE SICA

An unemployed man, his face a picture of shame and confusion, is caught and castigated by a crowd of men for stealing a bicycle; the cruel irony is that he was driven to the act by despair after the theft of his own bicycle, crucial to his newly obtained bill-posting job. De Sica's film is characteristic of the Italian neo-realist movement of the 40s, with its use of non-professional actors, in having been shot on real Roman locations, and with its simple story – depicting the search by the man and his young son for the stolen bike – inspired by the postwar plight of Italy's impoverished working-class. The concept of 'realism', however, is modified not only by the schematic, faintly contrived thrust of the narrative as it leads to the father's own sudden resort to theft, but by former matinee idol De Sica's

somewhat sentimental use of the cherubic boy to bear innocent witness to, and ensure our sympathies for, the man's predicament; indeed, he also made use of a child's perspective in *The Children Are Watching Us* (in which a woman's adultery leads to her husband's suicide) and in *Shoeshine* (about boyhood innocence eroded by the black market and reformatory life), while *Umberto D*, about a poverty-stricken old man, was arguably his darkest study of a lonely, broken spirit. Neo-realism's heyday, however, was short-lived, and by the late 50s De Sica, who had already adopted cloying, whimsical fantasy to treat the plight of the homeless in *Miracle in Milan*, seemed already to have lost any real sense of purpose, and was churning out undistinguished, utterly conventional farces and melodramas.

Vittorio De Sica b. 1902 Italy, d. 1974 France. **Bicycle Thieves** Italy 1948/ w Lamberto Maggioranni, Enzo Staiola, Lianella Carell, Gino Saltamerenda, Vittorio Antonucci. **Films include** *The Children Are Watching Us*, 1943; *Shoeshine*, 1946; *Miracle in Milan*, 1951; *Umberto D*, 1952; *Gold of Naples*, 1954; *Two Women*, 1961; *The Garden of the Finzi-Continis*, 1970. **See also** DASSIN, LOACH, PASOLINI, ROSSELLINI, TAVIANI BROTHERS

In a shimmering, silvery forest glade, the beautiful Titania (Anita Louise) gazes lovingly at Bottom (Jimmy Cagney), his head changed to that of an ass by the mischievous Puck, who has also cast a spell over the fairy queen's eyes; the scene is comic but magical, luminously shot by Hal Mohr. Though this unlikely Warner Bros adaptation is rightly co-credited to German theatre producer Max Reinhardt, for whom Dieterle had once worked as an actor, and though the director's filmography includes memorably dull biopics (Zola, Pasteur, Juarez and the discoverer of a cure for syphilis) his finest work reveals a flair for romanticism. The supernatural scenes in the Shakespeare film are light, lyrical and, thanks to Anton Grot's lavish art direction and vivid performances from an eccentric cast (Mickey Rooney as Puck, Joe E Brown as Flute, and an infant Kenneth Anger as the Changeling), charmingly fantastic. Similarly enthralling were a truly epic *The Hunchback of Notre Dame*, the expressionist Faustian fable *All That Money Can Buy* and two swooning romantic melodramas about the transcendent power of love, *Love Letters* and *Portrait of Jennie*; in each, Dieterle's emotional commitment and keen visual sense were successfully brought to bear on material which in clumsier hands might have seemed pretentious or nonsensical. Less typical but equally fine was *The Last Flight*, a dark, insightful study of the brittle devil-may-care romantic illusions of fliers in Paris after the Great War. Though a minor, erratic talent, Dieterle is deserving of more serious critical attention than he has so far received.

William (Wilhelm) Dieterle b. 1893 Germany, d. 1972 Germany. **A Midsummer Night's Dream** USA 1935/ w James Cagney, Dick Powell, Joe E Brown, Anita Louise, Victor Jory, Olivia de Havilland. **Films include** *The Last Flight*, 1931; *Fog Over Frisco*, 1934; *The Hunchback of Notre Dame*, 1940; *All That Money Can Buy*, 1941; *Syncopation*, 1942; *Love Letters*, 1945; *Portrait of Jennie*, 1949. **See also** ANGER, BORZAGE, CURTIZ, LAUGHTON, POWELL, RUDOLPH

WALT DISNEY

A wholesome, happy heroine has set up home with seven deftly stereotyped dwarfs: the cute, cosy, squeaky-clean domesticity of Disney's first feature (a travesty, like many of his adaptations, of the original tale) typifies his innovative technical sophistication – see the palpably solid, beautifully textured wood of the bed and roof timbers – and his reduction of the world to kitschy, childlike fantasy. Though he himself seldom directed the cartoons that emerged from what would become a huge entertainment empire, his naive, idealised, conservative vision was present in every frame. (The idea that Snow White might inadvertently celebrate polygamy would have been anathema to the proud purveyor of harmless fun for kids of every age.) The prettifying skills of his animators and writers cannot conceal his fundamentally lowbrow, banal, paternalistic notion of film art. Though his films used expressionist imagery to convey terror, from his Mickey Mouse shorts onwards they depicted the world as a sanitised correlative to WASP suburbia, with its magically soaring castles, rickety artisans' cottages and bucolic landscapes populated by winsome heroines, vapid, square-jawed heroes, cuddly anthropo-morphic fauna, and simplistically evil villains over whom good invariably triumphs. A stab at high culture with *Fantasia* largely resulted in saccharine 'illustrations' of classical music favourites, and Disney, pained by its failure, returned to more populist fables: the escapist formula has remained virtually unchanged at his studio ever since. His influence remains profound, on Hollywood film-making and on family entertainment worldwide.

Walt Disney b. 1901 USA, d. 1966 USA. **Snow White and the Seven Dwarfs** USA 1937. **Films include** *Steamboat Willie*, 1928; *Pinocchio, Fantasia*, 1940; *Dumbo*, 1941; *Bambi*, 1942; *Lady and the Tramp*, 1955; *Sleeping Beauty*, 1958; *Mary Poppins*, 1965; *The Jungle Book*, 1967. **See also** AVERY, FLEISCHER, JONES, MCCAY, PARK, SPIELBERG, STAREWICZ

STANLEY DONEN AND GENE KELLY

The luscious legs of temptress Cyd Charisse, the brooding erotic colours and expressionist shadows, and Kelly's heart-on-his-sleeve transparency of emotion are characteristic of Donen and Kelly's classic musical, a knowing, affectionately parodic comedy set in the Flapper Era when Hollywood made its awkward transition from silents to talkies. Together, Donen and Kelly directed some of the wittiest, most stylish and energetic musicals to emerge from MGM. Donen's elegant visual flair (his fluid camera was equally at home, as here, with studio artifice as with real locations, memorably and innovatively used in *On the Town*) was the perfect accompaniment to Kelly's dynamically balletic choreography; here in the 'Broadway Melody' ballet sequence, colour, composition, camera movement, music

and dance are as expressive of emotion as are the dialogue and cheerfully upfront performances in the more conventional narrative scenes. (Equally remarkable, as a portrait of carefree self absorption, was the deservedly famous number in which Donen's crane-shots follow Kelly splashing around a rain-soaked studio street to the strains of the film's title song.) Outside of their collaborations the pair's directing achievements were variable: Donen made several superior musicals (*Seven Brides for Seven Brothers*, *The Pajama Game* and, best of all, *Funny Face*) before proceeding to light, forgettable thrillers and comedies, while Kelly's only film of note was the ambitious but pretentious all-ballet triptych *Invitation to the Dance*. The joint offerings, however, exude brio, style, and intelligent, appealing optimism.

Stanley Donen b. 1924 USA **Gene Kelly** b. 1912 USA, d. 1996 USA. **Singin' in the Rain** USA 1952/ w Gene Kelly, Donald O'Connor, Debbie Reynolds, Jean Hagen, Cyd Charisse, Millard Mitchell. **Films include** *On the Town*, 1949; *Royal Wedding* (Donen), 1951; *Seven Brides for Seven Brothers* (Donen), 1954; *It's Always Fair Weather*, 1955; *Invitation to the Dance* (Kelly), 1956; *Funny Face* (Donen), *The Pajama Game* (Donen), 1957; *Damn Yankees* (Donen), 1958; *Charade* (Donen), 1963; *Hello, Dolly!* (Kelly), 1969. **See also** BERKELEY, DEMY, LUHRMANN, MAMOULIAN, MINNELLI

ALEXANDER DOVZHENKO

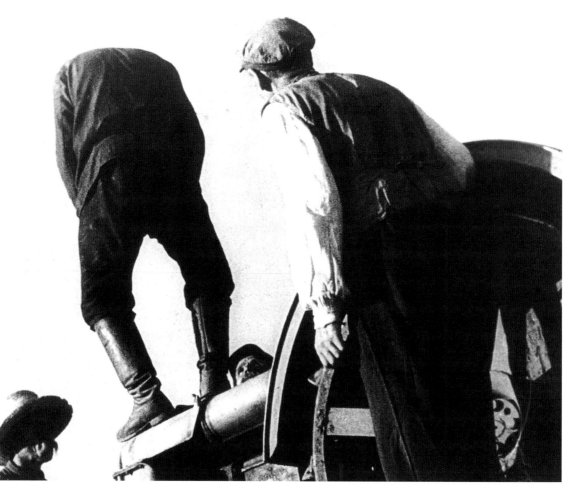

Delighted with their new tractor, Ukrainian peasants replenish its overheated radiator by urinating into it. Though Dovzhenko's film charts hostility between peasants and reactionary kulaks as the former collectivise their farms, it offers a far more poetic account of political strife than the propaganda of Soviet directors like Eisenstein, Vertov or Pudovkin. The slight story is essentially a framework for a celebration of village life and the peasants' age-old attachment to the land; the images are either static, as in the opening shots of a grandfather dying happily surrounded by ripe apples, or dynamically choreographed, as when the young farmer leading the collective dances drunkenly homewards, only to be shot by kulaks. Either way, Dovzhenko's painterly eye produces compositions of radiant pastoral beauty:

fields of grain sway under enormous, lowering skies, lovers sit staring at a brilliant moon, a coffin is borne past trees and sunflowers in bloom, symbolising the endless cycle of life and death. Just as his lyrical hymns to nature suggest an almost pantheistic attitude to life (in *Arsenal*, a horse being abused by its owner responds by explaining that it's not him but the Czar he should be beating), so Dovzhenko's experimental approach to narrative was sometimes so eccentric and intricate as to defy easy analysis; the elliptical tales within tales of *Zvenigora*, for example, mix realism and fantasy, past and present, comedy and drama, legend and history. At the same time, the robust sensuality of his imagery and his evident love of the Ukraine ensure that his idiosyncratic cinematic poetry remains moving and memorable.

Alexander Dovzhenko b. 1894 Ukraine, d. 1956 USSR. **Earth** USSR 1930/ w Semyon Svashenko, Stepan Shkurat, Mikola Nademsky, Yelena Maximova, Piotr Masokha. **Films include** *Zvenigora*, 1928; *Arsenal*, 1929; *Ivan*, 1932; *Aerograd*, 1935; *Shchors*, 1939; *Michurin*, 1948. **See also** EISENSTEIN, KIAROSTAMI, PARADZHANOV, TARKOVSKY, TAVIANI BROTHERS, VERTOV

The beauty of this image from Dreyer's extraordinary film lies in its tranquil simplicity: the luminous white of the room and the dead woman contrasted with the black coffin and clothes of her mourners. The scene precedes one of cinema's most devastatingly moving moments, when the woman's brother-in-law, whose eccentric behaviour and religious utterances have ensured that he's viewed by his family as demented, enters and brings about, through faith and love, her resurrection. Eschewing melodrama, special effects and rational explanation, Dreyer simply observes the miracle, and so renders it convincing. Though often characterised as a gloomy Dane preoccupied with spiritual matters, he made his subject the realm of human emotions: doubt, disenchantment, jealousy and, above all, love. If his

narratives, often assembled from long takes, were slow and his visual style spare, his method was the calm contemplation of gestures and faces; in *The Passion of Joan of Arc*, the girl's all-too-human suffering and her tormentors' cruelty are made intensely clear in a symphonic array of close-ups. Dreyer's pared-down style takes him beyond surface realism to something more mysterious and abstract: sounds or shadows (as in the truly eerie *Vampyr*) evoke the presence of unseen beings, landscape and architecture are invested, by lighting, design and composition, with supernatural force. Paradoxically, by rejecting anything superfluous to his purposes, this undisputed master of the cinema created some of its richest, most affecting and wondrously beautiful studies of the human condition.

Carl Theodor Dreyer b. 1889 Denmark, d. 1968 Denmark. **Ordet (The Word)** Denmark 1954/ w Henrik Malberg, Emil Hass Christensen, Birgitte Federspiel, Preben Lerdorff Rye. **Films include** *Leaves from Satan's Book*, 1919; *The Parson's Widow*, 1920; *Mikael*, 1924; *Master of the House*, 1925; *The Passion of Joan of Arc*, 1927; *Vampyr*, 1932; *Day of Wrath*, 1943; *Gertrud*, 1964. **See also** BERGMAN, BRESSON, GODARD, KIESLOWSKI, SJÖSTRÖM, OZU

ALLAN DWAN

Can Robin ever have seemed quite so merry, so uncomplicatedly optimistic a champion of the poor against feudal villainy as here, embodied by the unbridled athletic vigour of Douglas Fairbanks? True, that characterisation is primarily due to the actor-producer, and it would be absurd to argue *auteur* status for Dwan, whose several hundred films (if we include the one- and two-reel silents he made as one of Hollywood's most prolific pioneers) ranged from grade-A spectacles to Poverty Row chores. But there is something admirably lucid and robust about Dwan's best work: a joy in simple storytelling through visual means, evident in his imaginative deployment of Fairbanks' energetic prowess around the impressively massive sets and huge crowds of *Robin Hood*. Where possible, he favoured a mobile camera (indeed, he reputedly advised Griffith on how to mount the moving camera for the Babylonian sequences of *Intolerance*), though in later years his resources were often limited. He was adept with light, lively farce (*Up in Mabel's Room, Brewster's Millions*) and muscular action (*Sands of Iwo Jima*), and towards the end of his career worked very respectably in the western genre: *Cattle Queen of Montana* made lyrical use of mountain vistas, while the impressively taut *Silver Lode* was an intelligent, credible allegory that succeeded as a damning attack on the McCarthy witch-hunts. Dwan's talents may have been as modest as most of his budgets, but there is joy to be had from the infectious boyish delight he took in a good yarn, a decent cast, and dramatic sets and landscapes.

Allan Dwan b. 1885 Canada, d. 1981 USA. **Robin Hood** USA 1922/ w Douglas Fairbanks, Wallace Beery, Enid Bennett, Sam De Grasse, Alan Hale, Paul Dickey. **Films include** *Manhandled*, 1924; *The Iron Mask*, 1929; *Heidi*, 1937; *Suez*, 1938; *Up in Mabel's Room*, 1944; *Brewster's Millions*, 1945; *Driftwood*, 1947; *Sands of Iwo Jima*, 1949; *Silver Lode, Cattle Queen of Montana*, 1954; *Tennessee's Partner*, 1955; *Slightly Scarlet*, 1956. **See also** CURTIZ, GRIFFITH, LEWIS, WALSH, WELLMAN

The image is at once mythic and anti-mythic, simple yet resonant. It merely shows two ageing gunmen – driven to embark on a bounty mission by poverty, friendship and, more or less incidentally, a sense of injustice at a man being allowed to go almost unpunished after mutilating a whore – and a young upstart who hopes to make his name as a fearsome killer. The scene is typical of Eastwood's best work as director in that it both evokes and interrogates his starry status as a classic hero; here, his resolve and abilities as a gunmen are seen to be fading with age. Initially famous for acting (in an inimitably restrained style) in westerns and rogue-cop thrillers, Eastwood has steadily extended his range not only as a performer but as a director, refining genre conventions in work like *The Outlaw Josey Wales*, *Unforgiven* and *A Perfect World*, and virtually abandoning them altogether in *Honkytonk Man*, *Bird* and *White Hunter, Black Heart*, in which he subordinates narrative drive to unfussy character study. There is an engaging directness to his visual style as he focuses on the essentials of people and place: he simply observes characters interacting with each other and the landscape through which they pass. Hence, in *The Bridges of Madison County* (the best 'weepie' of recent times) a climactic scene in which Meryl Streep tells her lover that she cannot leave her family is shot in a long static take, while *Midnight in the Garden of Good and Evil* is notably less concerned with solving a murder mystery than with celebrating the individuality of a city. Simplicity need not lack subtlety, and Eastwood's finest work is compassionate, rich in insights, and quietly adventurous.

Clint Eastwood b. 1930 USA. **Unforgiven** USA 1992/ w Eastwood, Morgan Freeman, Gene Hackman, Richard Harris, Jaimz Woolvett, Frances Fisher. **Films include** *Play Misty for Me*, 1971; *High Plains Drifter*, 1973; *The Outlaw Josey Wales*, 1976; *Bronco Billy*, 1980; *Honkytonk Man*, 1982; *Bird*, 1988; *White Hunter, Black Heart*, 1990; *A Perfect World*, 1992; *The Bridges of Madison County*, 1995; *Midnight in the Garden of Good and Evil*, 1997; *True Crime*, 1999. **See also** FORD, HAWKS, LEONE, ANTHONY MANN, SIEGEL

SERGEI EISENSTEIN

The Odessa Steps sequence, in which Tsarist soldiers massacre the proletariat during the failed revolution of 1905, is one of the best known in cinema; what sticks in the mind is less its content (Soviet propaganda, as in all Eisenstein's work) than its dynamic 'montage', the rapid editing together of brief images (shot from so many different perspectives that attempts to fathom the exact topography of the scene are futile) to convey the conflict in almost abstract terms: the relentless descent of the oppressors, the shocked faces of the oppressed, a baby's pram careering down the steps. Eisenstein's early work (*Strike*, *Potemkin*, *October*, *The General Line*) is marked by his fascination both with 'montage theory' (whereby meaning derives less from individual images than from the way they 'collide') and with the idea of creating a cinema of and for the masses, focused on group action rather than heroic individuals; non-actors were cast according to physical 'typage'. The result, while technically impressive and exhilarating in its speed and scale, is strangely uninvolving emotionally, while the use of metaphorical inserts (a peacock denoting Kerensky's pride in *October*) is jarringly banal. As if aware that his complicated theories could only take him so far (they've had little influence on later mainstream film-making practice), he turned to more conventional epic pageantry in *Alexander Nevsky* and *Ivan the Terrible*; again, the epic scale and expressionist compositions were eye-catching, but the operatically stylised acting, the ponderous pace and the heavily allegorical stories have not endured well.

Sergei Eisenstein b. Latvia 1898, d. USSR 1948. **Battleship Potemkin** USSR 1925/ w Alexander Antonov, Vladimir Barsky, Grigori Alexandrov, Mikhail Gomorov, Beatrice Vitoldi. **Films include** *Strike*, 1924; *October*, 1928; *The General Line*, 1929; *Alexander Nevsky*, 1938; *Ivan the Terrible (Parts 1 & 2)*,1944-46. **See also** DOVZHENKO, KOZINTSEV, VERTOV, VON STERNBERG

VICTOR ERICE

The painter Antonio López inspects and enjoys the exquisite aroma of the fruit he is painting, in slow, painstaking detail, in his garden in Madrid. A documentary about the working methods, daily life and idealistic aspirations of an artist trying to cope with the transience of the world (López is so meticulous that over the months the tree begins to droop before his canvas), the film is nonetheless characteristic of (and indeed reflects) Erice's style and concerns. His first two features, made ten years apart, were Freudian fictions shown from the perspective of a curious child bemused by the mysteries around her: *The Spirit of the Beehive*, set just after the Civil War, explores a girl's fears in relation to her fascination with Frankenstein's monster, while *The South*, set in the 50s, charts a daughter's

troubled relationship with a father mooning over a film-star ex-lover. Myth, the movies and Spain's history inflect these tales, but what distinguishes their telling is Erice's painterly use of the camera, his ability to capture a precise moment in time while showing how it resonates through memory and fantasy; in his measured, elliptical stories, a change in light or subtle shift in perspective, a slow dissolve or scenes rhymed with one another through colour or composition convey mood and meaning. The tone is quiet, tantalisingly poetic, but grounded in reality, so that *The Quince Tree Sun*, itself made almost ten years after *The South*, may be seen in part as a self-portrait of the artist as a perfectionist, trying against all odds to reproduce the world on his own cinematic canvas.

Victor Erice, b. 1940 Spain. **The Quince Tree Sun** Spain 1992/ w Antonio López, Maria Moreno, Enrique Gran, José Carrtero.
Films include *The Spirit of the Beehive*, 1973; *The South*, 1983. **See also** ANGELOPOULOS, BOTELHO, BUÑUEL, DAVIES, HOU, KIAROSTAMI, SAURA

RAINER WERNER FASSBINDER

The scene is sumptuous, sensual, blatantly 'staged'. An intensely claustrophobic study of an emotionally sado-masochistic triangle involving a fashion-designer, her slavish assistant and a young wife with whom the former embarks on an affair, Fassbinder's film is heartfelt yet profoundly ironic, theatrical but 'minimalist', perceptive and deliberately provocative. The prolific German's work was remarkable for its variety – he progressed from static, Straub-like understatement to garishly colour-coded, fluidly shot histrionics evocative of Sirk and Godard, while working in crime films, literary adaptation, melodrama, domestic drama, satire and movies that defy categorisation – but a constant theme was the erosion of personal happiness, freedom and love by the demands of society (especially those of Germany as it underwent its postwar economic revival). Foregrounding divisions of class, sex, race and politics, most of his films depict and analyse the tensions arising from greed, jealousy, prejudice and exploitation within a small group or community. The victims might be a foreign labourer (*Katzelmacher*), a shy fruitseller (*The Merchant of Four Seasons*), a widow and her Arab lover (*Fear Eats the Soul*), a noble's wife (*Effi Briest*) or a besotted town dignitary (*Lola*); whatever the milieu, Fassbinder's unsentimental sympathy for the down-trodden was balanced by an astute grasp of wider political issues. With a highly artificial style partly inspired by but clearly opposed to the reassuring clichés of American cinema, he was one of the most talented, original and important film-makers of the 70s.

Rainer Werner Fassbinder b. 1946 W Germany, d. 1982 W Germany. **The Bitter Tears of Petra von Kant** W Germany 1972/ w Margit Carstensen, Hanna Schygulla, Irm Hermann, Eva Mattes. **Films include** *Katzelmacher*, 1969; *The Merchant of Four Seasons*,1971; *Fear Eats the Soul, Martha*, 1973; *Effi Briest*, 1974; *Fox*, 1975; *Chinese Roulette*, 1976; *The Marriage of Maria Braun*, 1978; *In a Year with 13 Moons*, 1978; *Berlin Alexanderplatz*, 1980; *Lola, Veronika Voss*, 1981; *Querelle*, 1982. **See also** ALMODÓVAR, GODARD, KAURISMÄKI, SALLES, STRAUB, SIRK, VON STERNBERG

Film director Guido (Marcello Mastroianni), plagued by anxieties both about his ability to complete his next movie and about his relationships with his wife, mistress and colleagues, imagines himself menaced by an enormous, voluptuous woman. Fellini's semi-autobiographical account of the creative process is a typically extravagant affair, interweaving reality and fantasy with gleeful abandon, and simultaneously courting and attempting to forestall charges of indulgence as it traces Guido's progress through a world of grotesque caricatures born of his febrile imagination. Indulgent the film certainly was, like all but his earliest work, but it is impossible to deny his visual inventiveness, which time and again created strikingly strange images. Less impressive were his narrative sense – after the

sprawling epic satire of modern decadence in *La Dolce Vita*, his films degenerated into rambling, mostly inconsequential rag-bags made up of comic anecdote, facile metaphor, nostalgic reminiscence and flamboyant set-pieces – and his banal, sentimental vision, half sorrowing, half celebratory, of the world as a ludicrous freak-show. Always, at the film's core, one sensed the presence of Fellini himself, protesting both his confusion at life's chaotic absurdity and his affection for the voluble, larger-than-life fools on view. Whether it was the world he loved or simply the fruits of his very public fantasy is open to debate; whatever, while his work was extremely uneven, he evidently saw himself as a great artist, whereas a more accurate assessment might describe him as a magnificent showman.

Federico Fellini b. 1920 Italy, d. 1993 Italy. **8 1/2** Italy 1963/ w Marcello Mastroianni, Claudia Cardinale, Anouk Aimée, Sandra Milo, Rossella Falk, Guido Alberti. **Films include** *The White Sheik*, 1952; *I Vitelloni*, 1953; *La Strada*, 1954; *Nights of Cabiria*, 1956; *La Dolce Vita*, 1959; *Fellini-Satyricon,* 1969; *Fellini's Roma*, 1972; *Amarcord*, 1973; *Fellini's Casanova*, 1976; *And the Ship Sails On*, 1983; *Ginger and Fred*, 1985. **See also** ALLEN, GILLIAM, GREENAWAY, KUSTURICA, LUHRMANN, MORETTI, RUSSELL

LOUIS FEUILLADE

The fiancée of a journalist investigating murders and jewel-robberies committed by a mysterious masked gang – the Vampires – performs a ballet in a slinky, winged black bodysuit reminiscent of that occasionally worn by priestess of crime Irma Vep; in seconds, the dancer will collapse, poisoned by a ring given her by the gang's leader. A pioneer of popular serials about seductively ingenious master criminals threatening bourgeois society, Feuillade delighted in complex narratives featuring all manner of sinister devices: subterranean hideaways, secret passages, rooftop escapes, obscure codes, fiendishly cunning disguises and severed heads. Yet he shot his exterior scenes on the streets of Paris and the Riviera, so that realism and fantasy combine to create a surreal, dreamlike universe where the familiar is literally and convincingly invaded by the extraordinary. The result is some of the most mesmerisingly lyrical, wittily imaginative imagery in film, playing on our fear of, and fascination with, anarchy, adventure and the impossible. Though there are travelling shots involving car-chases towards the end of *Les Vampires*, Feuillade mostly filmed face-on in static medium- or long-shot; that he recorded unlikely events in a realist, almost documentary style only enhances their entrancing strangeness. Crucial to the films' plausibility is the atypically low-key naturalism of the performances: the sensually charismatic Musidora's furtive glances, discreet gestures and elegant movements ensured Irma Vep a lasting place in cinema history.

Louis Feuillade b. 1873 France, d. 1925 France. **Les Vampires** France 1915-16/ w Musidora, Edouard Mathé, Jean Aymé, Louis Leubas, Stacia Napierkowska. **Film serials include** *Bébé*, 1910-13; *Life As It Is*, 1911-1913; *Fantômas*, 1913-14; *Judex*, 1916; *Tih Minh, Vendemiaire*, 1918; *Barrabas*, 1919. **See also** BUÑUEL, FRANJU, LANG, LUMIÈRE, MÉLIÈS, RESNAIS, RIVETTE

Four friends prepare to spend the night within a pentacle as the climax of their battle against Satanism. Most notable about the image, perhaps, is its almost classical sense of balance: the juxtaposition of darkness and light, the square arrangement of characters, candles, cushion and occult paraphernalia countered by the chalk circle, the stark, ascetic emptiness of the library about to be invaded by all manner of temptations and terrors. Fisher, who worked for horror-specialists Hammer for most of his career, was notable for the narrative and visual restraint he brought to potentially sensationalist material. He tended mostly to avoid shock-cutting and close-ups, preferring to create an unsettling atmosphere through decor and brooding colours (he particularly favoured saturated blacks, blues and reds). Indeed, were it not for his visual insistence that Evil is often more seductively attractive than Good, his rather ponderous narratives might seem too pedantic and bloodless to produce frissons of fear. In film after film, the conflict between the forces of Light and Darkness is played out as a struggle of wills with rational expertise battling irrationality and the sensual appetite. Following in the English Gothic tradition, many of Fisher's (unconsciously) Freudian films are set in the Victorian era, so concerned with issues of life and death, restraint and abandon, propriety and sex, order and chaos. Fisher was never an adventurous, innovative or profound film-maker, but to a genre often considered disreputable, he brought welcome intelligence, sobriety and pictorial elegance.

Terence Fisher b. 1904 England, d. 1980 England. **The Devil Rides Out** GB 1968/ w Christopher Lee, Charles Gray, Nike Arrighi, Leon Greene, Patrick Mower. **Films include** *So Long at the Fair*, 1950; *The Curse of Frankenstein*, 1957; *Dracula*, 1958; *The Mummy, The Hound of the Baskervilles*, *The Stranglers of Bombay*, 1959; *The Curse of the Werewolf*, 1961; *Dracula, Prince of Darkness*, 1965; *Frankenstein Must Be Destroyed*, 1969. **See also** BAVA, BROWNING, CRONENBERG, POWELL, ROMERO, WHALE

ROBERT FLAHERTY

The lovable 'primitive', cheerful despite the icy hardships he has to face in his daily search for food and shelter, laughs at the intrusion of modern technology into his igloo. The image, from the first completed feature by the 'father of documentary', speaks not only of Flaherty's pioneering spirit as an explorer-turned-film-maker (he was among the first to recognise the exotic appeal of unfamiliar cultures for Western film-goers), but of his complex interactive relationship with the subjects of his films. Whether dealing with an Eskimo family in *Nanook*, Samoan rituals in *Moana*, a traditional Irish fishing community in *Man of Aran* or bayoux invaded by oil-drillers in *Louisiana Story*, Flaherty used prettily lyrical camerawork to paint, time and again, respectful but naively romantic portraits of the innocent

'noble savage'; not only did he prefer to visit pre-industrialised societies, but he would stage actions for the camera in an effort to reveal a more dramatic 'truth', persuading Nanook to wear more 'genuine' Eskimo costumes and to adopt a more picturesque method of seal-hunting, or getting Irishmen to brave tempestuous seas and fish for basking sharks, which they hadn't done for half a century. Politics and economics were conspicuously absent from Flaherty's determinedly poetic brand of ethnography, which focused on man's struggle against Nature and the Machine. As 'documentary', his films may be too manipulative and narrow in their concerns for modern tastes; as heartfelt hymns to partly imagined worlds, however, they can exude the engaging charm of Nanook's smile.

Robert Flaherty b. 1884 USA, d. 1951 USA. **Nanook of the North** USA 1922. **Films include** *Moana*, 1926; *Tabu*, 1931; *Man of Aran*, 1934; *Elephant Boy*, 1936; *The Land*, 1942; *Louisiana Story*, 1948. **See also** HERZOG, MARKER, MORRIS, PENNEBAKER, RIEFENSTAHL, SCHOEDSACK AND COOPER

MAX AND DAVE FLEISCHER

Betty Boop and her friends Koko the clown and Bimbo the dog are menaced by a wicked queen (recently transformed by her magic mirror into a dragon), a giant disembodied hand and a decidedly phallic-looking monstrosity. Initially, the Fleischers' work was more darkly mischievous and surreally fantastic than Disney's. Starting with the graphically inventive *Out of the Inkwell* series – in which Koko, living in a world explicitly acknowledged as a drawn figment of the animator's imagination rather than a reflection of reality, was repeatedly confounded by objects turning into something different – the brothers proceeded to their greatest invention, half-child, half-vamp Betty, whose adventures arose from her charmingly bizarre blend of innocence and flirtatious eroticism. The Fleischers' eccentric

characters were 'rubbery' and smoothly flexible in shape and movement (Max had patented the Rotoscope, whereby animated motion was traced from live-action footage of real people, most memorably jazz singer Cab Calloway in this film and *Minnie the Moocher*), while backgrounds, filmed on three-dimensional sets, were unusually detailed. But it was the taste for innuendo, the macabre and the grotesque that defined their best work; if eroticism was to the fore in the Boop films, the later *Popeye* series revelled in aggression and violence. As Disney's popularity grew, they softened and sweetened their stories and characters, with disappointing results; while their first feature, *Gulliver's Travels*, has several impressively animated sequences, a second, *Mr Bugs Goes to Town*, was a commercial and critical failure.

Max Fleischer b. 1883 Austria, d. 1972 USA. **Dave Fleischer** b. 1894 USA, d. 1979 USA. **Snow White** USA 1933. **Films include** *Out of the Inkwell*, 1915; *Dizzy Dishes and Barnacle Bill*, 1930; *Minnie the Moocher*, 1932; *Popeye the Sailor Meets Sinbad the Sailor*, 1936; *Popeye the Sailor Meets Ali Baba's Forty Thieves*, 1937; *Gulliver's Travels*, 1939; *Mr Bug Goes to Town, Superman*, 1941. **See also** AVERY, DISNEY, HANNA AND BARBERA, JONES, MCCAY, PARK, SVANKMAJER

Famously, Ford made westerns. And while he worked in other genres and others made westerns, this image is immediately identifiable as Fordian: the lonely homestead, the lonely riders, the lonely butte rising against a limpid sky in his beloved Monument Valley. It has a simple, mythic permanence: men isolated from society by their heroic status (the film charts John Wayne's long, obsessive search for a niece abducted by Indians), their determination as rock-solid as the harsh landscape which they – endangering their own pioneer ways – are helping to turn from a wilderness into a garden of civilisation. Ford's work, which as a whole constitutes a poetic, propagandist history of American progress, depicts a world of moral imperatives; even though *The Searchers* atypically hints that Wayne's quest to right wrongs may

be rooted in crazed, vengeful xenophobia, there is seldom any doubt about what a man's gotta do – defend the sanctity of home, family and the pioneer community from lawlessness and (native American) savagery, by any means necessary. Accordingly, in many of his films the heroes are shown as figures of destiny, those they protect (notably women) are sentimentalised, and tradition hallowed. Away from the West, in *How Green Was My Valley* or *The Quiet Man*, Ford's conservatism seemed maudlin fluff, but below the stark mesas of the Cavalry Trilogy, in the dusty townships of *My Darling Clementine* and *The Man Who Shot Liberty Valance*, or in the leafy Arcadia of *Young Mr Lincoln*, the nostalgic celebration of American courage, while naive and reactionary, often assumed a genuinely epic dimension.

John Ford b. 1895 USA, d. 1973 USA. **The Searchers** USA 1956/ w John Wayne, Jeffrey Hunter, Vera Miles, Ward Bond, Natalie Wood, Harry Carey Jr. **Films include** *The Iron Horse*, 1924; *Judge Priest*, 1934; *Stagecoach, Young Mr Lincoln*, 1939; *The Grapes of Wrath*, 1940; *My Darling Clementine*, 1946; *Fort Apache*, 1948; *She Wore a Yellow Ribbon*, 1949; *Rio Grande*, 1950; *The Sun Shines Bright*, 1953; *The Man Who Shot Liberty Valance*, 1962; *Seven Women*, 1966. **See also** BOETTICHER, EASTWOOD, HAWKS, LEONE, ANTHONY MANN, MILIUS

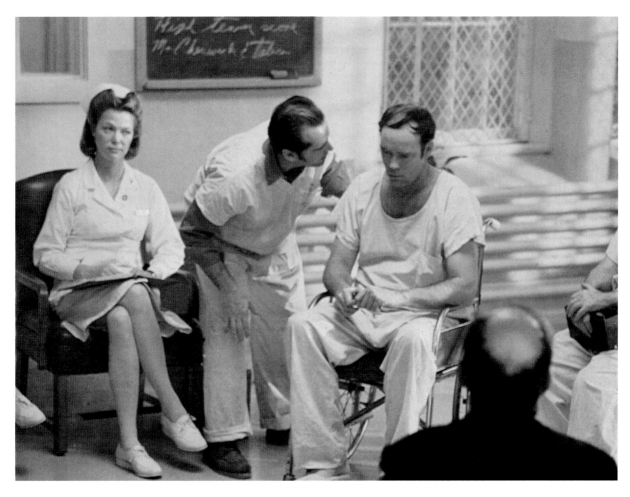

The scene is simple: in a mental hospital, nurse Louise Fletcher watches disapprovingly as unruly inmate Jack Nicholson flouts the rules by taking control of a group therapy session with his own rebellious brand of advice on how to become a happier individual. Perhaps most telling about the shot, in terms of style, are the angle and framing: the casual informality is more suggestive of documentary than of a polished Hollywood satirical drama. In his early films, particularly those made in his native Czechoslovakia (*A Blonde in Love*, *The Firemen's Ball*) where he often worked with non-professional actors, Forman told simple stories of ordinary people whose eccentricity gradually became apparent in scenes of group activity – a party, say – usually observed from a slight distance with a telephoto lens. The seemingly spontaneous 'candid camera'-style result was at once funny, warm, realistic and non-judgmental, so that any allegorical thrust (*The Firemen's Ball* is a satire on absurd social hierarchies, *Cuckoo's Nest* an attack on oppressive conformism) never looked contrived but seemed to arise naturally from the microcosm on view. Sadly, after the enormously successful (if at times emotionally manipulative) *Cuckoo's Nest*, which though acted by professionals elicited a memorably robust performance from Nicholson that matched the freshness of Forman's early work, the director opted for more conventional fare: slick adaptations of books and stage hits, and the bombastic *The People Vs Larry Flynt*, far less witty, perceptive and sympathetic than the subtle, ironic comedies with which he first made his name.

Milos Forman b. 1932 Czechoslovakia. **One Flew Over the Cuckoo's Nest** USA 1975/ w Jack Nicholson, Louise Fletcher, William Redfield, Will Sampson, Brad Dourif. **Films include** *Talent Competition*, 1963; *A Blonde in Love*, 1965; *The Firemen's Ball*, 1967; *Taking Off*, 1971; *Hair*, 1979; *Ragtime*, 1981; *Amadeus*, 1984; *Valmont*, 1989; *The People Vs Larry Flynt*, 1996. **See also** ALTMAN, ANDERSON, LEIGH, RENOIR, TRUFFAUT

GEORGES FRANJU

A young woman (Edith Scob), her flayed face concealed beneath a frozen mask of icy beauty, consorts with a fearsome guard-dog: she will loose the beast against her surgeon father who, wracked by guilt over a car-crash which left her scarred, has been trying to repair her face with flesh cut from kidnapped girls. Franju's 'horror thriller' is in fact a cool, elegant, profoundly poetic study of insanity and obsession in which normality is overturned: the doctor's cruel experiments and imprisonment of his daughter, his assistant's abduction of innocent girls, and Scob's setting the dog on her father are all acts born from devoted love. Few directors have used black and white so beautifully: darkness and light coexist as harmoniously in *Eyes Without a Face* as cruelty and compassion, or as the white doves that accompany Scob's final walk into the night, their gentle flutterings symbolising both her freedom and her madness. Franju, a former documentarist, was both an admirer of silent cinema (besides a film about Méliès, he also paid tribute to Feuillade with the nostalgic crime fantasy *Judex*), and a natural surrealist adept at juxtaposing images of violence and tenderness: *Le Sang des Bêtes* documents the workings of an abbatoir, *Hôtel des Invalides* intercuts shots of Napoleon's tomb and crippled war-veterans, *La Tête Contre les Murs* focuses on the ignorance of the doctors and a man who conspire in keeping the latter's delinquent son in an asylum. If sentimentality has no place in Franju's work, his awareness of humanity's hypocrisy and cruelty is admirably balanced by a sympathy for its victims.

Georges Franju b. 1912 France, d. 1987 France. **Eyes Without a Face (Les Yeux sans Visage)** France 1959/ w Pierre Brasseur, Alida Valli, Edith Scob, Juliette Mayniel. **Films include** *Le Sang des Bêtes*, 1949; *Hôtel des Invalides, Le Grand Méliès*, 1952; *La Tête Contre les Murs*, 1958; *Thérèse Desqueyroux*, 1962; *Judex*, 1963; *Thomas l'Imposteur*, 1965; *The Sin of Father Mouret*, 1970; *Shadowman*, 1973. **See also** BRESSON, BUÑUEL, COCTEAU, FEUILLADE, MÉLIÈS, VIGO

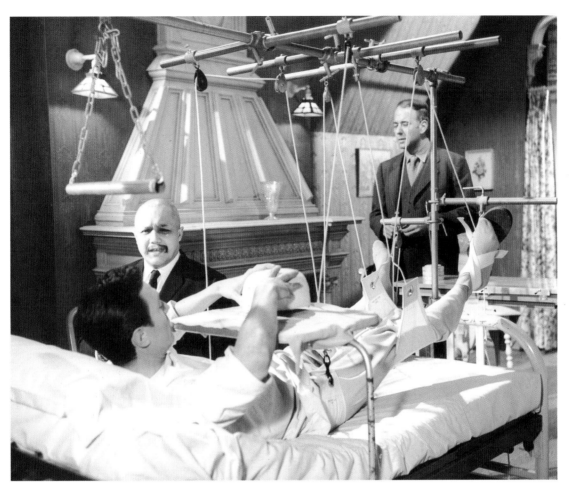

The composition is busy, baroque, beguiling: why are these weird-looking men speaking to this man in his weird contraption? There is in fact nothing wrong with his body – it is his mind that is sick, ever since the Communists brainwashed him during the Korean War, programming him to become a political assassin on his return to America. Frankenheimer's sadly prophetic conspiracy thriller-cum-political satire mirrors the web of intrigue that is its plot with unsettlingly rich and strange imagery; using frames within frames (TV screens and posters are everywhere) to supply a wealth of visual information, mixing 'realism' with grotesque caricature and alternating extreme close-up with long shot, quick zoom with static camera, Frankenheimer emphasises the complexity of a world in which technology, the media and political posturing ensure that appearances are invariably deceptive. Here and in his finest earlier films (*All Fall Down*, *The Birdman of Alcatraz*, *Seven Days in May*), Frankenheimer's restless visual style complemented the psychological subtlety of his precision-built stories; later, with less engaging material, it declined into florid, fashionable flashiness so that only the offbeat, patchily amusing crime spoof *99 and 44/100% Dead* and the gritty, harrowing *French Connection II* were of any real interest. Elsewhere, his work seemed so lazy, hysterical and pretentious that it hardly seemed credible he had once been considered one of America's most important film-makers; indeed, in retrospect, even his early films, however ambitious, audacious and inventive, now seem tainted by faddishness.

John Frankenheimer b. 1930 USA. **The Manchurian Candidate** USA 1962/ w Laurence Harvey, Frank Sinatra, Angela Lansbury, Janet Leigh, James Gregory. **Films include** *The Young Savages*, 1961; *All Fall Down*, *The Birdman of Alcatraz*, 1962; *Seven Days in May*, 1964; *Seconds, Grand Prix*, 1966; *I Walk the Line*, 1970; *99 and 44/100% Dead*, 1974; *French Connection II*, 1975; *52 Pick-Up*, 1986; *Ronin*, 1998. **See also** DE PALMA, KUBRICK, LUMET, PENN, STONE

SAMUEL FULLER

A prostitute, head shaven, naked except for shoes, skirt and bra, takes the cash she is owed from the pimp she has just knocked out – an attention-grabbing opening sequence typical of Fuller's punchy tabloid camera and cutting style. A former crime reporter, he envisaged his viscerally dynamic camerawork and hard-hitting stories in terms of cinematic headlines: here, as the woman beats the man, she flails at the camera (and, therefore, the audience itself). Fuller's B-movies, usually in the western, war and crime genres, chart conflict, internal and external with dazzling backing shots and rapid editing: characters are at war with each other and with themselves, so that heroism and cowardice, hatred and love, understanding and intolerance, self-interest and altruism vie for control. Moreover, much of his work is reminiscent of muck-raking exposé: when the prostitute starts life anew as a nurse in a seemingly decent small town, she finds corruption and hypocrisy – even her rich, respectable fiancé is, it transpires, a paedophile. Though seldom subtle, Fuller's films were dramatically powerful and, thanks to their dark ironies, complex in depicting America as a melting pot constantly boiling over into insane, violent aggression. In particular, few film-makers have been so brutally explicit about racial tensions; in his late masterpiece *White Dog*, about a dog trained to attack blacks, he foregrounded the very colour of skin as a visual and thematic motif to argue that racism is a product of conditioning. In short, Fuller's sensibility was inherently cinematic, and the meaning of his work is embodied in its raw confrontational style.

Samuel Fuller b. 1911 USA, d. 1996 USA. **The Naked Kiss** USA 1964/ w Constance Towers, Anthony Eisley, Michael Dante, Virginia Grey, Patsy Kelly. **Films include** *Fixed Bayonets*, 1951; *Park Row*, 1952; *Pickup on South Street*, 1953; *Run of the Arrow, Forty Guns*, 1957; *Verboten!*, 1958; *Underworld USA, Merrill's Maurauders*, 1961; *Shock Corridor*, 1963; *The Big Red One*, 1980; *White Dog*, 1982.
See also ALDRICH, GODARD, HOPPER, LEE, PARKER, NICHOLAS RAY, SCORSESE, SIEGEL, STONE

As Bonaparte's army invades Italy, Gance's epic homage to 'a man of destiny' (see the suitably visionary portrait of the aquiline Albert Dieudonné) reaches its climax, expanding into his innovatory 'Polyvision' to present a triptych as patriotic as the *Tricolore* flag. As hagiography, the film, for all its length and detail, is dramatically conventional, psychologically simplistic and politically suspect, celebrating Bonaparte's relentless rise to imperial power. Cinematically, however, it remains a triumph of audacious technique. The immediate impression is of scale: not just the image's width (only the film's final sequences are in Polyvision) but the number of extras, symptomatic of Gance's perfectionist desire to recreate historical events as accurately as possible. But he also made memorable use of tableaux staged with highly dramatic lighting to suggest Napoléon's heroic, superhuman status; a remarkably mobile camera; colour tinting; and montage sequences edited so rapidly that their actual content is sometimes virtually indecipherable: one is carried along by the energy of the spectacle, rather than by its dramatic meaning. During the silent era, when he aligned himself with the French avant-garde, Gance was consistently innovative – in *La Folie du Docteur Tube*, for example, he used distorting lenses to convey a world of psychological fantasy – though his narratives rarely transcended bombast and melodrama. But with the advent of sound and after the poor reception of *La Fin du Monde*, his career went into gradual decline. He was, however, a technical pioneer of huge ambition, his enthusiasm for the cinematic medium unquestionable.

Abel Gance b. 1889 France, d. 1981 France. **Napoléon** USA 1927/ w Albert Dieudonné, Gance, Antonin Artaud, Gina Manès, Wladimir Roudenko. **Films include** *La Folie du Docteur Tube*, 1915; *Mater Dolorosa*, 1917; *J'Accuse*, 1919; *Le Roue*, 1922; *La Fin du Monde*, 1931; *Un Grand Amour de Beethoven*, 1936; *La Vénus Aveugle*, 1941; *Cyrano et d'Artagnan*, 1964. **See also** DeMille, Eisenstein, Griffith, Riefenstahl, Vertov, Vigo

In a huge, gloomy 'surgery' shaped like a giant beehive a doctor, with a grotesque baby-mask perched on his head, begins to torture an old friend who has dared to challenge the insane bureaucratic system of the 1984-style society in which they live. Formerly an animator and member of the Monty Python comedy team, Gilliam has exercised his free-wheeling imagination to become one of cinema's most fertile fantasists. Structurally and visually, *Brazil* is in many ways reminiscent of Orwell's satire on oppressive authority; set in a shabby, futuristic yet 40s-style world of governmental secrecy, monumental architecture, primitive valve computers and guerrilla terrorism, it tells of a mild man's doomed attempts to win himself love, freedom and trouble-free plumbing… typically for Gilliam, nightmare terror is mixed with bizarre, irreverent humour. His dynamic, fluid images combine surrealism, expressionism, the epic, mythical and mundane; amazingly, despite inventive but wayward stories which, appropriately, centre on romantic/idealist dreamers who find their needs rejected by conventional society, the films achieve a dark coherence, thanks in no small part to his bold visual sense. Few contemporary directors are as adept at creating, through lavish design, impossible worlds, let alone rendering them credible through a crazed internal logic. And few seem as anarchic: his distaste for the conformism of modern life and for the bright, tidy narratives favoured by the mainstream are evident in his every film. Erratic they may be, but they are consistent in their capacity to challenge, amuse and surprise.

Terry Gilliam b. 1940 USA. **Brazil** GB 1984/ w Jonathan Pryce, Kim Greist, Ian Holm, Robert De Niro, Bob Hoskins, Michael Palin. **Films include** *Jabberwocky*, 1976; *Time Bandits*, 1981; *The Adventures of Baron Munchausen*, 1988; *The Fisher King*, 1991; *12 Monkeys*, 1995; *Fear and Loathing in Las Vegas*, 1998. **See also** BOROWCZYK, JEUNET AND CARO, LYNCH, MÉLIÈS, QUAY BROTHERS, SVANKMAJER

JEAN-LUC GODARD

Gun at the ready, square-jawed detective and intergalactic agent Lemmy Caution (Eddie Constantine) takes respite from the loveless computerised world of *Alphaville* by reading Chandler's *The Big Sleep*. Few films show their heroes reading, but Godard was ever prone to drop literary allusions, or indeed cinematic ones: his work, despite its later woolly pretensions to political analysis, takes as its subject cinema itself. So Lemmy is at once a comic-strip hero, heir to Chandler's Marlowe and a sci-fi Orpheus bent on rescuing a Eurydice (Godard's then muse and wife Anna Karina) from a futuristic metropolis strangely suggestive of 60s Paris by night. The New Wave's *enfant terrible* explored his love-hate relationship with Hollywood cinema through inventive pastiche, undermining genres through jump-cuts, gags, digressions,

direct-to-camera monologues, deliberate amateurism (notably in the daft musical numbers of *Une Femme est Une Femme*), references, homages and, increasingly, slogans marked by portentous punning wordplay. Eventually, his restless experimentalism and growing concern with politics (not to mention an oft-voiced disenchantment with film-making, perverse given that he continued to work prolifically) led him to abandon conventional narrative structure altogether, so that his later 'essays' often seem merely obscure, indulgent meditations on the ways in which sound and image can be combined. Nevertheless, his fertile imagination and playful enthusiasm for his chosen medium initially produced stylistic innovations which can only be described as revolutionary; his influence is immense.

Jean-Luc Godard b. 1930 France. **Alphaville** France 1965/ w Eddie Constantine, Anna Karina, Howard Vernon, Akim Tamiroff, Laszlo Szabo. **Films include** *A Bout de Souffle*, 1959; *Une Femme est une Femme*, 1961; *Vivre Sa Vie*, 1962; *Les Carabiniers, Le Mépris*, 1963; *Bande à Part*, 1964; *Pierrot le Fou*, 1965; *Deux ou Trois Choses Que Je Sais d'Elle*, 1966; *Weekend*, 1967; *Sympathy for the Devil*, 1968; *Vent d'Est*, 1969; *Tout Va Bien*, 1972; *Sauve Qui Peut*, 1980; *Passion*, 1982; *Prénom Carmen*, 1983; *Histoire(s) du Cinéma*, 1989-99. **See also** BERTOLUCCI, FASSBINDER, HARTLEY, MARKER, MAKAVEJEV, OSHIMA

A film still could hardly be more reminiscent of a painting; the meticulously lit tableau, reeking of artifice with its statuesque nudes, massed nobility and carefully positioned furniture, evokes the work of Venetian masters like Bellini or Titian. That there is also literally a frame within the frame creates an impression of *trompe d'oeil*, wholly appropriate to this modernist reworking of Shakespeare's *The Tempest*: the film's narrative has Prospero 'compose' the play's text so that its characters are the product of his imagination (Gielgud speaks the lines not only of Prospero but all the other characters) and the story becomes an account of its own genesis. Greenaway is the most intellectually erudite and ambitious of film-makers (he also works in many other art forms), drawing, like Prospero, from the books dreamt up for his library, on all manner of arcane or apocryphal knowledge, and eschewing conventional drama and manipulation of the audience's emotional responses for more cerebral methods. Both the tone and content of his films are cool (his dark tales of devious scheming and deadly revenge and insistence on the vulnerability of human flesh have provoked charges of misanthropy), but the stately tracking shots, ornate compositions, barbed, witty dialogue and endless allusions can be enthralling: watching a Greenaway film is akin to seeing a bizarre encyclopaedia come to life. Ironically, while he parades his knowledge of history and aesthetics, his use of state-of-the-art technology, like his analytical attitude to human behaviour, suggests an almost scientific approach to the future of cinema.

Peter Greenaway b. 1942 England. **Prospero's Books** Netherlands 1991/ w John Gielgud, Michael Clark, Michel Blanc, Tom Bell, Isabelle Pasco, Mark Rylance. **Films include** *A Walk Through H, Vertical Features Remake*, 1978; *The Falls*, 1980; *The Draughtsman's Contract*, 1982; *The Belly of an Architect,* 1986; *Drowning by Numbers*, 1988; *The Cook, the Thief, his Wife and her Lover,* 1989; *The Pillow Book*, 1995; *8¹/₂ Women*, 1999. **See also** Buñuel, Fellini, Resnais, Ruiz, Syberberg

D W GRIFFITH

A young farmer cradles the orphaned servant he has saved from certain death on an ice-floe about to plummet over a waterfall; she had been turned out into the freezing countryside by his father, who had discovered she had given birth to an illegitimate child after being seduced and abandoned. The image is simple, poetic and poignant, the romantic climax to one of Griffith's most famous last-minute-rescue sequences, in which his careful editing together of close-ups and long shots filmed on location with library and studio footage provides a suspenseful finale to a pastoral melodrama. Griffith is best known for lavish historical spectacles like *Judith of Bethulia*, *Birth of a Nation* (a truly impressive Civil War epic marred by its racist depiction of blacks and celebration of the Ku Klux Klan) and the four-part *Intolerance*.

However his early shorts were profoundly influential in exploring and establishing the classical film syntax of close-ups, cross-cutting and camera-movement, and he frequently worked in smaller, more intimate romances notable for their lyrical photography, evocative sets and unusually subtle performances. Lillian Gish, shown here with Richard Barthelmess, was the finest of a group of actors that included her sister Dorothy, Bobby Harron, Mae Marsh and others. Often the stories were sentimental, moralistic and featured stereotype characters straight out of Victorian melodrama, but Griffith's natural flair as a storyteller, his assured control of mood and his affection for the final chase ensured that most succeeded as engrossing yarns. The advent of sound, however, effectively put paid to a once illustrious career.

David Wark Griffith b. 1875 USA, d. 1948 USA. **Way Down East** USA 1920/ w Lillian Gish, Richard Barthelmess, Lowell Sherman, Burr McIntosh, Kate Bruce. **Films include** *Judith of Bethulia*, 1914; *The Birth of a Nation*, 1915; *Intolerance*, 1916; *Hearts of the World*, 1918; *True Heart Susie*, 1919; *Broken Blossoms*, 1919; *Orphans of the Storm*, 1921; *America, Isn't Life Wonderful?*, 1924; *Abraham Lincoln*, 1930. **See also** DWAN, FORD, GANCE, PORTER, VON STROHEIM

YILMAZ GÜNEY

In a remote, run-down village, two men are arrested by heartless members of Turkey's armed militia. Though shot by Serif Gören, *Yol* was undoubtedly the creation of matinee idol-turned-director Güney, who, as often, wrote the film in prison (for murdering a judge, a charge resulting from repeated run-ins with a government furious at his calls for social and political change), and who gave his former assistant precise instructions on how it should be made. About five prisoners given a week to visit their homes, the film charts how hope is eroded by an oppressive society in which freedom is an illusion: not only are the people at the mercy of the state but traditional morality itself prevents fulfilment of individual needs – a man expected to punish his wife's infidelity with death is driven to take her away from their village into an empty, snowy wilderness. Güney's depiction of his country and its landscape is raw, bleak and unsentimental; if his sympathies clearly lie with the poor, weak and uneducated rather than the rich and powerful, his crisp unadorned camerawork never conceals the harsh, unforgiving ways of peasant life. In *The Herd* (shot by Zeki Ökten, again according to the incarcerated Güney's detailed script), a nomadic family taking its sheep on an epic odyssey to Ankara falls prey both to the corruption of a modern industrialised city and to their own superstitions, ignorance and hostile prejudices; the prison-drama *The Wall*, made in exile in France, makes even clearer his thesis, spelt out in typically simple, direct images: that Turkey itself was a prison, in which warders and inmates alike were victims.

Yilmaz Güney (Putun) b. 1937 Turkey, d. 1984 France. **Yol (The Way)** Turkey 1981/ w Tarik Akan, Halil Ergun, Serif Sezer, Necmettin Cobanoglu, Meral Orhousoy. **Films include** *Hope*, 1970; *Elegy*, 1972; *The Enemy*, 1979; *The Herd*, 1979; *The Wall*, 1982. **See also** CHAHINE, PONTECORVO, ROSI, ROSSELLINI

ROBERT HAMER

There is something quintessentially English about this image of Edwardian courtship: the fussy furniture and costumes, the polite distance between the lovers, Joan Greenwood's modest posture, and Dennis Price's cool, calm, confident gaze. Cool or cold? What the picture alone cannot reveal is not only the elegant verbal wit of Hamer's eminently civilised black comedy but the fact that Price is a ruthless murderer, a social outcast determined to remove the eight human obstacles – his aristocrat relatives, all played by Alec Guinness – that stand in the way of his becoming a Duke and winning over the likewise ambitious (and, as it happens, married) Greenwood. Counterpointing the buttoned-up bourgeois formality of his characters' public behaviour with the callously self-serving, destructive nature of their desires, Hamer uses exquisite irony and exposes the gulf between what is said and what is shown to mount a sharp critique of English hypocrisy – an acerbic satire far more biting than the cosy anti-establishment populism that was Ealing Studios' trademark. Indeed, Hamer's skills were best put to use in dark thrillers like *Pink String and Sealing Wax*, *It Always Rains on Sunday* and the haunted mirror episode in *Dead of Night*, each of which probed the troubled, repressed and violent passions that seethe beneath the surface of everyday middle-class respectablility, with protagonists reacting against a feeling of entrapment and injustice. Sadly, Hamer's heyday was all too short-lived; nevertheless, his finest work is an eloquent reminder that not all postwar British cinema was strait-laced.

Robert Hamer b. 1911 England, d.1963 England. **Kind Hearts and Coronets** GB 1949/ w Dennis Price, Alec Guinness, Joan Greenwood, Valerie Hobson, Miles Malleson. **Films include** *Dead of Night*, *Pink String and Sealing Wax*, 1945; *It Always Rains on Sunday*, 1947; *The Spider and the Fly*, 1949; *Father Brown*, 1954; *School for Scoundrels*, 1960. **See also** BUÑUEL, CHABROL, HITCHCOCK, LOSEY, MACKENDRICK, MANKIEWICZ, POWELL

87

MICHAEL HANEKE

Paul, an uninvited visitor to a family's holiday home, places a cushion cover over the son's head. He and his friend Peter have politely announced they intend to kill the family, and by tormenting the boy try to make his parents choose who must die first. Crucially, in Haneke's nightmare scenario (the third of his rigorous, disturbing studies of motiveless murder), virtually no violence appears on screen. Rightly insisting that violence served up as 'entertainment' blinds us to its horrific realities, he suggests it by off-screen sound, reaction-shots and reticent depictions of its aftermath. (After the boy's death, an uncut ten-minute long-shot portrays, with almost unbearable honesty, the parents' traumatised inability to grasp their predicament.) Influenced by Kafka and Bresson, Haneke's austere, modernist style is elliptical and fragmentary in both narrative structure and visual framing: scenes and compositions show only what is essential to meaning. Even his feature debut *The Seventh Continent*, a mosaic of mundane, seemingly insignificant events leading to a family's communal suicide, mostly comprises shots of hands, feet and objects, as if showing characters in full would provide too facile and reassuring an explanation for their acts. Haneke provokes viewers to think for themselves: in *Funny Games* Peter and Paul – their names, part of their deadly 'game', emphasise their unknowable Other-ness – turn to ask the audience what it thinks about the film and the events depicted. That none of the family survives indicates Haneke's seriousness, intelligence and integrity in refusing to pander to audience expectations and desires.

Michael Haneke b. 1942 Germany. **Funny Games** Austria 1997/ w Susanne Lothar, Ulrich Mühe, Arno Frisch, Frank Giering, Stefan Clapczynski. **Films include** *The Seventh Continent*, 1988; *Benny's Video*, 1992; *71 Fragments in a Chronology of Chance*, 1994; *The Castle*, 1997. **See also** BRESSON, GODARD, KIAROSTAMI, KITANO, OSHIMA

WILLIAM HANNA AND JOSEPH BARBERA

The ferociously irate cat towers menacingly over the mouse: an archetypal moment in the frantic battle between two of cinema's best known, best loved characters. Though the violence in Hanna-Barbera's seemingly unlimited variations on the cat-and-mouse theme is unremitting and extreme – Tom, especially, is battered, flattened and twisted into impossibly grotesque shapes again and again – a sweet symbiosis exists between the two enemies: it is as if the pair understand that they need each other just to exist (as indeed, dramatically, they did). And since this is MGM family entertainment, cute little Jerry, initially the under-dog, remains safe and usually triumphant: his shrewdness and his capacity for mischief, barely concealed by a cheekily cherubic appearance, is more than a match for the less imaginative, more psychotically driven Tom. Theirs is a ritualistic war, waged in a familiar but faintly unreal arena usually limited to the confines of a lounge, kitchen and, now and then, a garden: if humans are present, only feet and legs are visible. The weaponry, therefore, consists of household fittings, furniture and utensils, so that Tom, beaten with a frying pan, will briefly mirror its shape before emerging unscathed and normal again in the next scene. Less anarchic than Avery, less surrealistic and intellectually knowing than Jones, Hanna-Barbera finally came to depend on a well-worn formula, and their later television works shows a coarsening in the animation. Tom and Jerry themselves, however, remain unforgettable comic creations, as complementary to one another as Laurel and Hardy.

William Hanna b. 1910 USA. **Joseph Barbera** b. 1911 USA. **A Mouse in the House** USA 1947. **Films include** *Puss Gets the Boot*, 1940; *Yankee Doodle Mouse*, 1943; *Mouse Trouble*, 1944; *Quiet Please*, 1945; *The Cat Concerto*, 1946; *Professor Tom*, 1948; *Two Mouseketeers*, 1951; *Mouse for Sale*, 1955. **See also** AVERY, DISNEY, FLEISCHER, JONES, PARK, TASHLIN

A woman brandishes a kitchen knife at her daughter, while the latter's boyfriend looks on impassively. In Hartley's films, the search for love, peace of mind and self-knowledge, often played out within dysfunctional families, is expressed through flat, not quite naturalistic performances, as characters intone aphoristic, allusive dialogue and stand carefully positioned like objects of furniture or features in a landscape. Though his plots' elements are often those of the melodrama or thriller, Hartley prefers to avoid conventional dramatic climaxes, just as he explores serious themes (*Trust* is partly about parental abuse, child-kidnapping, teenage pregnancy, abortion and psychopathic despair) within an overall format that is essentially comic. The tone, both verbal and visual (he favours a slightly unreal use of bright colours), is cool, ironic, faintly absurdist, and delights in artifice: in *Amateur* the lead characters are an ex-nun trying to establish a career as a writer of pornography and a gentle amnesiac with a history of sadism and violent crime. By foregrounding the films' formal qualities (*Flirt* tells the same story three times over in different cities, with actions and dialogue re-ordered or given to different characters in each), he adopts an experimental approach to cinematic narrative and focuses more directly on ideas; at the same time his droll wit and generous attitude to his characters' quest for love ensures that his films are not merely dry, formal exercises but funny and emotionally affecting, making him one of the most distinctive young American film-makers at work today.

Hal Hartley b. 1959 USA. **Trust** USA 1990/ w Adrienne Shelly, Martin Donovan, Merritt Nelson, John MacKay, Edie Falco, Matt Malloy. **Films include** *The Unbelievable Truth*, 1989; *Surviving Desire*, 1991; *Simple Men*, 1992; *Amateur*, 1994; *Flirt*, 1995; *Henry Fool,* 1997; *The Book of Life*, 1998. **See also** BOTELHO, GODARD, JARMUSCH, KAURISMÄKI, SOLONDZ

In the witty, breakneck-paced verbal sparring that characterises editor Cary Grant's ruthlessly manipulative efforts to win back his ex-wife and top reporter Rosalind Russell, in order to gain a scoop about murder and political corruption, can be found Hawks' abiding themes: the importance of professionalism, self-respect and responsibility; the on-going battle between the sexes; the need to discover and use one's talents. Hawks' visual style was classical, restrained, unpretentious – camera at eye-height, unobtrusive editing, a sparing use of close-ups, camera-movements and emphatic angles – so that the focus was firmly on the often dazzling interplay of words and gestures between characters defined by their actions; hence Russell, clearly a career-woman in her 'masculine' pin-stripe suit and thus fated to remain in the male-dominated world of journalism, gives the determined, deviously jaunty Grant a run for his money as they endlessly try to outwit each other, while their leaning towards one another subtly hints at their intimacy and mutual attraction. But for all the frantic overlapping dialogue and the threat of execution of an innocent man that serves as the dark backdrop to their sparring, *His Girl Friday* – the fastest and, perhaps, funniest talkie ever made – is like most Hawks films, be they comedies or adventures, a strangely relaxed affair: the actors really seem to be enjoying themselves as they go about the 'fun and business' of making a movie – the director's own modest description of his seemingly effortless, supremely humane and entertaining art.

Howard Hawks b. USA 1896, d. USA 1977. **His Girl Friday** USA 1940/ w Cary Grant, Rosalind Russell, Ralph Bellamy, John Qualen, Gene Lockhart. **Films include** *A Girl in Every Port*, 1928; *Scarface*, 1932; *Twentieth Century*, 1934; *Bringing Up Baby*, 1938; *Only Angels Have Wings*, 1939; *To Have and Have Not*, 1945; *The Big Sleep*, 1946; *Red River*, 1948; *Gentlemen Prefer Blondes*, 1953; *Rio Bravo*, 1959; *Hatari!*, 1962. **See also** CARPENTER, HILL, MICHAEL MANN, MELVILLE, RENOIR, WALSH

TODD HAYNES

Seventies glamrock star Brian Slade contemplates the price of fame, of losing all sense of self in the pursuit of art and the effort to satisfy audience expectations. Haynes' fictional rise-and-fall biopic is not merely a nostalgic celebration of an era of musical invention and sexual liberation; characteristically, it is also an exploration of the gulf between public image and private reality (with an investigative flashback story modelled on *Citizen Kane*), and a study of how transgressive sexuality is viewed by society. The leading director to emerge from the New Queer Cinema, Haynes repeatedly examines the fraught relationship of the individual to society: how conventions (or the rejection of them) form, constrain or liberate personality and experience. *Superstar* reveals how Karen Carpenter's wholesome image may have contributed to her death from anorexia, *Poison* how sexuality considered 'abnormal' is demonised as monstrous; *[Safe]* examines oppressive attitudes to illness in a world that assumes there is a rational explanation for everything. Haynes' strengths are not only his astute, provocative analyses of the way the personal and political intersect but his readiness to adopt whatever cinematic style suits his material: the Barbie dolls used to represent the Carpenters were both a budgetary necessity and a comment on their image, *[Safe]* employed muted colours and claustrophobic framing to suggest its protagonist's entrapment, *Velvet Goldmine* mirrored glamrock's baroque artifice. Audacious and imaginative, Haynes is undeniably one of today's most radical, intelligent film-makers.

Todd Haynes b. 1961 USA. **Velvet Goldmine** GB/USA 1998/ w Jonathan Rhys Meyers, Ewan McGregor, Toni Collette, Christian Bale, Eddie Izzard. **Films include** *Superstar: The Karen Carpenter Story*, 1987; *Poison*, 1990; *Dottie Gets Spanked*, 1993; *[Safe]*, 1995.
See also CAMPION, FASSBINDER, GODARD, JARMAN, LUHRMANN, NICHOLAS RAY, SALLES, SIRK, WELLES

The Spanish conquistador Aguirre (Klaus Kinski), driven to megalomaniac madness by his obsessive quest for the legendary El Dorado, surveys one of the few surviving subjects of the vast wilderness of an empire he has proclaimed his own. Herzog's fable about greed, power and insanity is a typically apocalyptic, often surreal study of man's capacity for delusion and self-destruction. The Spaniards fall prey not only to a strange landscape (ravishingly shot in long, often hand-held takes by Thomas Mauch) and its hostile, largely unseen inhabitants, but to their own murderous power-struggles as they vainly attempt to bring their irrelevant European ideology – religion, war, the acquisition of wealth – and social hierarchies to the Amazon jungle. Kinski's brooding, aggressive intensity was a regular feature in Herzog's various tales of misguided obsession; also characteristic are dreamlike images (a boat suspended at the top of a tree in *Aguirre*, bizarre landscapes in *Fata Morgana* and *The Enigma of Kaspar Hauser*), a dark, cruelly ironic wit, and a partly Romantic, partly ethnographic interest in exotic or primitive cultures. Herzog is also a very fine documentarist (even in his non-fiction films, again often about obsession and suffering, the imagery is frequently startling in its strangeness), and many of his films reflect on their own making. Fond of shooting in difficult locations, he can seem as eccentric and driven as one of his heroes. Recently he appears to have found it difficult to continue making films, but his visionary work of the 70s constitutes a high point of the modern cinema.

Werner Herzog (Werner Stipetic) b. 1942 Germany. **Aguirre, Wrath of God** W Germany 1972/ w Klaus Kinski, Cecilia Rivera, Ruy Guerra, Helena Rojo, Del Negro, Peter Berling. **Films include** *Signs of Life*, 1967; *Even Dwarfs Started Small, Fata Morgana* 1970; *Land of Silence and Darkness*, 1971; *The Enigma of Kaspar Hauser*, 1974; *Heart of Glass*, 1976; *Stroszek*, 1977; *Nosferatu the Vampyre, Woyzeck*, 1979; *Fitzcarraldo*, 1982, *Cobra Verde*, 1988; *Lessons of Darkness*, 1992. **See also** ANGELOPOULOS, DOVZHENKO, MALICK, PARADZHANOV, SYBERBERG

The faces are fixed, serious; clearly, these men are prepared to do what they gotta do. As the James-Younger gang journeys to its fateful bank raid in Northfield, Minnesota, they almost look as if they know they are riding into history; certainly, they are ready to face danger. The laconic heroes of Hill's finest action movies are defined not by psychological complexity but by their expertise, courage and strength of will when facing stress – traditional male virtues, just as the films themselves are steeped in tradition. In re-telling the story of the legendary Jesse James, Hill emphasised the mythic themes of loyalty and family honour by casting real-life brothers (the Keaches, Quaids and Carradines) as the outlaws, and revelled in recreating, in stark but elegant, eloquent images, scenes of social rituals (dances, fights,

funerals) reminiscent of Ford's westerns. Genre is central to Hill's work: the heist movie *The Driver* is as taciturn and moodily stylised a study in cunning and betrayal as Melville's pared-down *noir* thrillers, *The Warriors* relocates the story of Xenophon's *Anabasis* to a nocturnal New York populated by rival gangs as bizarrely garbed as tribes from a sci-fi epic, and *Southern Comfort*, echoing America's doomed foray into Vietnam, melds the macho traditions of the war film and the western. Hill's own later forays into comedy and pastiche – *48 HRS*, *Streets of Fire*, *Red Heat* – led to a loss of focus and a coarsening of narrative and characterisation; only two westerns – *Geronimo* and *Wild Bill* – avoid cliché and match the quiet but impressive intensity and taut dramatic lines of his early work.

Walter Hill b. 1942 USA. **The Long Riders** USA 1980/ w James and Stacey Keach, David, Keith and Robert Carradine, Dennis and Randy Quaid. **Films include** *Hard Times*, 1975; *The Driver*, 1978; *The Warriors*, 1979; *Southern Comfort*, 1981; *48 HRS*, 1982; *Streets of Fire*, 1984; *Brewster's Millions*, 1985; *Red Heat*, 1988; *Geronimo*, 1993; *Wild Bill*, 1995. **See also** BOETTICHER, FORD, HAWKS, LEONE, MELVILLE, MICHAEL MANN, MILIUS, PECKINPAH

ALFRED HITCHCOCK

Robert Walker demonstrates the art of strangulation to a society matron: a party trick – or is it? Patricia Hitchcock looks anxious, as well she might, given that her resemblance to a woman Walker has recently murdered makes him forget it's only a game. Hitchcock, famously 'the master of suspense', mostly avoided shock-cuts, preferring to create an anticipation of danger by focusing on small, significant details: here, the girl's stare heightens our fear not only that Walker will kill the foolish dowager, but that his earlier crime may be discovered. (Hitch was adept at manipulating audience sympathies, so that allegiances constantly switch between innocent victim, seductively amoral villain and order-restoring hero.) His desire to make viewers squirm first saw him borrow and develop Expressionist imagery and sound

effects, but as he became increasingly experimental and confident in his notions of 'pure cinema', he adopted a richer, more flexible style. Slow tracking-shots might alternate with rapid montage, extreme close-ups with long shots, unusual angles and distorted perspectives with classical framing, conventional naturalism with symbolism, expressionist colour, Gothic romanticism and even, in the Dali-designed dream sequence for *Spellbound*, surrealism. Likewise, he regularly injected moments of macabre humour into his tautly structured, almost mechanically efficient stories. Though he seemingly cared little if backdrop scenery was obviously artificial, he was a superb technician, expert at orchestrating the irruption of menacing, life-changing chaos into a complacent, deceptively safe and ordered world.

Alfred Hitchcock b. 1899 England, d. 1980 USA. **Strangers on a Train** USA 1951/ w Robert Walker, Farley Granger, Ruth Roman, Leo G Carroll, Patricia Hitchcock. **Films include** *The Lodger*, 1926; *Blackmail*, 1929; *The 39 Steps,* 1935; *The Lady Vanishes*, 1938; *Rebecca*, 1940; *Notorious*, 1946; *Rope*, 1948; *Rear Window*, 1954; *Vertigo*, 1958; *North by Northwest*, 1959; *Psycho*, 1960; *The Birds*, 1963; *Marnie*, 1964; *Family Plot*, 1976. **See also** CHABROL, CLOUZOT, DE PALMA, KUBRICK, LANG, POLANSKI, SPIELBERG, TRUFFAUT

DENNIS HOPPER

The thrill of speed, the security of male friendship, the romance of the open road, the quest for freedom, the pioneering spirit of America: Hopper's massive cult hit about two hippy bikers (Hopper and Peter Fonda, the film's producer) using the proceeds from a cocaine deal to travel from California to New Orleans drew on a range of time-honoured clichés to lend its anti-heroes' odyssey a mythic dimension. Not that the film is a simplistic celebration either of America, which is depicted as being, at least in the South, riven by narrow-minded prejudice, or of its protagonists' romantic rebellion against conformity and the Establishment; the Fonda character is laid-back to the point of indolence, his buddy barely articulate in his drug-fuelled reveries, though they are sufficiently self-aware to acknowledge,

just before being gunned down for no good reason by rednecks, that they 'blew it' in their search for freedom. Like his acting, Hopper's direction tends to be raw, edgy, ambitious and undisciplined. Sometimes, as in the LSD sequence in a New Orleans cemetery or in the entirety of *Out of the Blue*, a dark drama about a severely dysfunctional family, his restless experimentalism is genuinely eloquent in conveying unsettling moods through jagged editing and expressionist images; elsewhere, as in the film-making allegory *The Last Movie* or the hyperbolic thriller *The Hot Spot*, it results in pretentiousness and incoherence. *Colors*, about cops struggling to deal with LA's gang wars, is arguably his most controlled film, and like his best work reveals an ability to pinpoint the mood of the times.

Dennis Hopper b. 1936 USA. **Easy Rider** USA 1969/ w Hopper, Peter Fonda, Jack Nicholson, Karen Black, Phil Spector, Antonio Mendoza, Robert Walker. **Films include** *The Last Movie*, 1971; *Out of the Blue*, 1980; *Colors*, 1988; *Catchfire*, *The Hot Spot*, 1990.
See also FULLER, MILIUS, PECKINPAH, PENN, NICHOLAS RAY

HOU HSIAO-HSIEN

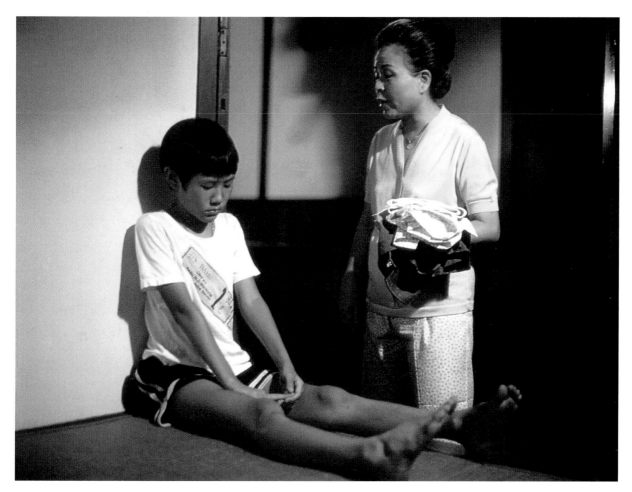

A young boy sulks, ignoring his grandmother; for all the everyday familiarity of the image, it is pregnant both with his stillness and with a sense of his inner, unspoken emotional turmoil. Hou's films are full of such moments; emotions and events are hinted at rather than shown as he observes the minutiae of human behaviour. His contemplative style is at times reminiscent of Ozu, with its generally static camera and simple compositions (though he usually favours far longer takes), and his early films likewise portray tensions in the family; here, a boy and his young sister are sent to stay with their grandparents while their mother is in hospital, and between playing games, bear witness to an adult world of violence, crime and sexual longing they barely comprehend. Hou's quiet, impressionistic narratives build steadily to an emotional pay-off that is often devastating when it finally comes: in *The Time to Live and the Time to Die*, when the carefree complacency of childhood is shattered by a death in the family, the hitherto impassive young protagonist erupts into physically uncontrollable grief, all the more effective for having been preceded by scenes of restrained repose. In later, more complex films like *A City of Sadness*, *Good Men, Good Women* and *The Flowers of Shanghai*, the predicaments of the characters are marked by and clearly reflect the social history of Taiwan and mainland China; much of his work concerns the identity crisis resulting from the countries having been separated. Indeed, perhaps Hou's greatest strength is his ability to combine the personal and political so poetically.

Hou Hsiao-hsien (Xiaoxian) b. 1947 China. **A Summer at Grandpa's** Taiwan 1984/ w Wang Qiguang, Gu Jun, Mei Fang, Lin Xiuling. **Films include** *The Time to Live and the Time to Die*, 1985; *Dust in the Wind*, 1986; *Daughter of the Nile*, 1987; *A City of Sadness*, 1989; *The Puppetmaster*, 1993; *Good Men, Good Women*, 1995; *Goodbye South, Goodbye*, 1997; *The Flowers of Shanghai*, 1998. **See also** ANTONIONI, ERICE, IM KWON-TAEK, OZU, YANG

In a monumentally bleak landscape, villainous Ming dynasty agents ambush a group of Buddhist monks: as the latter fend off the attack, the screen turns into a spectacular flurry of acrobatic action, with bodies and swords flying in a kinetic whirl of sumptuous colours, heightened sound effects and rapid cutting. King Hu's epic is a masterpiece of the martial arts genre, embracing traditional ghost story, historical drama, political conspiracy and philosophical speculation as its complex narrative proceeds from realism to metaphysical fantasy. Working within the tradition of Chinese sword-play movies, the Hong Kong actor-turned-writer-director deployed humour, fantasy and convoluted stories to bring a fresh perspective to familiar material. Most distinctive was the dazzling expertise brought to the balletic action sequences, in which he and fight-arranger Han Ying-Chieh choreographed conflict in the pyrotechnical style of Peking Opera. Characters fly through the air with gravity-defying grace and speed, thanks partly to the performers' superb timing and athletic prowess, partly to skilful editing and imaginative camera placement which together render astonishing physical feats strangely plausible within the context of the fable-like stories. Costume, decor and landscape, too, contributed to the dreamlike mood, with colour, especially, used to create visual coups; memorably, in *A Touch of Zen* a stabbed monk's blood runs gold. The combination of virtuoso technique and visually inventive details throughout his films placed King Hu at the forefront of martial arts cinema.

King Hu (Hu Jinquan) b. 1931 China, d. 1997 Taiwan. **A Touch of Zen (Xia Nu)** Taiwan 1969/ w Hsu Feng, Shih Chun, Pai Ying, Tian Feng, Roy Chiao. **Films include** *Come Drink with Me*, 1965; *Dragon Gate Inn*, 1967; *The Fate of Lee Khan*, 1973; *The Valiant Ones*, 1974; *Raining in the Mountains*, *Legend of the Mountain*, 1979. **See also** CHEN, KUROSAWA, WONG, ZHANG

Two gold-prospecting partners stand alone in deadly confrontation in the Mexican mountains: a stark image of hopes dashed by greed, fear and the fragility of friendship, typical of Huston's story telling talent at its most witheringly cynical. He loved larger-than-life yarns (*Sierra Madre* has the simplicity of a parable), and there's no denying the gleeful hamminess of the performances of Bogart's increasingly paranoid Fred C Dobbs, Tim Holt's young innocent and, as the wily old buzzard who tempts them into joining his search for gold, the director's father, Walter. But the film, unlike much of Huston's work, also succeeds in visual terms: the classical framing is to the point, stressing the growing conflict between the trio and reflecting their moral, mental and spiritual degeneration in the arid landscape.

Huston, who favoured working from literary sources, seldom made films that seemed at all personal. Ambitious but erratic, he preferred to ignore the restraints of genre but rarely produced anything original or emotionally involving; often he seemed content to shoot character actors in exotic locations, unsure as to the thematic substance, weight or tone of his material. That said, his finest work (the influential early noir *The Maltese Falcon*, *Sierra Madre*, *The Asphalt Jungle*, *Moby Dick*, *Fat City* and *The Man Who Would Be King*) casts a beady eye over human aspiration, with the allure of power and an easy life inevitably wrecking the best-laid plans. Finally, in a sensitive adaptation of Joyce's *The Dead*, he treated the theme of lost love and dashed dreams with unprecedented tenderness.

John Huston b. 1906 USA, d. 1987 USA. **The Treasure of the Sierra Madre** USA 1948/ w Humphrey Bogart, Tim Holt, Walter Huston, Bruce Bennett, Barton MacLane. **Films include** *The Maltese Falcon*, 1941; *Key Largo*, 1948; *The Asphalt Jungle*, 1950; *The African Queen*, 1952; *Beat the Devil*, 1954; *Moby Dick*, 1956; *The Misfits*, 1960; *Reflections in a Golden Eye*, 1967; *Fat City*, 1972; *The Man Who Would Be King*, 1975; *Wise Blood*, 1979; *Prizzi's Honor*, 1985; *The Dead*, 1987. **See also** CIMINO, CURTIZ, MELVILLE, WALSH, WELLMAN, WILDER, ZINNEMANN

IM KWON-TAEK

A young orthodox monk cradles the body of an older colleague discovered in the snow; the dead man's hands, frozen in prayer, reflect the devout wisdom that was belied by his iconoclastic fondness for alcohol and sex. The empty, snowy landscape is typical of Im's predilection for reflecting emotions through seasonal imagery, and of his fascination with nature as a symbol of timeless values. Im's films centre on questions concerning Korea's cultural, political and spiritual identity, and are structured around polarised oppositions: the traditional and the new, the transient and the eternal, spirituality and sensuality, and (with regard to the socially traumatic division of the country into separate northern and southern entities) Confucianism, communism and materialism. Though characters often represent contradictory responses to life's dilemmas, Im's expertise with actors never allows them to become mere historical or political cyphers: his vision is quietly but determinedly humanist, with an acute, elegiac awareness of suffering (particularly that of women in patriarchal society) caused by ideological conflict, intolerance and oppression.

At the same time, suffering may lead, as here, to enlightenment or, as in *Sopyonje* (about the impoverished plight of traditional wandering musicians in an increasingly indifferent, westernised world), to transcendent artistry. Im's visual style is classical in its restraint and directness; his pacing is measured, while his images, lyrical yet never florid, make evocative use of the Korean landscape to suggest the primacy of the individual's natural needs and emotions over social considerations.

Im Kwon-Taek b. 1936 Korea. **Mandala** South Korea 1981/ w Chun Mu-Song, Ahn Sung-Kee, Pang Hui, Ki Jong-Su.
Films include *The Genealogy*, 1978; *The Hidden Hero*, 1979; *Ticket, Surrogate Mother*, 1986; *Adada*, 1988; *Come, Come, Come Upward*, 1989; *The General's Son*, 1991; *Sopyonje*, 1993; *The Taebaek Mountains*, 1994; *Festival*, 1996. **See also** CHEN, HOU, KUROSAWA, MIZOGUCHI, YANG, ZHANG

In a picture-postcard woodland glade, the twittish Cecil (Daniel Day-Lewis) pursues his courtship of Lucy (Helena Bonham Carter),whose heart has secretly been awakened by another more passionate but less socially acceptable suitor. Produced and adapted from E M Forster's comedy of buttoned-up Edwardian manners by his regular collaborators Ismail Merchant and Ruth Prawer Jhabvala, Ivory's film is typical of their countless literary adaptations with its solid, rather pernickety performances, its meticulous approach to costume and decor, its unimaginative camerawork and its consuming tastefulness. With some justification, it has been suggested that Merchant-Ivory's films are for those who seldom read books or see movies; that they are simplistic textual illustrations, bereft of genuine cinematic style, illuminating insights and vitality. In *A Room with a View* Forster's wit is coarsened; easy comic targets like snobbishness and prudery and a dismally broad skinny-dipping scene are substituted for the novel's subtler ironies. Time and again, Merchant-Ivory choose to adapt tales of individuality and passion repressed by social convention, yet the films themselves are passionless and academic (in a determinedly middle-brow way), deadened by the emphatic, pretty design and discreet intimations of inner frustration. The murky realities of life barely impinge on the tidy, untroubling studies of human decency; there is no sense of a world beyond the frame or of darker, complex emotions lying beneath the films' bland, unruffled surfaces. That said, in spite or because of these shortcomings, they remain very popular.

James Ivory b. 1928 USA. **A Room with a View** GB 1985/ w Maggie Smith, Helena Bonham Carter, Denholm Elliott, Julian Sands, Daniel Day-Lewis, Simon Callow. **Films include** *Shakespeare Wallah*, 1965; *Savages*, 1972; *The Wild Party*, 1975; *Heat and Dust*, 1983; *The Bostonians*, 1984; *Maurice*, 1987; *Howards End*, 1992; *The Remains of the Day*, 1993; *Surviving Picasso*, 1996; *A Soldier's Daughter Never Cries*, 1998. **See also** LEAN, LEWIN, VISCONTI, WYLER, ZINNEMANN

MIKLÓS JANCSÓ

The vast Russian steppes in the aftermath of the 1917 Revolution: government soldiers and revolutionaries are lined up against one another, but in this typically geometric, even abstract image not only is no single hero foregrounded but it's almost impossible to tell which side is which. Jancsó's finest films – starkly poetic accounts of historical events – focus on the ceaseless struggle for power of massed forces: on flat, featureless plains, groups of people sweep by on horses, arrange themselves in patterns, win and lose futile skirmishes, torture, kill and die. The very long takes (*Red Psalm* comprises only 26 shots) are elegant, fluid but strangely detached: the camera's swoops and zooms are not a mere aesthetic trope but a reflection of the action, of the continual and transient shifts in power.

Narrative details, inevitably, are not always easily comprehensible in Jancsó's mechanistic, largely dialogue-free depictions of human conflict, and if the precisely choreographed movement is in itself virtually a celebration of revolutionary endeavour, the reduction of individuals to mere pawns, figures in a landscape, can sometime smack of mannerism, especially in later, more ornate but less rigorous works such as *Private Vices, Public Virtues*, which equates sexual and political revolt in a visually gorgeous but dramatically listless retelling of the Mayerling story. At its best, however, in work like *The Round Up*, *The Confrontation* and *Elektreia*, his unique, balletic style is entirely in harmony with the dialectics of the films' dramatic and political meaning.

Miklós Jancsó b. 1921 Hungary. **The Red and the White** Hungary 1967/ w Jószef Madaras, András Kozák, Tibor Molnár, Jácint Juhász, Anatoli Yabbarov. **Films include** *My Way Home*, 1964; *The Round Up*, 1965; *The Confrontation*, 1969; *Red Psalm*, 1971; *Elektreia*, 1975; *Private Vices, Public Virtues*, 1976; *Hungarian Rhapsody*, 1979. **See also** ANGELOPOULOS, ANTONIONI, PASOLINI, TAVIANI BROTHERS

DEREK JARMAN

The shot is both classically derived – the martyrdom of Saint Sebastian is familiar from countless artworks – and intentionally homoerotic. Jarman imagines Sebastian as a Roman soldier whose harrowingly painful demise comes about through the vengeful cruelty of a captain in whom he has inspired unrequited passion. As an openly gay film-maker, he was inevitably a maverick of the British cinema, but his eccentric, low-budget stylistic strategies placed him still further outside the mainstream: not only was *Sebastiane* unusual in its lush, rapturous photography and explicit physicality, but its dialogue was in Latin (with English subtitles). Jarman was both naturally anti-establishment and nostalgic: in *Jubilee*, Elizabeth I is led through the ravaged, violent, punk landscape of a vaguely futuristic Britain; a version of

The Tempest was camped up to playful effect; *The Last of England* was a fragmented, deeply personal attack on Thatcher's Britain. Yet he was also a very English Romantic with an abiding interest in art: *Caravaggio*, *War Requiem*, in which Britten's mass was accompanied by documentary and fictional images showing the dreadful waste of war, and an updated version of Marlowe's *Edward II* were as painterly as *Sebastiane*, and more accessible than much of his work, the experimentalism of which sometimes seemed aimed to appeal primarily to a coterie of friends and admirers. *Blue*, made shortly before his death from AIDS, was arguably his most radical film, his blindness evoked by a frame of unchanging blue, accompanied by a poetic narration charting his thoughts, feelings and experiences.

Derek Jarman b. 1942 England, d. 1994 England. **Sebastiane** GB 1976/ w Leonardo Treviglio, Barney James, Neil Kennedy, Richard Warwick, Lindsay Kemp. **Films include** *Jubilee*, 1978; *The Tempest*, 1979; *The Angelic Conversation*, 1985; *Caravaggio*, 1986; *The Last of England*, 1987; *War Requiem*, 1988; *The Garden*, 1990; *Edward II*, 1991; *Wittgenstein*, *Blue*, 1993. **See also** ANGER, COCTEAU, HAYNES, PASOLINI, POWELL, RUSSELL, WARHOL

The pensive, impassive faces of two Japanese rock 'n' roll fans, alone in a seedy Memphis hotel (chief location for the film's three separate but subtly interconnecting stories, all of which take place on the same night) on their pilgrimage to the home of Elvis, embody Jarmusch's fascination with dreamers and strangers in a strange land. The lipstick smear left incongruously on the bored young rocker's lips after his girlfriend has kissed him is typical of the writer-director's tendency to a gently absurdist, understated comedy, which affectionately punctures the cool, hip pretensions and delusions of his self-consciously laconic loners. The compositions are uncluttered, often static and oddly formal, stressing the essential solitude of characters seemingly obsessed with self-definition; the sparing dialogue, generally minimalist performances and a preference for long takes evoke lives plagued by problems of communication, misunderstanding, rootlessness and inertia. At the same time, Jarmusch's elliptical, dedramatised, episodic narrative style is symptomatic of his restlessly experimental interest in the method and structure of cinematic story-telling. Crucially, however, this interest in formalism – which makes him unlikely ever to join the Hollywood mainstream – is balanced by subtle wit, the warmth he clearly feels for his characters and a bemused, intelligent interest in the unfamiliar backroads of American life (the underrated *Dead Man* was a decidedly different western), so that he remains one of the most accessible, original and influential of that country's independent film-makers.

Jim Jarmusch b. 1954 USA. **Mystery Train** USA 1989/w Masatoshi Nagase, Youki Kudoh, Screaming Jay Hawkins, Nicoletta Braschi, Joe Strummer, Steve Buscemi. **Films include** *Permanent Vacation*, 1981; *Stranger Than Paradise*, 1984; *Down By Law*, 1986; *Night on Earth*, 1991; *Dead Man*, 1996; *Ghost Dog: The Way of the Samurai*, 1999. **See also** BRESSON, DREYER, GODARD, HARTLEY, KAURISMÄKI, OZU, WENDERS

JEAN-PIERRE JEUNET AND MARC CARO

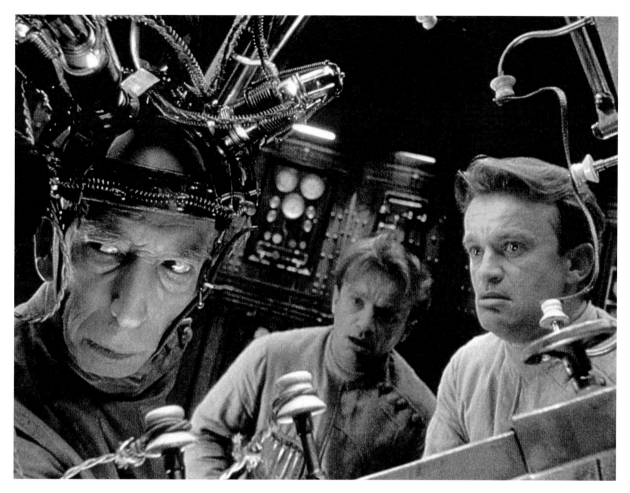

A futuristic yet strangely old-fashioned laboratory: absolutely identical brothers (two, in fact, of six such clones) look on as another, Krank, his face grotesquely and prematurely aged due to his inability to dream, dons a contraption which will allow him to 'steal' the dreams of orphans he has kidnapped from a Dickensian, sea-girt city. Like their earlier *Delicatessen*, Jeunet and Caro's fantasy thriller is notable not only for the surrealistic world in which it is set, but for its intensely imaginative, semi-comic fairy tale, peopled by eccentric characters reminiscent of myth. Unlike many fantasists, Jeunet and Caro devise stories according to an immensely detailed logic of cause and effect: hence, Krank and his narcoleptic brothers, not to mention their pint-sized mother and a migraine-ridden brain suspended in a tank, are all the botched inventions of a mad scientist. The plot's rationale is thus akin to the bizarre workings of dream, and the pseudo-scientific contraptions, expressionist cityscapes and sinister-looking characters, often shot with wide-angle lenses, evoke the volatile mood of childhood nightmare; indeed, *City*'s imperilled protagonist (if any one character can be described as such; the films follow the fortunes of a wide variety of grotesques) is a greedy, gleefully belching infant, while *Delicatessen* focuses mainly on an ex-circus clown of childlike innocence. Their more sophisticated sense of narrative notwithstanding, Jeunet and Caro may be seen as the modern French cinema's equivalent to Méliès; their films display the same unbridled delight in pure invention.

Jean-Pierre Jeunet b. 1953 France **Marc Caro** b. 1956 France. **The City of Lost Children** France 1995/ w Ron Perlman, Dominique Pinon, Daniel Emilfork, Judith Vittet, Jean-Claude Dreyfus. **Films include** *Delicatessen*, 1991; *Alien Resurrection* (Jeunet only), 1997. **See also** Coen Brothers, Gilliam, Lynch, Méliès

CHUCK JONES

Duck Amuck

©1951 Warner Bros.

Naive as a child, Daffy Duck vainly attempts to pass as the valiant hero of a swashbuckling saga: the image, suitably grand and sumptuously colourful, shows Jones' sharp talent for parody. Soon, however, Daffy's endearingly absurd dreams of fame and fortune will turn to nightmare as he meets his nemesis: not the expected dastardly medieval villain, but the paintbrush and eraser of a mischievous unseen animator (finally revealed to be Bugs Bunny), who changes Daffy's costumes, anatomy and scenic backdrops at will, overlays inappropriate sound effects, and alters the frame's position, size and shape so suddenly that the hapless would-be movie star's identity and existence are threatened. During his glory days at Warners, Jones excelled both at investing his various animal characters with vivid (but never cute) human personalities, and at injecting a wealth of allusive, intellectual gags into his cartoons' terse, perversely logical seven-minute stories; high culture (as in the magnificent Wagnerian parody *What's Opera, Doc?*) was a frequent reference point, though no film was as inventively self-reflexive as *Duck Amuck* with its gleefully deconstructive trashing/exploration of film syntax. While the initially realistic images are often steadily and systematically invaded by weird, fantastic angularity verging on abstraction in the *Roadrunner* series, the epic, Sisyphean dimension of Wile E Coyote's endless, absurd battles with an indestructibly fleet bird was brought home by being staged in a desert so stark, harsh and vast that it seemed uniquely located somewhere between surrealism and expressionism, proof that Jones was a sophisticated major artist in his own right.

Charles Martin Jones b. 1912 USA. **Duck Amuck** USA 1953. **Films include** *For Scent-Imental Reasons*, 1949; *So Much for So Little*, 1950; *The Scarlet Pumpernickel*, *The Rabbit of Seville*, 1950; *Rabbit Seasoning*, 1952; *Duck Dodgers in the 24 1/2 Century*; *One Froggy Evening*, 1956; *Steal Wool*; *What's Opera Doc?*, 1957; *High Note*, 1960; *The Dot and the Line*, 1965; *The Phantom Tollbooth*, 1969. **See also** AVERY, DISNEY, FLEISCHER, HANNA AND BARBERA, MCCAY, PARK

AKI KAURISMÄKI

An unemployed man checks his appearance before setting out for a job interview, while his devoted wife and dog look on, displaying neither hope nor appreciation… nor indeed anything but a morose acceptance of life's inevitable problems. In Kaurismäki's darkly comic world, communication is restricted to a few furtive glances and even fewer words; life's vicissitudes – poverty, injustice, unwanted pregnancy, nagging families, loneliness, love's torments– hang heavily over his characters, who take refuge in vodka and suicidal impulses. At the same time, Kaurismäki's finest work – *Ariel, Leningrad Cowboys Go America, The Match Factory Girl, Take Care of Your Scarf, Tatjana, Drifting Clouds, Juha* – celebrates resilience and (more rarely) the supportive power of love, while sharply but gently

acknowledging through detailed, deadpan comic observation the absurdity of vanity. Seldom moving his camera, encouraging his actors never to show explicit emotion, focusing on their minutest gestures and glances, he hones his films down to narrative essentials; even the stark sets and colour (*Drifting Clouds* is full of moody blues, suggesting the twilight world his couple are trapped in after being simultaneously made redundant) direct attention to the sad plight of his melancholy loners and losers. Nor does sentimentality dilute the dark tone: as if aware of his material's melodramatic potential, he undercuts 'dramatic' moments with an ironic use of music, be it tango, Tchaikovsky or Shostakovich. What distinguishes his best work from mere black comedy, however, is his very real compassion for his characters.

Aki Kaurismäki b. 1957 Finland. **Drifting Clouds** Finland 1996/ w Kati Outinen, Kari Vaananen, Elina Salo, Sakari Kuosmanen, Markku Peltola, Pietari the dog. **Films include** *Crime and Punishment*, 1983; *Shadows in Paradise*,1986; *Hamlet Goes Business,* 1987; *Ariel*, 1988; *Leningrad Cowboys Go America, The Match Factory Girl*, 1989; *I Hired a Contract Killer*, 1990; *Take Care of Your Scarf, Tatjana*, 1993; *Juha*, 1999. **See also** BERGMAN, DREYER, JARMUSCH, KEATON, KITANO

In this shot from Kazan's film of Tennessee Williams' stage hit, our eyes are inexorably drawn to that sweat stain on Brando's T-shirt: it signifies dirty, gritty realism, the brute physicality of the Stanley Kowalski character, and, by its very proximity to the faded, fragile elegance of Vivien Leigh's Blanche Dubois, a heady whiff of sex. Kazan, who augmented his prestigious career as a theatre director with a series of worthy genre pieces noted for their 'realism', finally hit his stride with *Streetcar*, which introduced the steamy intensity of his stage productions to the cinema. The performance was the thing – Brando's itchy, twitchy, mumbling Method mannerisms in an electric encounter with Leigh's more conventional classicism – and while Kazan's camerawork was unable to transcend the piece's stage origins, the designs at least contributed a claustrophic, feverish atmosphere. In works like *Viva Zapata*, *On the Waterfront*, *East of Eden*, *Baby Doll* and *Wild River* (his quietest and best film), he abandoned the studio for location shooting, but retained the services of Actors Studio stars like Brando, Dean and Steiger, effectively revolutionising film acting; in retrospect, however, many of the performances look less naturalistic than overwrought, just as the direction, despite the focus on 'serious' issues, often seems overemphatic (making Brando's informer a Christ-like martyr in *Waterfront* was especially misguided). Thereafter, save for the autobiographical *America, America*, Kazan's work steadily declined into hysterical melodrama and a tired adaptation of Fitzgerald's *The Last Tycoon*.

Elia Kazan b. 1909 Turkey. **A Streetcar Named Desire** USA 1951/ w Marlon Brando, Vivien Leigh, Kim Hunter, Karl Malden, Rudy Bond. **Films include** *Panic in the Streets*, 1950; *Viva Zapata!*, 1952, *On the Waterfront*, 1954; *East of Eden*, 1955; *Baby Doll*, 1956; *A Face in the Crowd*, 1957; *Wild River*, 1960; *Splendor in the Grass*, 1961; *America, America*, 1964; *The Last Tycoon*, 1976. **See also** ALDRICH, CASSAVETES, FULLER, LUMET, PENN, NICHOLAS RAY, SCORSESE

The as-ever unsmiling gaze is bemused but stoically resolute; the recreation of period and place accurate, discreetly beautiful and (with city-slicker Buster straddling an inadequate pony as he attempts to negotiate a violent, technologically primitive Old South) faintly absurd. Keaton was both a genius of understated comic acting and a masterful film-maker whose often technically innovative direction – which deployed a superbly mobile camera and inventive editing – paid painstaking attention to historical detail, both visual and social, in its evocation of a chaotic, dangerously volatile world where survival is achieved not by feats of super-human heroism but by resilience, determination and cool-headed pragmatism. That he himself performed, amazingly, all but one of his stunts is authenticated by his preference for long, fluid takes, but while he was graceful and athletic in motion and a master of the chase sequence, he eschewed slapstick for a quiet comic style in which subtle glances and furtive gestures convey a wealth of psychological and emotional information — here, his determination to survive a ludicrous, long-standing family feud of which he is the innocent victim. Buster's weapons in his fight against both life's injustices and his own inability to fit in with the world were not, as with Chaplin's *Tramp*, childlike malice, but intelligence, resourceful invention and unsentimental optimism: qualities which not only define his superb storytelling skills in master-pieces like *Sherlock Junior*, *Seven Chances*, *The General*, *Steamboat Bill Junior* and *The Cameraman*, but lend his work an unusually modern, timeless appeal.

Joseph Francis Keaton b. 1895 USA, d. 1966 USA. **Our Hospitality** USA 1923/ w Keaton, Joe Roberts, Natalie Talmadge.
Films include *The Three Ages*, 1923; *Sherlock Junior, The Navigator*, 1924; *Seven Chances*, 1925; *The General*, 1926; *College*, 1927; *Steamboat Bill Junior, The Cameraman*, 1928, *Spite Marriage*, 1929. **See also** CHAPLIN, JONES, KAURISMÄKI, KITANO, LESTER, TATI

ABBAS KIAROSTAMI

And Life Goes On...

A boy wanders aimlessly amidst the rubble of a mountain village devastated a year earlier by an earthquake. The image may arouse expectations of reportage or gritty neo-realism, but the films of Iranian master Kiarostami, while succeeding partly as oblique but illuminating reflections of his country's recent history, occupy a more fertile territory somewhere between documentary and self-reflexive, modernist drama. In this, the second part of a loose trilogy made in and around the village of Koker, the boy's film director father sets out to discover if the locals he cast in the first movie, *Where Is My Friend's Home?*, have survived the quake; the man is played by an actor, just as in the subsequent *Through the Olive Trees* (which depicts the making of *And Life Goes On...*) another actor plays the director of

the second film. The sophisticated Chinese-boxes structure of the trilogy is typical of Kiarostami's explorations of the relationship between reality, artifice and the film-making process; *Close-Up* intercuts a man's impersonation of film-maker Mohsen Makhmalbaf with his subsequent trial for fraud, so that the temporal shifts and use of different film styles and points of view ensure that we can never take for granted the authenticity of what we are seeing: the only evident 'truth' is the confusion of the defendant (who 'plays' himself) regarding fact and falsehood. Behind this playful, philosophical veneer, Kiarostami's humane compassion for his characters shines bright, his simple compositions and stories and long takes a mark of deep respect for their quiet integrity and strength of spirit.

Abbas Kiarostami b. 1940 Iran. **And Life Goes On...** Iran 1992/ w Farhad Kheradmand, Buba Bayour. **Films include** *The Traveller*, 1974; *The Report*, 1977; *Where Is My Friend's Home?*, 1988; *Homework*, 1989; *Close-Up*, 1990; *Through the Olive Trees*, 1994; *The Taste of Cherry*, 1997. **See also** ERICE, GODARD, MAKHMALBAF, MORRIS, MORETTI, ROSSELLINI

KRZYSZTOF KIESLOWSKI

A woman in bed with her lover next to a window looks almost to be underwater: an apt image for a tale of grief (her husband and daughter have recently died in a car crash she survived) in which a sense of guilt, injustice and self-protection lead her to withdraw from the world. Former documentarist Kieslowski's early features were noted for their simple, robust realism, but in his later work (*No End*; *Dekalog*; *The Double Life of Véronique*; the *Three Colours Trilogy*), he developed a more ornate, expressionist style, directing attention with painstaking precision to the immediate physical reality of his characters' lives, in order to illuminate an inner world of emotion, thought and premonition. Though primarily concerned with metaphysical and spiritual questions, his films were firmly rooted in everyday existence: the camera renders people, places and objects pregnant with meaning through subtle lighting, coded colours, faintly distorted perspectives, shallow depth of field, gliding camera movements and lingering, dramatic close-ups. Moreover, heightened sound effects, musical leitmotifs and associative editing create strange, resonant links between characters, while the intersecting strands of his elliptical narratives suggest a hidden but very real ordering intelligence at work behind the seeming chaos of the universe. Indeed, Kieslowski's use of a materialistic medium, limited to depicting visual surfaces, to explore the mysterious, immaterial forces – chance, coincidence, destiny, fate – that affect everyday experience, was masterful.

Krzysztof Kieslowksi b. 1941 Poland, d. 1996 Poland. **Three Colours: Blue** France/Poland/Switzerland 1993/ w Juliette Binoche, Benoît Régent, Florence Pernel, Charlotte Véry. **Films include** *Factory*, 1970; *Hospital*, 1976; *Camera Buff*, 1979; *Talking Heads*, 1980; *Blind Chance*, 1981; *No End*, 1984; *Dekalog*, 1988; *The Double Life of Véronique*, 1991; *Three Colours: White, Three Colours: Red*, 1994. **See also** BERGMAN, BRESSON, DREYER, LOACH, WAJDA, WELLES

KITANO TAKESHI

Yakuza hitman 'Beat' Takeshi (Kitano's performing name) fires at rivals in a bar, showing neither concern for a wounded colleague nor fear for himself. As an actor Kitano is a master of impassive cool, his blank expression suggesting the disenchantment of a man determined only to do his job and die with dignity. His direction is equally economic: dialogue is kept to a minimum, the static, immaculately framed compositions are often shot from directly in front of the characters, and the cutting is elliptical yet to the point. In *Sonatine*, roughly divided into three musical movements (tempestuous, comic, sombre), he regularly subverts the stylistic conventions of the crime thriller by filming acts of violence, or even conversations, from an unusual perspective, by using jokey camera tricks to depict the gangsters' silly beach games as they hide from a rival mob, and by completely omitting to show a long-awaited final shoot-out (the camera remains at a distance outside the hotel where the battle occurs, so that we see only the light of gunfire flashing through a window). The inventive playfulness may be disarmingly witty, but Kitano's attitude to his characters is, in his best work, fundamentally serious: *A Scene at the Sea*, *Kids Return* and *Hana-Bi* feature protagonists preoccupied with the question of how to remain true to oneself, their visual gags and occasional brutality (the latter two films are again partly set in the world of crime) deftly counterpointed by lyrical images of taciturn tenderness. A true original, Kitano is one of the most exciting, adventurous and distinctive film-makers at work today.

Kitano Takeshi b. 1947 Japan. **Sonatine** Japan 1993/ w Kitano, Kokumai Aya, Watanabe Tetsu, Katsumura Masanobu, Terashima Susumu. **Films include** *Violent Cop*, 1989; *Boiling Point*, 1990; *A Scene at the Sea*, 1991; *Getting Any?*, 1994; *Kids Return*, 1996; *Hana-Bi*, 1997; *Kikujiro*, 1999. **See also** HAWKS, JARMUSCH, KAURISMÄKI, KEATON, MELVILLE, OZU, PECKINPAH

As the king and the blinded Edgar stumble over a pitilessly arid, rocky terrain, they are followed and watched by Lear's subjects, impoverished victims of a cruel feudal state which the monarch, in his madness, has unwittingly helped to destroy, thus ensuring a kind of redemption for himself. Kozintsev's epic, stately film of Shakespeare's play is an exemplary cinematic adaptation, its grim grey images of a world in turmoil an imaginative correlative to the original text. Lear (Yuri Yarvet), small and wily rather than a towering tyrant, is a distinctly human protagonist caught up in the dynamics of society at large, which is peopled by Breughelesque peasants, cripples and vagabonds. Though the film is open to Marxist interpretation as an analogy of the modern world, it also succeeds as a subtle study of a man who through suffering comes to recognise his tyrannical folly. Though Kozintsev's early films, made in collaboration with Leonid Trauberg with whom he founded the Factory of the Eccentric Actor, dealt with typically Soviet subjects – slum clearance in *The Devil's Wheel*, the Paris Commune in *The New Babylon* – his work was notable for its lively wit, deft characterisations and imaginative visual effects; even *The Maxim Trilogy*, charting the life of a revolutionary hero from 1910 to 1918, was humorous, free from didacticism and unusually intimate in its observations. It was, however, the three majestic literary adaptations made without Trauberg (the others were the exquisite *Don Quixote* and *Hamlet*, scored like many of Kozintsev's films by Shostakovich) which crowned an impressive career.

Grigori Kozintsev b. 1905 Russia, d. 1973 USSR. **King Lear** 1971 USSR/ w Yuri Yarvet, Elsa Radzinya, Galina Volchek, Valentina Shendrikova, Karl Sebris, Oleg Dal. **Films include** *The Devil's Wheel*, 1926; *The Cloak*, 1926; *The New Babylon*, 1929; *The Maxim Trilogy*, 1935-39; *Don Quixote*, 1957; *Hamlet*, 1964. **See also** DOVZHENKO, EISENSTEIN, GANCE, VERTOV

As Alex and his droogs advance towards us, we are probably less aware of the threat they represent than of the striking design of their make-up and costumes, the statuary and the lighting. Style, for the meticulous perfectionist Kubrick, is insistent, a delight in technique and technology for their own sake. In films like *The Killing*, *Paths of Glory* and *Dr Strangelove*, it complemented story and characterisation, but as time passed and his projects became more painstakingly grandiose, his interest in humans (as distinct from his dismay at the follies of Humanity) diminished, so that what remained were cinematic set-pieces more notable for their 'look' than for any insights into life as we know it. *2001: A Space Odyssey* set the tone, a woolly-minded hypothetical fantasy about mankind's evolution which set more store by match-cuts, a singing computer, massive but seemingly weightless spacecraft and a spectacular psychedelic light-show than by its few human pawns, while the trite, muddled study of crime, punishment and free will in *A Clockwork Orange* viewed violence with both uncomprehending paranoia and gloating relish. However much Kubrick may have preferred to treat Big Issues, as an artist he seemed cold, aloof, humourless, and content to play with wide-angle lenses, film speeds, clever lighting, an ironic use of music and an overblown sense of scale which hints at the work's epic status. Clearly, the memorably vivid images he created are those of a superb craftsman; sadly, they tend to shout rather than speak, so that overall the exact meaning of his films often lacks subtlety and clarity.

Stanley Kubrick b. 1928 USA, d. 1999 England. **A Clockwork Orange** GB 1971/ w Malcolm McDowell, Patrick Magee, Michael Bates, Warren Clarke, Adrienne Corri, John Clive. **Films include** *Killer's Kiss*, 1955; *The Killing*, 1956; *Paths of Glory*, 1957; *Lolita*, 1962; *Dr Strangelove*, 1963; *2001: A Space Odyssey*, 1968; *Barry Lyndon*, 1975; *The Shining*, 1980; *Full Metal Jacket*, 1987; *Eyes Wide Shut*, 1999. **See also** COPPOLA, FELLINI, GANCE, HITCHCOCK, WELLES

KUROSAWA AKIRA

The lord Washizu crouches defeated yet stubbornly defiant in the face of certain death. Kurosawa's imaginative transposition of *Macbeth* to medieval Japan is typically distinguished by its rich blend of Noh acting, dynamic movement and dramatic imagery: Washizu's castle is forever shrouded in rolling mists accentuated by the high-contrast black and white photography; the witches are replaced by an old woman spinning in a magical forest glade; the usurper's pride is literally punctured by a hail of arrows. Lauded in the West for his sentimental brand of liberalism, Kurosawa was in fact at his best with spectacular action fare. *Seven Samurai* (inspired by his love of westerns) is arguably the finest example, a genuine epic with expertly staged battles that make stirring use of mud, rain, and thundering horses, the samurais' blend of animalistic energy and sword-fighting grace, and rapid montage that alternates tracking and panning shots, crowded long-shots and sudden close-ups, and unexpected moments of contemplative repose. Indeed, Kurosawa was always a superb technician and a natural storyteller adept at vivid characterisation; but (save for the very affecting *Living*) when he aimed for philosophical significance his films seemed hollow and portentous. *Rashomon* shows several versions of the same rape and murder to prove, simplistically, the subjectivity of 'truth', whereas late works like *Dreams*, *Rhapsody in August* and *Madadayo* are indulgent, ponderous essays in half-baked humanism. That said, his best work is notable for its energy, atmosphere, and muscular, poetic visuals; as a popular entertainer, his reputation seems assured.

Kurosawa Akira b. 1910 Japan, d. 1988 Japan. **Throne of Blood (Cobweb Castle)** Japan 1957/ w Mifune Toshiro, Yamada Isuzu, Chiaki Minoru, Shimura Takashi, Namira Chieko. **Films include** *Rashomon*, 1950; *Living (Ikiru)*, 1952; *Seven Samurai*, 1954; *The Lower Depths*, 1957; *The Hidden Fortress*, 1958; *Yojimbo*, 1961; *Sanjuro*, 1962; *Dodeskaden*, 1970; *Derzu Uzala*, 1975; *Kagemusha*, 1980; *Ran*, 1985; *Dreams*, 1990; *Madadayo*, 1993. **See also** FORD, HU, MILIUS, MIZOGUCHI, OZU, RENOIR

EMIR KUSTURICA

A spectacular gypsy festival, at which the film's innocent teenage hero meets his sweetheart: an image of celebration, community and purification, its water, flames and floating statues evocative of a pagan mass. Yet, in accompanying a crooked gypsy boss to Italy, unknowingly to recruit refugee child-prostitutes and thieves, the boy loses his innocence, returning to a loveless marriage and a divided community. Kusturica's abiding theme is the contradictions and conflicts within Balkan life. *When Father Was Away on Business* is a relatively quiet, child's-eye view of hardship and betrayal in the early Tito years. *Underground* is an epic, semi-comic allegorical fantasy, in which the experiences of two friends – one gullibly kept in a subterranean bomb shelter long after war has ended, the other staying above ground to

become a corrupt national hero – mirror Yugoslavia's murderous animosities and its inhabitants' abiding lust for life. From film to film, Kusturica's style has become increasingly grandiloquent: crowd scenes predominate, with the camera swirling in long, complex takes among ceaselessly vociferous characters indulging in sex, song, dance, drink, petty crime and violent argument. The expertly choreographed chaos sometimes suggests that Kusturica is easily carried away by his desire to concoct extraordinary, surreal images, so that the precise lines and direction of the narrative are left obscure. Ironically, while he has been accused of political bias, his characters' unglamorous actions are usually motivated by baser appetites, reflecting his own immersion in the sensual and visceral excesses of his style.

Emir Kusturica b. 1954 Yugoslavia. **Time of the Gypsies** Yugoslavia 1989/ w Davor Dujmovic, Bora Todorovic, Ljubica Adzovic, Husnija Hasmovic. **Films include** *Do You Remember Dolly Bell*, 1981; *When Father Was Away on Business*, 1985; *Arizona Dream*, 1993; *Underground*, 1995; *Black Cat, White Cat*, 1998. **See also** BERTOLUCCI, BUÑUEL, FELLINI, FORMAN, RUSSELL

Seldom has an image from a movie so eloquently conveyed the fear and claustrophobia of entrapment as this shot of Peter Lorre, the child-murderer being hunted by police and underworld alike in Lang's magnificent first talkie; moreover, few directors can have created so many images of entrapment as did Lang during his long, distinguished career. Repeatedly, his protagonists are imprisoned not only by an uncaring society or by their own flawed nature, but by Destiny itself: Lang's stories, which regularly return to the theme of crime and punishment, have the rigorous logic of a philosophical theorem. Hence his visual style is best seen not only as expressionism (though his early films were made as that movement was flourishing in Germany) but as abstraction: his dark studio-built cities are a distillation of urban anxiety, where a single slip, through desire, greed or vengefulness, leads inexorably to downfall and, often, death. Like his imagery, his narrative style was austere, economic, focused on essentials; few directors have shown such seriousness of purpose. And yet his work never lacked compassion: though aware of *M*'s terrible crimes, we see that he cannot help himself, and find him no less pathetically human than his pursuers. Likewise, in *Fury* a good man is warped by the need to wreak revenge on a world that adopts the methods of the lynch mob, while in *Scarlet Street* a meek cashier kills simply out of a misplaced desire for a little love in his life. In Lang's world, however, the Law, individual guilt, an unforgiving world and the workings of Fate combine to ensure there's little hope of escape.

Fritz Lang b. 1890 Austria, d. 1976 USA. **M** Germany 1931/ w Peter Lorre, Otto Wernicke, Ellen Widmann, Inge Landgut, Gustav Grundgens, Theodor Loos. **Films include** *Destiny*, 1921; *Dr Mabuse*, 1922; *Metropolis*, 1927; *Fury*, 1936; *You Only Live Once*, 1937; *Hangmen Also Die*, 1943; *The Woman in the Window, Ministry of Fear*, 1944; *Scarlet Street*, 1945; *Secret Beyond the Door*, 1948; *Rancho Notorious*, 1952; *The Big Heat*, 1953; *Beyond a Reasonable Doubt*, 1956. **See also** CHABROL, CLOUZOT, HITCHCOCK, MURNAU, PABST, SIODMAK, WIENE

Rogue preacher Robert Mitchum prepares to murder his recently-wed wife Shelley Winters for the stolen money her late husband hid away; she, wishing to be purified for the sin of having driven the latter to crime, offers no resistance. At first sight, the chiaroscuro lighting might suggest that Laughton's sole movie as director (sadly, a further project, *The Naked and the Dead*, never came to fruition) is a *film noir*; on closer inspection, however, the strange, slightly unreal symmetry of the composition, coupled with the unexpected serenity of the actors' postures, suggests a more eccentric style. Indeed, Laughton's film is one of the most bizarre, original and hauntingly beautiful works to emerge from Hollywood, an allegorical blend of fairy-tale, American pastoral and thriller in which the forces of good and evil (Lillian Gish's protective spinster and Mitchum's deranged parson) battle for the souls of Winters' innocent children during the Depression. The imagery ranges from shadowy expressionism to rural lyricism that echoes Griffith's dramas, from dreamy surrealism (the children's flight downriver watched by animals in huge close-up) to outright theatrical artifice – cameraman Stanley Cortez lit this scene as a triangle after remembering Sibelius' *Valse Triste*. And while the script makes frequent Biblical allusions, with its heightened performances, deliberately 'naive' visuals, polarised characters and narrative simplicity, the film is best seen as a determinedly poetic attempt to convey the cares, confusions and terrors of childhood: an attempt that is memorably and uniquely successful.

Charles Laughton b. 1899 England, d. 1962 USA. **The Night of the Hunter** USA 1955/ w Robert Mitchum, Lillian Gish, Shelley Winters, Billy Chapin, James Gleason, Sally Ann Bruce. **See also** BORZAGE, FORD, GRIFFITH, LANG, WHALE

Immaculately framed against a stunning backdrop of yellow sand and clear blue sky, a handsome Englishman improbably clad in Arab garb senses his destiny as he tests his expertise with a dagger. Lean's portrait of T E Lawrence was deeply romantic yet riven by contradictions: a poet-warrior, a liberator but an agent of British imperialism. But the abiding impression left by the film is of scale, evoking the hero's relationship to his environment: Lean's later works were without exception determinedly epic affairs, packed with striking images of crowds and picturesque landscapes, as if size guaranteed substance. Notoriously a pernickety perfectionist, he favoured weighty historical and literary subjects but regularly succumbed to visual grandiosity: in the self-consciously romantic *Doctor Zhivago*, the clumsy, unconvincing *Ryan's Daughter* and a pedantic but muddled adaptation of Forster's *A Passage to India*, his preference for the epic mode is aligned to stories requiring subtler, more intimate observation. Indeed, his early, more modest films are his best, notably his versions of Dickens' *Great Expectations* and *Oliver Twist*, where his feel for design and sharp editing combine to create lively, intelligent entertainments in which the characters are not yet overshadowed by milieu. After the success of *The Bridge on the River Kwai*, however – an ambitious, ironic but befuddled and overextended mix of anti-war message and conventional heroics – Lean seemed seduced by a sense of himself as a Great British Artist, and his films became longer, duller and more staidly academic in their staging of lavish spectacle.

David Lean b. 1908 England, d. 1991 England. **Lawrence of Arabia** GB 1962/ w Peter O'Toole, Alec Guinness, Anthony Quinn, Jack Hawkins, Omar Sharif, Anthony Quayle. **Films include** *In Which We Serve*, 1942; *This Happy Breed*, 1944; *Brief Encounter*, 1945; *Great Expectations*, 1946; *Oliver Twist*, 1948; *The Sound Barrier*, 1952; *The Bridge on the River Kwai*, 1957; *Doctor Zhivago*, 1965; *Ryan's Daughter*, 1970; *A Passage to India*, 1984. **See also** IVORY, KUBRICK, MILIUS, REED, SPIELBERG, VISCONTI

Life on the streets: as young and old banter with each other on a hot summer's day in Brooklyn, tensions between blacks and whites in the 'hood rise to boiling point. If Lee is best known for his sometimes provocative studies of racial prejudice and conflict, the value of his films arguably lies less in political commentary (which can tend towards the simplistic) than in his having given a cinematic voice to contemporary African-Americans. Not only is he adept at portraying the fabric, texture and sheer variety of the black American experience but his style, often neglected in favour of the films' content, is idiosyncratic and assured. Here, the old-timers on the sidewalk act as a Greek chorus, commenting on the film's characters and reminding us wittily of generational divisions in the community; the bright red backdrop evokes both the vibrancy of African-American culture and the bloody outcome of the day's interracial conflict; while everywhere around them, characters move as if choreographed in a musical, the camera swooping from one heated encounter to another to show how every action is linked in the chain of events leading to the climactic riot. Lee has never been a realist: from the playful Godardian narrative of *She's Gotta Have It* and the dance routines of *School Daze* to the subtle changes in lighting, tone, costume, colour and composition of *Malcolm X* and the microcosm of black masculinity in *Get on the Bus*, he has repeatedly (if erratically) adopted different styles according to his purpose – styles whose fluency and vitality nevertheless remain clearly identifiable as his own.

Spike Lee b. 1956 USA. **Do the Right Thing** USA 1989/ w Lee, Danny Aiello, Ossie Davis, Giancarlo Esposito, John Turturro, Rosie Perez, Bill Nunn. **Films include** *She's Gotta Have It*, 1986; *School Daze*, 1988; *Mo' Better Blues*, 1990; *Jungle Fever*, 1991; *Malcolm X*, 1992; *Crooklyn*, 1994; *Clockers*, 1995; *Girl 6*, 1996; *Get on the Bus*, 1997; *He Got Game*, 1998; *Summer of Sam*, 1999. **See also** FULLER, GODARD, SCORSESE, STONE

A lower-middle-class birthday party: it should be a happy family affair, but tensions, resentments and revelations will inevitably arise – the fact that the black girl, welcomed as a workmate of Brenda Blethyn, is in fact her recently rediscovered illegitimate daughter from a long-forgotten fling is only one of the deceits revealed at the film's end. Perhaps unsurprisingly, given that Leigh worked extensively for the stage, it's a theatrical climax; that background had an influence not only on his stories, many of which are interior-set comedy-dramas about small groups of family and friends, but on his use of camera (here, typically, he places everyone on the far side of the table) and the occasional larger-than-life acting which pushes naturalism into caricature. Leigh at his best is an acute, incisive observer of working- and lower-middle-class behaviour and mores. Working closely with his casts, who in lengthy discussions, improvisation and rehearsals produce many characteristics and lines that shape the final script, he aims at a serio-comic realism that will reflect the aspirations, anxieties and experiences of undereducated, unglamorous, far from sophisticated people seldom seen centre-screen; sadly, the allure of easy laughs can lead him to use such broad strokes that well-intentioned portraits may emerge as patronising or sentimental. That said, *Meantime*, *Naked* (his most irascibly honest, revealing and cinematically sophisticated film) and much of the admittedly very affecting *Secrets and Lies* succeed gloriously as perceptive, witty, warts-and-all studies of a particular way of London life.

Mike Leigh b. 1943 England. **Secrets and Lies** GB 1995/ w Brenda Blethyn, Marianne Jean-Baptiste, Timothy Spall, Phyllis Logan, Claire Rushbrook. **Films include** *Bleak Moments*, 1972; *Meantime*, 1983; *High Hopes*, 1988; *Life Is Sweet*, 1991; *Naked*, 1993; *Career Girls*, 1997; *Topsy-Turvy*, 1999. **See also** ANDERSON, CAPRA, DAVIES, LOACH, SOLONDZ

MITCHELL LEISEN

The scene is clearly conspiratorial, and pure vintage Hollywood: a chorine (Claudette Colbert) whispering with an aristocrat (John Barrymore)! Small wonder they look concerned: the teaming – he's invited her to his chateau to tempt a gigolo away from his wife, she's posing as a countess in order to hook a rich husband – is so unlikely, they're bound to be found out. The plot, by Billy Wilder and Charles Brackett, is typical screwball farce, but the underrated Leisen brought to it not only superbly sophisticated comic timing but real heart; no one else, save Cukor, would have been so generous to the broken Barrymore, let alone revelled so gleefully in the absurd, escapist sight of the rich at play. His best work may have depended on good writers (Brackett and Wilder also wrote *Arise My Love* and *Hold Back the*

Dawn, while Preston Sturges scripted *Easy Living* and *Remember the Night*), but the gentle romanticism, the silvery visual elegance, and the relaxed performances in those films are proof of his own light touch. He was expert at combining comedy, melodrama and a touch of social comment (many of his movies concern class and money), and, as a former costume designer and art director, alert to the importance of decor, whether in the supremely camp Freudian musical *Lady in the Dark* (he was openly gay) or, more subtly, in *Kitty*, a tender comedy-drama about another lowly girl breaking into society – in Gainsborough's London! Later, his work declined (though *No Man of Her Own* is superior *noir*); nevertheless, he deserves reappraisal as one of Hollywood's most sophisticated directors of comedy.

Mitchell Leisen b. 1898 USA, d. 1972 USA. **Midnight** USA 1939/ w Claudette Colbert, Don Ameche, John Barrymore, Mary Astor, Francis Lederer, Hedda Hopper. **Films include** *Murder at the Vanities*, 1934; *Hands Across the Table*, 1935; *Easy Living*, 1937; *Remember the Night, Arise My Love*, 1940; *Hold Back the Dawn*, 1941; *Lady in the Dark*, 1944; *Kitty*, 1945; *To Each His Own*, 1946; *No Man of Her Own*, 1950.
See also CUKOR, LUBITSCH, MINNELLI, SIRK, STURGES, WILDER

A gunfight, with two mortal enemies embracing their destiny: after years of biding his time, Charles Bronson exacts revenge on the sadistic Henry Fonda, who long ago forced him to participate in the killing of his father. Leone's style is at once operatic, ironic and elegiac, and *Once Upon a Time in the West*, set largely in Ford's Monument Valley, is as much a commentary on western movie lore as it is about the West itself. Working against traditional concepts of heroism, his darkly troubled protagonists are driven by greed, revenge, sheer malice or a rough sense of justice, while his epic, flashback-heavy tales – here, personal histories are set against the bringing of the railroad to the wilderness – are often dominated by set-piece tableaux of deadly conflict. Shoot-outs, set to the sometimes cacophonous, sometimes achingly romantic sound of Ennio Morricone's music, consist simply of almost abstract shots of eyes, hands and guns in massive close-up alternated with elegantly symmetrical long shots – seldom have the vast expanses of the CinemaScope screen been used so dramatically. Leone's baroque style was nevertheless anti-mythic: from the 'Dollars Trilogy' onwards, men battle, amid the grandeur of the baked Western landscape, over money and power, reflecting the ruthless rise of capitalism. Haunted memories, too, motivate their futile odysseys, and became the central motif of his masterpiece, *Once Upon a Time in America*, a sombre, melancholy gangster epic of Proustian dimensions in which time, eventually, heals the wounds of love and betrayal committed and suffered by a group of small-time hoodlums.

Sergio Leone b. 1929 Italy, d. 1989 Italy. **Once Upon a Time in the West** Italy 1968/ w Henry Fonda, Charles Bronson, Jason Robards, Claudia Cardinale, Frank Wolff, Keenan Wynn. **Films include** *A Fistful of Dollars*, 1964; *For a Few Dollars More*, 1965; *The Good, the Bad and the Ugly*, 1966; *A Fistful of Dynamite*, 1971; *Once Upon a Time in America*, 1984. **See also** EASTWOOD, FORD, MANN, MELVILLE, PECKINPAH

A girl new to London and two admirers carry a bed found in a junkyard through the centre of the city. Vaguely offbeat, faintly comic, the image typifies the 'wacky' humour pioneered by Lester in the Swinging Sixties. The story, about a womaniser instructing inexperienced friends in the art of seduction, is a sentimental, moralistic cautionary tale that reflected and exploited Britain's tentative moves towards sexual liberation; the style, presaging later pop promos, is relentlessly kinetic and gimmicky, making use of rapid editing, jump-cuts, different camera speeds and scenes assembled from shots taken from a bewildering if redundant variety of angles. As the title of his first short, *The Running, Jumping and Standing Still Film*, suggests, Lester specialised in frantic, slapsticky action: in two features

with the Beatles, *A Hard Day's Night* and *Help!*, he stressed their youthful energy with repeated scenes of the four running around either as an expression of boyishly innocent pleasure taken in action for action's sake, or as a means of escape from hysterical fans. At the same time, the group's innocuous irreverence found an ally in Lester's affection for surreal, Goonish humour, as seen in his two intermittently amusing but modish parables about mankind's insanity, *How I Won the War* and *The Bed Sitting Room*. Lester's best films, in fact, are calmer affairs – *Petulia*, *Robin and Marian* and *Butch and Sundance: The Early Days* – where characterisation takes precedence over upfront visual technique. Mostly, however, his post-60s work has been undistinguished, bereft even of the insistent liveliness that was once his trademark.

Richard Lester b. 1932 USA. **The Knack… and how to get it** GB 1965/ w Rita Tushingham, Ray Brooks, Michael Crawford, Donal Donnelly. **Films include** *A Hard Day's Night*, 1964; *Help!*, 1965; *How I Won the War*, 1967; *Petulia*, 1968; *The Bed Sitting Room*, 1969; *The Three Musketeers*, 1973; *The Four Musketeers*, 1975; *Robin and Marian*, 1976; *Butch and Sundance: The Early Days*, *Cuba*, 1979; *Superman II*, 1980. **See also** GODARD, RUSSELL, SENNETT, TATI

There is something fastidious, even fussy about the decor of Bel Ami's garret, with its bizarre bric-a-brac, ornate lamps, odd stove, pictures and ceiling. This is typical of producer-turned-writer-director Lewin's penchant for 'arty', literary subjects (*Bel Ami* is an intelligent, largely faithful adaptation of Maupassant's novella about an impoverished ex-soldier who makes his living partly as a gossip-mongering journalist, partly by ruthlessly trading on his appeal to a series of women) and of his tendency to recreate historical settings with painstaking accuracy. (Paintings were often a reference point: in this film, Ernst's *The Temptation of Saint Anthony*, while for his equally meticulous adaptation of Wilde's *The Picture of Dorian Gray*, he used Technicolor inserts of Ivan Le Lorraine Allbright's portrait of the morally decaying protagonist.) Though his work has often been dismissed as vulgar, pretentious and overly verbose, Lewin was a master of witty, epigrammatic dialogue – it is hardly surprising that Sanders, the image of supercilious cynicism, appeared in his first three films – and invested his characters with psycholgical subtlety and depth. Bel Ami is no mere scoundrel but, as this pensive moment of doubt shows, consciously the victim of his own opportunism. Nor were Lewin's strengths solely literary: his elegant, atmospheric evocation of 19th-century London and Paris in *The Moon and Sixpence*, *Dorian Gray* and *Bel Ami* were followed by the almost surreal, lavishly florid images – at once mythic and melodramatic – of *Pandora and the Flying Dutchman*, one of the most exotically romantic films made by an American.

Albert Lewin b. 1894 USA, d. 1968 USA. **The Private Affairs of Bel Ami** USA 1947/ w George Sanders, Angela Lansbury, Ann Dvorak, Frances Dee, Albert Basserman, John Carradine. **Films include** *The Moon and Sixpence*, 1943; *The Picture of Dorian Gray*, 1945; *Pandora and the Flying Dutchman*, 1951; *Saadia*, 1953; *The Living Idol*, 1957. **See also** CUKOR, GREENAWAY, IVORY, MANKIEWICZ, STILLMAN

JOSEPH H LEWIS

Pursued by the law, two bank-robbers take refuge in a swamp, trapped like animals. B-movie maestro Lewis was adept at making a little go a long way. Here, the misty marsh allows him not only to stage his final scene without extras (we merely hear the posse's gunfire) but to develop the theme of his criminal couple as lovers whose bestial need for one another ensures they are unable to obey society's moral codes: for their first meeting, when they recognise their shared passion for guns, Lewis had the actors circle and inspect each other like dogs in heat. He brought an imaginative eye even to his earliest, lowly programme-fillers, making inventive use of props or shooting from odd angles, but as he progressed to more fruitful subjects – the Hitchcockian *My Name Is Julia Ross*, the psychological whodunnit *So Dark the Night*, the gangster thriller *The Big Combo* – he became still more audacious: the last, a stunningly shot *film noir*, features torture by hearing-aid and a scene in which, as the deaf man is shot, we simply see guns flashing silently towards the camera, while *Gun Crazy*'s centrepiece is a bank-robbery shown in one long take shot from the back of the getaway car. Complementing such visual ambition, Lewis's stories were often psychologically and dramatically perverse: besides the phallic play with guns in *Gun Crazy*'s study of *amour fou*, *The Big Combo* included gay hitmen and masochistic obsession, *The Halliday Brand* was an Oedipal western and *Terror in a Texas Town* ended with a Swedish immigrant farmer killing the villain, in the climactic face-off, with a harpoon.

Joseph H Lewis b. 1907 USA. **Gun Crazy** USA1949/ w John Dall, Peggy Cummins, Berry Kroeger, Marros Carnovsky, Nedrick Young.
Films include *My Name Is Julia Ross*, 1945; *So Dark the Night*, 1946; *The Undercover Man*, 1949; *A Lady Without Passport*, 1950; *Cry of the Hunted*, 1953; *The Big Combo*, 1954; *7th Cavalry*, 1956; *The Halliday Brand*, 1957; *Terror in a Texas Town*, 1958. **See also** CORMAN, FULLER, SIEGEL, SIODMAK, TOURNEUR, ULMER

A boy and his bird: a typically simple, unglamorous image from Loach, who more than any other British film-maker has made it his task to document the everyday textures of working-class lives. But he has never been content merely to show; his low-key stories serve as a framework in which he analyses how those lives are shaped by class, money and politics. *Kes* charts the spiritual rebirth of a boy, dismissed as a ne'er-do-well by his mother, brother, neighbours and teachers alike, when he finds and trains a young falcon; sequences of the bird in flight make it a poetic symbol of freedom, of the possibility of the boy's hobby igniting an interest in pursuing an education and a future away from the dangerous mines on which the town's stunted economy depends. But, as in *Family Life*, *Riff-Raff*, *Raining Stones*

and *My Name Is Joe*, dreams of a better life are thwarted by the social and political realities of peer pressure, poverty and powerlessness: the boy's elder brother, angry over stolen money, kills the bird, destroying the boy's hesitantly growing sense of ambition. Loach rarely romanticises his characters, but shows how frustration can lead to in-fighting and crime. Nevertheless, such actions are depicted as the result of a wider malaise in which the empowered – politicians, employers, institutions in general – neglect the poor. The emotional force of his films is ensured by superbly naturalistic performances, an unadorned camera style, a gritty, almost documentary approach to dialogue, milieu, and the mundane fabric of daily existence, rendered dramatic by Loach's clear political commitment.

Ken Loach b. 1936 England. **Kes** GB 1969/ w David Bradley, Lynn Perrie, Freddie Fletcher, Colin Welland, Brian Glover, Bob Bowes. **Films include** *Poor Cow*, 1967; *Family Life*, 1971; *Looks and Smiles*, 1981; *Fatherland*, 1986; *Hidden Agenda*, 1990; *Riff-Raff*, 1992; *Raining Stones*, 1993; *Ladybird, Ladybird*, 1994; *Land and Freedom*, 1995; *Carla's Song*, 1997; *My Name Is Joe*, 1998. **See also** DAVIES, DE SICA, LEIGH, ROSSELLINI, SAYLES

JOSEPH LOSEY

A playboy (James Fox) and his Cockney valet (Dirk Bogarde) are distorted in a mirror's reflection – a metaphor for how their relationship is warping into reverse, so that the scheming manservant will dominate his indolent master. In all but Losey's early films – modest, taut crime thrillers about temptation, trust and betrayal – a baroque visual sensibility, particularly attuned to decor, vies with a rather academic, heavy-handed penchant for symbolism and allegory. Moving to England after being blacklisted during the HUAC witchhunts, he became preoccupied by questions of class and the conceit of a disruptive intruder catalysing tensions between lovers, friends or members of a family: here, Bogarde, with a girlfriend's help, seduces Fox away from his own lover (the homosexual attraction between the two men is implied rather than explicit), and wrests control of his house, whose lavish furnishings and staircases Losey deploys to mirror shifts in power. Together with films like *Eve*, *King and Country*, *Accident* and *The Go-Between*, *The Servant* (scripted, like the latter two films, by Harold Pinter) might indicate a leftist antipathy towards the rich and the powerful, but overall Losey's work is more suggestive of a sour, cynical misanthropy; certainly, in films as diverse as *Secret Ceremony*, the fittingly titled *Figures in a Landscape* (the most transparently metaphorical of his movies) and *Steaming*, the characters seem cyphers rather than individuals. Whereas in the 60s Losey was regarded as a serious artist, for the most part his overwrought style and gloomy narratives now seem mannered, passionless and pretentious.

Joseph Losey b. 1909 USA, d. 1984 England. **The Servant** GB 1963/ w Dirk Bogarde, James Fox, Wendy Craig, Sarah Miles, Catherine Lacey, Richard Vernon. **Films include** *The Prowler*, *M*, 1951; *The Criminal*, 1960; *The Damned*, *Eve*, 1962; *King and Country*, 1964; *Accident*, 1967; *Secret Ceremony*, 1968; *Figures in a Landscape*, 1970; *The Go-Between*, 1971; *Mr Klein*, 1976; *Don Giovanni*, 1979; *Steaming*, 1985. **See also** BOORMAN, CHABROL, RESNAIS, ROEG, VISCONTI

ERNST LUBITSCH

How knowing, how amoral are the smiles of con-artists Miriam Hopkins and Herbert Marshall as they casually share cash and mutual passion in a Parisian cab! Former silent comedian Lubitsch was famous as a director of light 'Continental' comedy, and while this shot sadly doesn't show Hans Dreier's elegant Art Deco designs, nor lets us hear Samson Raphaelson's mellifluous, innuendo-laden dialogue, it's still clear from Marshall's suave demeanour and Hopkins' receptive response that they're only out for money, sex and the sheer fun of fleecing a widow for whom they work. Lubitsch's brittle, brilliantined comedies of the 30s served up an escapist, light-hearted world of endless champagne, daring deceits, constant flirtation and illicit liaisons behind closed doors – narrative ellipsis was his hallmark, suggestive of delicious brief encounters unratified by the censors. While the wit might be exquisite – and it must be said that *Trouble in Paradise* has endured better than, say, *Bluebeard's Eighth Wife* – the insistently smart, heartless tone can become tiresome. The later, atypical *The Shop Around the Corner* (a truly moving romantic comedy that never plays down the pain and confusion of passion) and *To Be or Not to Be* (a black farce set in Nazi-occupied Warsaw) are considerably greater achievements, more affecting and finally more adult than the self-conscious naughtiness of the earlier films. That said, compared to most modern comedies (one need only see the difference between *The Shop Around the Corner* and Nora Ephron's 'remake', *You've Got Mail*), Lubitsch's sly but open-minded attitude to sex seems mature indeed.

Ernst Lubitsch b. 1892 Germany, d. 1947 USA. **Trouble in Paradise** USA 1932/ w Miriam Hopkins, Herbert Marshall, Kay Francis, Charlie Ruggles, Edward Everett Horton, C Aubrey Smith. **Films include** *The Marriage Circle*, 1924; *The Love Parade*, 1929; *Monte Carlo*, 1930; *Design for Living*, 1933; *The Merry Widow*, 1934; *Bluebeard's Eighth Wife*, 1938; *Ninotchka*, 1939; *The Shop Around the Corner*, 1940; *Heaven Can Wait*, 1943; *Cluny Brown*, 1946. **See also** Cukor, Leisen, Mamoulian, Von Sternberg, Wilder

GEORGE LUCAS

A square-jawed action-hero; a boyish, enthusiastic, similarly all-American innocent; a wise sage; and a ferocious-looking simian with a heart of gold. Lucas's hugely successful space opera not only drew upon the hallowed clichés of old movie and TV serials but with its comic-strip 'goodies' battling the evil Empire, it offered a range of identification-figures for young and old alike – there was even a feisty, determinedly modern Princess for female viewers. Besides setting new standards in special effects, the film was a supremely shrewd marketing exercise: simple, pacy and visually spectacular enough for children, sufficiently knowing and tongue-in-cheek for those raised on *Flash Gordon*, *Star Trek* and old westerns (*Star Wars*' story was partly inspired by *The Searchers*), and populated with cute, cardboard

characters ripe for transformation into toys. Lucas, who artistically, if not in business terms, has 'grown up' even less than Spielberg, is one of the greatest influences on modern American film-making, fostering a vision of cinema that's technically impressive, visually spectacular, and intellectually and emotionally uninvolving in its devotion to dynamic but light-hearted action. Though his first feature, *THX 1138*, was also visually innovative (if dystopian) sci-fi, and suggested some promise for Lucas as a serious film-maker, with the deft rites-of-passage comedy *American Graffiti*, he already displayed his penchant for cosy, undemanding nostalgia. His talents as a businessman and popular entertainer are undisputed; as an artist, his ambitions seem woefully limited.

George Lucas b. 1944 USA. **Star Wars** USA 1977/ w Mark Hamill, Harrison Ford, Carrie Fisher, Alec Guinness, Peter Cushing, Peter Mayhew. **Films include** *THX 1138*, 1971; *American Graffiti*, 1973; *Star Wars: The Phantom Menace*, 1999. **See also** CAMERON, COPPOLA, DANTE, DISNEY, MILIUS, SPIELBERG

After a tempestuous 'rumble' at Verona Beach, Romeo (Leonardo DiCaprio) cradles his dying friend Mercutio (Harold Perrineau) in his arms, while the unrepentant culprits look on. Were it not for the costumes, the scene might almost be from a Leone film, so splendidly epic and perfectly positioned is that framing ruined arch. Luhrmann's dazzlingly inventive version of Shakespeare's play, relocated to a teeming, vaguely futuristic metropolis, draws to amazingly coherent effect on various styles and genres: punk, disco, expressionism, surrealism, sci-fi, delinquent youth movies, musicals, comic-strip and camp baroque. While bravely but successfully retaining the Elizabethan dialogue, his main achievement in bringing the play to relevant, vibrant life is in finding a rich, visually imaginative equivalent for the original poetry: the Montagues and Capulets, families controlling rival conglomerates, pass through billboarded streets filled with flash limos, police helicopters, and leather-clad gangs packing pistols. While the action scenes are rapidly edited MTV-style, and prologue and epilogue are wittily reworked as a TV newscast, Luhrmann never neglects the romantic heart of the story: long takes and lavish design lend tender lyricism to Romeo and Juliet's trysts. Luhrmann's strength lies in making familiar material fresh; *Strictly Ballroom*, a brash but touching romantic comedy set in the world of Australian ballroom dancing, depicted both its gaudily narcissistic milieu and its ill-starred lovers with gently mocking irony and celebratory affection. He is a promising and distinctive young film-maker.

Baz Luhrmann b. (date unknown) Australia. **William Shakespeare's Romeo & Juliet** USA 1996/ w Leonardo DiCaprio, Claire Danes, Harold Perrineau, Pete Postlethwaite, Miriam Margolyes, Brian Dennehy. **Films include** *Strictly Ballroom,* 1992. **See also** ALMODÓVAR, CAMPION, DEMY, HAYNES, POWELL

Eleven good men and true (or are they? Henry Fonda, appropriately at their centre, has tested his colleagues' various weaknesses and, after long discussion, swayed their opinions) stare at the last member of the jury (an offscreen Lee L Cobb) who refuses – inevitably out of prejudice born of personal experience – to accept that a boy accused of murder might be innocent. It's a classic image from a Hollywood message-movie: populated by a carefully delineated cross-section of ordinary folk, gently conscience-pricking in directing the men's stares towards (but not directly at) the audience, and faintly complacent – in the end, almost everyone has some good in them. Lumet has worked in many genres with variable success (including errors of judgement like *Murder on the Orient Express* and *The Wiz*), but his abiding interest

is in crime and punishment, the fragility of justice and the knotty complexity of the legal system. In contrast to his other, ponderous 'big issue' dramas like *Fail-Safe*, *The Pawnbroker* or *Network*, his films about the law are often intelligent, engrossing and open to ironic ambiguity: *The Offence*, *Dog Day Afternoon* and *Q&A* are marked by an ambivalence towards characters that transcends knee-jerk liberalism, while *Prince of the City*'s exhaustive study of a guilt-stricken cop torn between fear of the state and loyalty to corrupt colleagues is masterly. Perhaps inevitably, in attempting to unravel such tangled issues, Lumet (whose work has declined in recent years) has mostly restricted himself to simple, 'realist' visuals focused on milieu and performance – wisely, since he has repeatedly proved to be an expert director of actors.

Sidney Lumet b. 1924 USA. **Twelve Angry Men** USA 1957/ w Henry Fonda, Lee J Cobb, E G Marshall, Ed Begley, Jack Warden, Martin Balsam. **Films include** *Fail-Safe*, 1963; *The Pawnbroker*, 1965; *The Offence*, 1972; *Serpico*, 1973; *Dog Day Afternoon*, 1975; *Network*, 1976; *Prince of the City*, 1981; *The Verdict*, 1982; *Running on Empty*, 1988; *Q&A*, 1990. **See also** Frankenheimer, Kazan, Parker, Penn

AUGUSTE AND LOUIS LUMIÈRE

The title tells all: a train draws into a station. That's all that happens in the film, but while few modern moviegoers have seen it, it remains one of the most famous shots in cinema history, simply because those viewers who first saw it in Paris were reputedly so astonished by the sight of the iron monster actually approaching them that many swooned or even fled the screening. The Lumières are widely regarded (albeit with some dispute) as the fathers of cinema: inventors of the *cinématographe*, they certainly held the first public screenings for which tickets were sold, in December 1895. For the most part, they merely shot, with a static camera that occasionally panned, whatever was at hand: home-movies with no real 'story', let alone editing. Yet the films remain entrancingly beautiful and surprisingly moving: not only because they are the earliest moving images available to us (their first brief shot of workers leaving the brothers' photographic factory in Lyon feels almost miraculous to behold), but because the Lumières inadvertently anticipated both the relationship between the camera and actors (their subjects often 'act up') and that between the projected image and the viewer. The train's progress towards the camera produces suspense and fear; a baby being fed in *Le Déjeuner de Bébé* provokes affectionate sentiment; a gardener surprised when he is sprinkled by his hose in *L'Arroseur Arrosée* is the unwitting victim of the first film comedy. Famously, the Lumières pronounced that the cinema had no future, and returned to their photographic business; history proved them wrong, but we can only be thankful for their mistake.

Auguste Lumière b. 1862 France, d. 1954 France. **Louis Lumière** b. 1864 France, d. 1948 France. **L'Arrivée d'un Train en Gare** France 1895. **Films include** *La Sortie des Ouvriers de l'Usine Lumière, Le Déjeuner de Bébé, L'Arroseur Arrosée, Le Repas en Famille, La Démolition d'un Mur, La Vie et la Passion de Jésus Christe*, 1895-97. **See also** FEUILLADE, MÉLIÈS, PORTER, SENNETT, WARHOL

133

A couple (Lupino and Edmond O'Brien), evidently in love, hold hands on a crowded bus: a mundane, cosily familiar image, its very ordinariness extraordinary given that the film explores the taboo of bigamy. Lupino's treatment of a potentially sensationalist subject is subtle and sensitive, sympathetic both to travelling salesman O'Brien's genuine if confused love for two very different (but never stereotyped) wives and to the vulnerable status of women expected to choose between career and family, and honest in its unglamorous depiction of working-class life. Famed as an actress who specialised in playing strong-willed, independent women, Lupino was also the only female writer-director in Hollywood during the 40s and 50s. Because her first three films (*Never Fear*, *Outrage* and *Hard, Fast and Beautiful*) dealt respectively with an unmarried mother, a rape victim and a daughter forced into playing professional tennis by a domineering mother, she is often characterised as a proto-feminist film-maker. Yet her unsentimental generosity towards the bigamous husband, expressed in images more attuned to low-key realism than to melodrama, is humanist rather than ideological. Moreover, her subsequent *The Hitch-hiker* focused entirely on men: a tense thriller about two fishermen who inadvertently pick up a psychotic murderer, it's a taut, stylish *film noir* that plays more effectively with claustrophobia (the car) and agoraphobia (the desert) than most road-movies by male directors. Sadly, she directed only one more film (*The Trouble with Angels*); the consequent low-profile of her work behind the camera is in need of serious reappraisal.

Ida Lupino b. 1918 England, d. 1995 USA. **The Bigamist** USA 1953/ w Edmond O'Brien, Ida Lupino, Joan Fontaine, Edmund Gwenn, Jane Darwell, Kenneth Tobey. **Films include** *Never Fear, Outrage*, 1950; *Hard, Fast and Beautiful*, 1951, *The Hitch-hiker*, 1953; *The Trouble with Angels*, 1966. **See also** Arzner, Bigelow, Hawks, Walsh, Wellman

LEN LYE

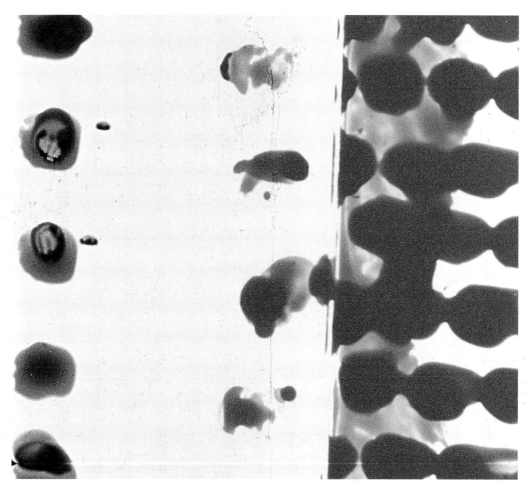

Blobs and squiggles, colours and shapes: Lye's fascination with the abstract, formal qualities of animation led him, in the five-minute *Colour Box*, to experiment with the then revolutionary practice of abandoning the traditional method of shooting with a camera by painting directly on to celluloid. A logical development of pioneering work done by artists like Eggeling, Leger, Duchamp, Richter, Walter Ruttmann and Oskar Fishinger, Lye's film, made for Britain's General Post Office Film Unit, was quite simply a graphic celebration of movement and colour, inevitably crude but imbued with real vitality as dots, lines, patterns and textures endlessly rearrange themselves on screen. Despite being aligned to some rather woolly philosophical, aesthetic and scientific theories, the painter and sculptor's techniques could result in work notable for its vibrant, quirky inventiveness. After the similarly abstract *Kaleidoscope*, for example, he experimented in *Rainbow Dance* and *Trade Tattoo* by subjecting images of the human form to unusual colour effects; visually at least, the result, with its bright hues, often anticipates pop art. There was, by his own admission, nothing to 'understand' in most of his films, although he also worked, less successfully, on live-action wartime propaganda shorts for the Ministry of Information. Regardless of whether one buys his strange, pretentious claims about images coming from the 'old brain' to the body's sense of 'kinetic presence', there is in his most enduring work an engaging vitality and sensuality.

Len Lye b. 1901 New Zealand, d. 1980 USA. **Colour Box** GB 1935. **Films include** *Kaleidoscope*, 1935; *Rainbow Dance*, 1936; *Trade Tattoo*, 1937; *Swinging the Lambeth Walk*, 1940; *Kill or Be Killed*, 1943; *Color Cry*, 1953; *Free Radicals*, 1958; *Particles in Space*, 1966. **See also** MCLAREN, QUAY BROTHERS

DAVID LYNCH

Sex, violence, fear: a chanteuse has forced an innocent youth she's found watching her from her closet to strip and make love to her at knifepoint; but is someone now watching them? In Lynch's surreal *film noir*, sado-masochistic relationships, voyeurism and psychopathic menace are the norm; at the same time, his off-kilter exploration of the twisted psyche of smalltown America is an adult fairy-tale – Kyle MacLachlan is a knight in tarnished armour whose curiosity about damsel-in-distress Isabella Rossellini impels him to risk his life rescuing her from demonic ogre Dennis Hopper, who abducted her husband and son in order to avail himself of her sexual favours. From his avant-garde debut, *Eraserhead*, onwards, Lynch has repeatedly imagined the American Dream as a nightmare of dangerous liaisons, unspeakable crimes, irrational obsessions, death, decay and delirious perversity: here Rossellini is so traumatised by her ordeal that she can only understand desire when it's accompanied by brutal violence. Lynch loves the grotesque, unsettling and inexplicable: accordingly, some of his films (*Wild at Heart*, *Fire Walk with Me*, *Lost Highway*) decline into barely coherent series of bizarre tableaux, while others (*Eraserhead*, *Elephant Man*, *Blue Velvet* and the early episodes of the TV soap fantasy *Twin Peaks*) are frighteningly evocative studies of psychological torment. Then, black humour, an ironic approach to genre and symbolism, an expressionist use of colour, architecture, music and sound, and painterly, sinister compositons combine to create some of the most inventively chilling American movies ever made.

David Lynch b. 1946 USA. **Blue Velvet** USA1987/ w Kyle MacLachlan, Isabella Rossellini, Dennis Hopper, Laura Dern, Dean Stockwell, Hope Lang. **Films include** *Eraserhead*, 1977; *The Elephant Man*, 1980; *Dune*, 1984; *Twin Peaks,* 1990-91; *Wild at Heart*, 1990; *Twin Peaks: Fire Walk with Me*, 1992; *Lost Highway*, 1997; *The Straight Story,* 1999. **See also** BOROWCZYK, BROWNING, BUÑUEL, CORMAN, GILLIAM, GRIFFITH, LANG, SVANKMAJER

In a 1950s parlour still decorated in the Edwardian style, little old ladies serve tea to a decidedly unusual-looking music quintet: in fact, the men are criminals whose leader – at the piano, naturally – rents a room upstairs. But why do the toughs look so stiffly uneasy (besides the fact that they are clearly ill-suited to such genteel surroundings)? They can't bring themselves to kill the sweet, innocent landlady who might ruin their plans, and will end up murdering each other instead. Mackendrick's film is a characteristically ironic, mordant affair blending almost grotesquely cosy English manners and black comedy. He had already darkened Ealing's usual comic whimsy in *Whisky Galore*, *The Man in the White Suit* and *The Maggie*, where idealism and the common weal fall foul of greed, envy, apathy and bureaucracy (the self-interested in-fighting may be seen as analogous to post-war British politics), not to mention *Mandy*, a poignant melodrama in which a father's well-meaning but blind refusal to accept his daughter's deafness denies her the support she needs. Perhaps unsurprisingly, Mackendrick, whose sceptical sensibility was at odds with Ealing's homely ethos, moved to America, where he made his masterpiece, *Sweet Smell of Success*: a cynical study in tawdry corruption, its dog-eat-dog columnists, agents and politicians shrouded in glittering images even darker than *noir*. Thereafter, while *Sammy Going South* and *A High Wind in Jamaica* offered intelligent, unusually bleak accounts of childhood's confusing cruelties, his work became more uneven, and, sadly, he soon retired from film-making.

Alexander Mackendrick b. 1911 USA, d. 1993 USA. **The Ladykillers** GB 1955/ w Alec Guinness, Katie Johnson, Cecil Parker, Herbert Lom, Peter Sellers, Danny Green. **Films include** *Whisky Galore*, 1949; *The Man in the White Suit*, 1951; *The Maggie*, 1954; *Sweet Smell of Success*, 1957; *Sammy Going South*, 1963; *A High Wind in Jamaica*, 1965; *Don't Make Waves*, 1967. **See also** Buñuel, Chabrol, Clouzot, Hamer, Wilder

DUSAN MAKAVEJEV

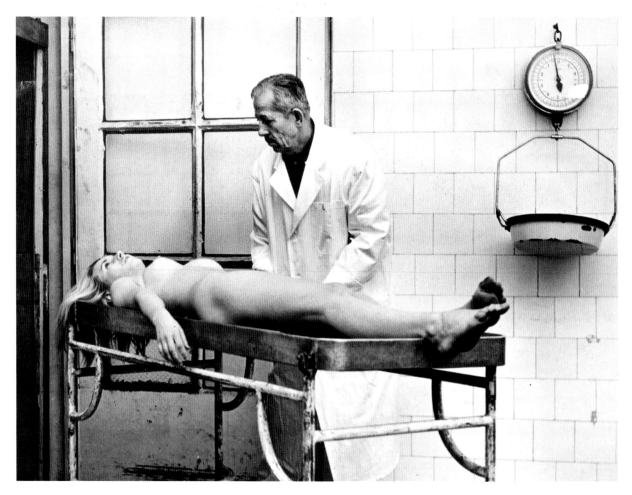

The autopsy of a young woman, drowned in a well: in the preceding scene we saw her in post-coital play with her lover, the sex act itself having been 'represented' by documentary footage of Communists demolishing church steeples. The prime method used by Makavejev in his witty, irreverent, quizzical explorations of the links between sexuality, power and politics, past and present, the individual and society, is collage. Like all his best films (*Man Is Not a Bird*, *Innocence Unprotected*, and *WR: Mysteries of the Organism*), *The Switchboard Operator* alternates fiction, documentary and archive footage so that the main 'story' – the doomed romance between a sexually liberated telephonist and a repressed rat-exterminator – serves as a paradigm of the human behaviour described and shown in lectures to camera by scientific 'experts', old newsreels and movies, political slogans, artworks and poems. For Makavejev, we are creatures of age-old impulses which society strives with varying success to contain: hence, the exterminator's sexual conservatism is inextricably linked – psychologically and within the film's jigsaw-like structure – with his membership of the Party. Often, Makavejev's films are like illustrated essays, their analytical commentaries juxtaposed with narrative sequences that are documentary-like in their naturalism yet sly and almost surreal in their easy-going, playful eroticism. Recently, his work has seemed more strained, mannered and inconsequential; perhaps the sexual curiosity, socio-political optimism and artistic experimentalism of the 60s and 70s were crucial to his own creativity.

Dusan Makavejev b. 1932 Yugoslavia. **The Switchboard Operator** Yugoslavia 1967/ w Eva Ras, Ruzica Sokic, Slobodan Aligrudic, Miodrag Andric, Dr Aleksander Kostic. **Films include** *Man Is Not a Bird*, 1966; *Innocence Unprotected*, 1968; *WR: Mysteries of the Organism*, 1971; *Sweet Movie*, 1974; *Montenegro*, 1981; *The Coca-Cola Kid*, 1985; *Manifesto*, 1988; *Gorilla Bathes at Noon*, 1993. **See also** BUÑUEL, GODARD, MARKER, MEYER, OSHIMA

MOHSEN MAKHMALBAF

Three girls from a nomadic tribe gather flowers to dye wool for a carpet ('gabbeh') which will show the story of one of the girls – Gabbeh – as her father delays her marriage. The image is painterly, tableau-like, radiantly colourful (embodying the theme that life is colour) and, in depicting the very process and apparatus of the carpet's making, self-reflexive. After several relatively straight-forward films about social hardship, Makhmalbaf adopted a more experimental aesthetic: here, the heroine simultaneously 'is' the carpet itself and the girl it depicts, a real or mythic figure situated both in and outside the film's story, who comments and urges on its progress as she relates it to an old couple who are per-haps her future self and her lover. Past and present, reality and legend, and digressions on storytelling (the girl's

uncle, delivering a lesson on colour, grabs and mixes hues from the landscape itself) are woven into the complex narrative fabric, whose modernist twists are counterbalanced by traditional natural symbolism (water, fire, eggs, apples); the tone is at once literal and metaphorical, poetic and deconstructive. Likewise, *A Moment of Innocence* explores the relativity of truth and the links between fact and fiction as it charts the making of a film recreating an incident from Makhmalbaf's past. Often, his films, unlike those of his compatriot Kiarostami, are too clever and contrived to persuade emotionally or philosophically; nevertheless, his fertile imagination and fascination with life's relationship to art make for rewarding, challenging viewing.

Mohsen Makhmalbaf b. 1957 Iran. **Gabbeh** Iran/France 1995/ w Shaghayegh Djodat, Abbas Sayahi, Hossein Moharami, Parveneh Ghalandari. **Films include** *Boycott*, 1985; *The Peddler*, 1986; *The Cyclist*, 1988; *Marriage of the Blessed*, 1989; *Once Upon a Time Cinema*, 1992; *Salaam Cinema*, 1994; *A Moment of Innocence*, 1996; *The Silence*, 1998. **See also** GODARD, KIAROSTAMI, MORRIS, RIVETTE

TERRENCE MALICK

Texan farm-workers search for locusts destroying the wheat-crop; in seconds, in the escalating panic, flames ignited by dropped lanterns will turn the land into a blazing inferno that matches the raging jealousy and anger arising from a romantic triangle built on fear, greed and deceit. The intense lyricism of Malick's brilliantly lit and framed compositions not only recalls the work of early directors like Murnau and Sjöström and American painters like Wyeth, Wood and Hopper, but serves as an eloquent externalisation of inner emotions. In *Badlands* and *Days of Heaven*, his sumptuous images were countered by intentionally naive voiceovers (narrated in oblique, inarticulate tones by innocent girls describing events they barely comprehend), evoking both the fundamental mysteriousness of individual motivation and the relationship of human ambition and achievement to the larger scheme of the universe: the second film, particularly, is almost Biblical in its elemental imagery. Returning to film-making 20 years later with the war epic *The Thin Red Line*, Malick deployed a whole host of voiceovers to express the various confusions, anxieties and spiritual and physical needs of soldiers facing death daily; here, his use of dreamlike natural imagery painted a terrifying yet strangely serene portrait of paradise lost, in which conflict and destruction are unfathomable yet eternal facets of the cosmos. Malick is the modern American cinema's great poet-philosopher, whose images, painstakingly perfectionist in their historical accuracy yet imbued with the timelessness of myth, speak of a fascination with – and, perhaps, a faith in – the transcendent.

Terrence Malick b. 1943 USA. **Days of Heaven** USA 1978/ w Richard Gere, Brooke Adams, Linda Manz, Sam Shepard, Robert Wilke. **Films include** *Badlands*, 1973; *The Thin Red Line*, 1998. **See also** DOVZHENKO, HERZOG, MURNAU, SJÖSTRÖM, WELLES

What could be more natural than an elderly man taking a shine to a pretty young croupier in a casino? Yet Burt Lancaster's dapper, impossibly white garb and status as Hollywood icon bring a level of unreality to the scene: he is, in fact, a guardian angel, a knight in slightly tarnished armour come to rescue damsel-in-distress Susan Sarandon from loneliness and the threat of a ruthless drugs gang. Malle's film is part crime thriller, part Beauty-and-the-Beast romance, part wistful comedy about social, economic and moral changes in America (Lancaster's kindly petty crook repeatedly alludes to the good old days of the great gangsters). If it's hard to discern a unifying theme or visual style in Malle's work, it is marked by his gentle, generous sympathy for loners, losers and dreamers and by the way his best films often straddle realism and fantasy, drama and non-fiction (he also made several fine documentaries). The taut thriller *Lift to the Scaffold* was set in a very recognisable nocturnal Paris, *Le Feu Follet* portrayed a man's moves towards suicide with an admirable lack of dramatic contrivance or sentimentality, *Lacombe Lucien* offered genuine insights into why an innocent adolescent might become a Fascist, and *Au Revoir les Enfants* was a subtly nuanced drama about unwitting but deadly betrayal lifted from Malle's childhood memories. His polished but unflashy camerawork generally favoured medium-shots, observing characters and milieu with a mix of affectionate interest and objective detachment; his eclectic choice of material, however, resulted in a body of work unusually variable in quality.

Louis Malle b. 1932 France, d. 1995 USA. **Atlantic City** USA 1980/ w Burt Lancaster, Susan Sarandon, Kate Reid, Michel Piccoli, Hollis McLaren, Robert Joy. **Films include** *Lift to the Scaffold, Les Amants*, 1957; *Zazie dans le Métro*, 1960; *Le Feu Follet*, 1963; *Viva Maria!*, 1965; *Phantom India*, 1968; *Lacombe Lucien*, 1973; *Pretty Baby*, 1978; *My Dinner with André*, 1981; *Alamo Bay, God's Country*, 1985; *Au Revoir les Enfants*, 1987; *Milou en Mai*, 1990. **See also** BECKER, DEMME, RENOIR, TRUFFAUT

ROUBEN MAMOULIAN

The threat posed by the bestial Hyde – sitting on Ivy's bed, aroused by her décolletage – is clearly sexual rather than simply murderous: understandable, given that his respectable other self, Jekyll, has expressed despair about his lengthy engagement to his fiancée and felt tempted by an earlier encounter with Ivy. Mamoulian is often regarded as a technical innovator with little to say, but the precise visual suggestion of sexual desire and its repression by Victorian society was daring, unusually true to Stevenson's novella, and typical of the director's determination to express meaning with all the cinematic tools at his command. The film's lengthy opening shot, filmed from Jekyll's point of view, both leaves us in suspense at to the protagonist's appearance (is it Hyde?) and aligns our sympathy with his frustrated predicament.

Similarly, the inventively eloquent use of song, costume, decor, rhyming dialogue, jokes, fluid camera movement, fast and slow motion and Eisensteinian montage makes *Love Me Tonight* not only one of the most delightfully lively musicals ever made but a truly cinematic fairy-tale about a sleeping beauty awakened by a none-too-princely tailor, while *Becky Sharp* – the first feature in full Technicolor – uses the enlarged palette for dramatic purposes, most famously in an overhead shot of a ballroom being swamped by blood-red tunics as soldiers prepare to leave for Waterloo. Such conflations of style and meaning are recurrent in Mamoulian's films; their elegance, delicate wit, cinematic sophistication and imaginative fertility make him one of the most enduringly appealing directors of Hollywood's Golden Age.

Rouben Mamoulian b. 1898 Russia, d. 1987 USA. **Dr Jekyll and Mr Hyde** USA 1931/ w Fredric March, Miriam Hopkins, Rose Hobart, Holmes Herbert, Halliwell Hobbes. **Films include** *Applause*, 1929; *City Streets*, 1931; *Love Me Tonight*, 1932; *Queen Christina*, 1933; *Becky Sharp*, 1935; *High, Wide and Handsome*, 1937; *The Mark of Zorro*, 1940; *Blood and Sand*, 1941; *Summer Holiday*, 1947; *Silk Stockings*, 1957. **See also** HAYNES, LUBITSCH, LUHRMANN, MINNELLI, OPHÜLS, POWELL, VON STERNBERG

JOSEPH L MANKIEWICZ

'Fasten your seatbelts – it's going to be a bumpy night.' So warns Bette Davis at a theatrical party as acerbic drama critic George Sanders introduces protégée Marilyn Monroe ('a graduate of the Copacabana school of acting') to Davis and Anne Baxter, a fan who ruthlessly works her way into the ageing actress's affections only to steal her lover and her stardom. Here for once, dialogue is quoted as central to Mankiewicz's brittle, witty style: the producer-turned-writer-director was famous for ironic epigrams, complex flashback structures, stories told from multiple perspectives, and his overall articulacy – the stagey positioning of the actors here, which suggests an invisible proscenium arch, typifies his lack of interest in using inherently cinematic methods to tell a story, delineate characters or express meaning.

That said, his finest films were intelligent, sophisticated entertainments, and in *All About Eve*, *A Letter to Three Wives*, *House of Strangers*, *People Will Talk* and *The Barefoot Contessa*, the verbal dexterity and sense of performance were fittingly aligned to tales of pretence, deceit and self-image: certainly, *Eve* is one of the most appealingly sardonic depictions of the pretensions, insecurities, ambitions and egotism of the theatre world. Elsewhere, though *The Ghost and Mrs Muir* – a romantic comedy about a genteel widow revitalised by her relationship with a dead sea captain – was affectingly tender and subtly shot and designed, Mankiewicz's stabs at visual style – in, say, *Guys and Dolls* or *Sleuth* – can seem forced and clumsy, and the tone heartless. His facility as a wordsmith, however, remains undisputed.

Joseph L Mankiewicz b. 1909 USA, d. 1993 USA. **All About Eve** USA 1950/ w Bette Davis, Anne Baxter, George Sanders, Celeste Holm, Gary Merrill, Thelma Ritter, Marilyn Monroe. **Films include** *The Ghost and Mrs Muir*, 1947; *A Letter to Three Wives*, *House of Strangers*, 1949; *People Will Talk*, 1951; *Five Fingers*, 1952; *Julius Caesar*, 1953; *The Barefoot Contessa*, 1954; *Guys and Dolls,* 1955; *Suddenly Last Summer*, 1959; *Cleopatra*, 1963; *Sleuth*, 1972. **See also** CUKOR, LEWIN, ROHMER, STLLMAN, WILDER

ANTHONY MANN

James Stewart – traditionally the embodiment of gentle, fair-minded decency – looks haunted, even manic as he draws against the men who would deprive him of the bounty he feels is his due after losing his land during the Civil War. After making a number of tense, claustrophobic *noir* thrillers in the 40s, Mann embarked on a series of westerns notable for their symbolic, expressive use of the rugged American landscape (his heroes' journeys are geographical and spiritual) and their psychological complexity. Here, Stewart's integrity has been eroded by an obsessive desire for revenge: he will do anything, from pretending to be a lawman to killing the partners he has enlisted in his hunt for a wanted man, to recover his farm and lost idealism. Mann was especially adept at filming exteriors, so that nature not only dwarfs his characters' petty but deadly rivalries, but allows them a chance to prove their heroic potential: in *The Naked Spur*, Stewart achieves his aim, and thereby comes to recognise the warped effects of his torment, by scaling the bluff of the title. Built around honour, betrayal and vengeance, Mann's films (notably *The Man from Laramie* and *Man of the West*) often featured oppressive father-figures; scenes of violence might resonate with Freudian overtones of patricide, castration and humiliation. At the same time, he was clearly fascinated by classical themes: *The Furies* is evocative of Greek myth, *Man of the West* of King Lear, while the epic *El Cid* – a western in disguise – is his finest study in heroism, ending with the knight's corpse riding off into the distant horizon and an assured place in legend.

Anthony Mann (Emil Anton Bundsmann) b. 1906 USA, d. 1967 W Germany. **The Naked Spur** USA 1953/ w James Stewart, Robert Ryan, Ralph Meeker, Millard Mitchell, Janet Leigh. **Films include** *Desperate*, *T-Men*, 1947; *Devil's Doorway*, *Winchester 73*, *The Furies*, 1950; *Bend of the River*, 1952; *The Far Country*, 1954; *The Man from Laramie*, 1955; *The Tin Star*, 1957; *Man of the West*, 1958; *El Cid*, 1961; *The Fall of the Roman Empire*, 1964. **See also** Boetticher, Eastwood, Ford, Leone, Peckinpah

MICHAEL MANN

FBI agents check forensic evidence they hope will lead to a serial killer; one, able to fathom the criminal mind, is anxious that his empathetic reasoning may drive him again to nervous breakdown. Mann's supremely stylish adaptation of Thomas Harris' thriller typically displays an almost obsessive fascination with professional procedure and, in the tradition of directors like Hawks and Melville, defines men according to their actions. Equally characteristic is Mann's expressionistic use of colour, architecture, movement and music to externalise the dark recesses of his protagonist's mind. Here, the hi-tech laboratory embodies the complex logistics of the agent's methods as he tracks the Tooth Fairy; the subterranean red suggests both the psychic hell of closing in on his prey, and the blood and fire associated with the killer's crimes. Mann is one of the modern crime movie's finest practitioners. Though expert with action scenes – for which he uses rapid, razor-sharp editing and a sinuously mobile camera – his chief virtue lies in his ability to probe the psychological complexity of his characters through lean but subtly telling dialogue and a precise visual exploration of their relationship to one another and the environment in which they work. At times form and content virtually merge: the paring down of the final chase at LAX airport in *Heat* to a nightmarish, near-abstract collage of thunderous sound, primary colours, flashing lights and creeping shadows eloquently evokes the almost mythic dimension of the struggle between a perfectionist cop and the master thief who is his alter ego.

Michael Mann b. 1943 USA. **Manhunter** USA 1986/ w William Petersen, Joan Allen, Brian Cox, Kim Greist, Dennis Farina, Tom Noonan. **Films include** *The Jericho Mile*, 1979; *Thief*, 1981; *The Keep*, 1983; *The Last of the Mohicans*, 1992; *Heat*, 1995. **See also** HAWKS, HILL, KITANO, LANG, MELVILLE, WALSH

CHRIS MARKER

Strange, ornamental cats in a suburban Tokyo temple consecrated to the creatures: Marker's camera misses little. Arguably the cinema's greatest essayist, he transcends traditional documentary with his exhilaratingly personal reports on the world, discursive filmed letters which – even in *Le Joli Mai*, a comparatively straightforward *cinéma verité* account of Parisians in 1962 – adopt the quizzical perspective of a stranger in a strange land. His concerns are time, place, politics (his fundamentally Leftist films were made with a collective he founded in the mid-60s), culture, and the relationship between the photographic image and memory; his impressionistic, collage-style 'narratives' are poetic, allusive and literary in tone; his visual style is at once discreet, as it observes people in their everyday lives, and acutely aware of how the camera affects whatever it captures (the reclusive Marker himself hates being photographed). His masterpiece, *Sans Soleil* offers a thought-provoking, wayward, but finally cogent commentary on various subjects – Japan, Africa, technology, pornography, religion, guerrilla warfare, guerrilla film-making, and the San Francisco locations of *Vertigo* – using a meditative voiceover, documentary footage, freeze-frames, electronic music and synthesised images to move between the universal and the personal: the cats here not only inspire thoughts on grief, faith and animism, but, like the repeated shots of birds and the clips from Hitchcock's film, testify to his own abiding obsessions. Marker is an idiosyncratic talent, experimental and endlessly curious, and has now apparently abandoned traditional film-making for work in the CD-Rom format.

Chris Marker (Christian François Bouche-Villeneuve) b. 1929 France (Mongolia?) **Sans Soleil (Sunless)** France/Japan 1982.
Films include *Olympia 52*, 1952; *Lettre de Sibérie*, 1958; *Description d'un Combat*, 1960; *Cuba Si!*, 1961; *Le Joli Mai, La Jetée,* 1963; *Loin du Vietnam*, 1967; *Le Train en Marche*, 1973; *Le Fond de l'Air est Rouge*, 1977; *AK*, 1985; *The Last Bolshevik*, 1993; *Level 5*, 1996.
See also GODARD, MAKAVEJEV, MORETTI, MORRIS, RESNAIS, VERTOV

WINSOR McCAY

A dinosaur chomping on a tram: long before *King Kong* or *Jurassic Park*, McCay discovered the appeal not only of seeing monstrously large creatures on screen, but of showing the impossible. The cartoonist, famous for his Little Nemo comic-strip in the *New York Herald*, may not have been the first movie animator – he was preceded by Stuart Blackton and Emile Cohl – but in the original *Gertie the Dinosaur*, he pioneered the affectionate anthropomophisation of animals. There was, inevitably, an air of novelty to that film – the animated sequences are introduced by live-action footage of McCay displaying his techniques to a group of businessmen – and no real story: in response to his (intertitled) suggestions, Gertie appears, dances, and takes his animated self for a ride. But there is immense charm not only in the simple,

elegant lines (which often resemble art nouveau in style) and easy-going movement, but in Gertie's character as she regularly ignores orders to eat palm trees and boulders, bursts into tears or tosses a passing mammoth into a lake from which she guzzles. Clearly, McCay understood animation's potential for depicting what live-action cannot: besides the delightful *The Story of a Mosquito* (in which massive close-ups and strange angles create almost abstract images of an insect gleefully drinking blood from a drunkard's head), the lyrical *The Centaurs* and the witty *The Dream of a Rarebit Fiend*, he also recreated a contemporary disaster in *The Sinking of the Lusitania*, in which more 'realistic' images are tinged, typically, with touches of authentic visual poetry.

Winsor McCay b. 1871 USA, d 1934 USA. **Gertie on Tour** USA c. 1918. **Films include** *Gertie the Dinsoaur*, 1909; *Little Nemo*, 1910, *Jersey Skeeters*, 1911; *The Story of a Mosquito*, 1912; *The Sinking of the Lusitania*, 1918; *Flip's Circus, The Centaurs*, 1918-21; *The Dream of a Rarebit Fiend*, 1921. **See also** AVERY, DISNEY, HANNA AND BARBERA, JONES, PARK, STAREWICZ

NORMAN McLAREN

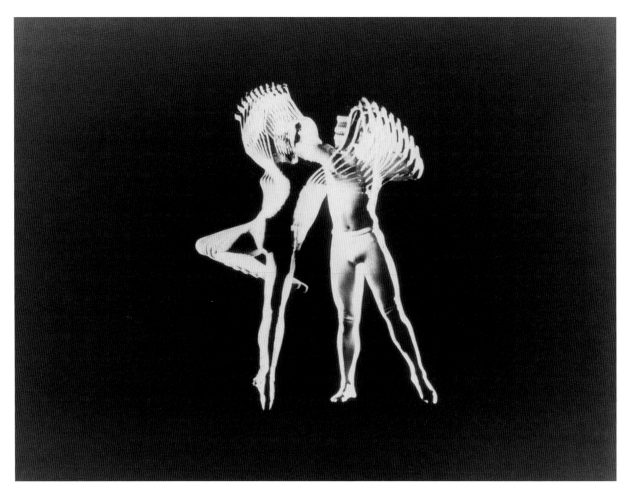

Dancers' gracefully choreographed limbs begin to multiply, swirling like feathers to the music. Mostly made for the National Film Board of Canada, McLaren's animated films are technically innovative and often thrillingly beautiful; *Pas de Deux* uses high-contrast black and white photography, slow motion and staggered multiple superimpositions created in the printing process to develop a swooningly lyrical, semi-abstract accompaniment to a plaintive melody. Experimentation with sound and image was his forte: inspired by Len Lye's technique of painting directly on film, in shorts like *Boogie Doodle* and *Begone Dull Care* he began to paint and engrave lengthways on film, overcoming the tyranny of the frame and finding a visual equivalent for jazz in riotous movements of colour, dots, lines and sharply rhythmic editing. Not all his work was abstract or drawn; in *Neighbors* and *The Blackbird*, he experimented, respectively, with pixillated shots of human beings for a philosophical satire, and animated cut-outs for a poetic fable; *A Phantasy*, meanwhile, combines a surreal, Tanguy-inspired animated landscape with sequences of dots in symmetrical motion, while a kind of *musique concrète* derives from marking the optical soundtrack. Though *Neighbors*, the Keatonesque pixillation *A Chairy Tale* and *Blinkity Blank* are comic, most of McLaren's work is designed not to tell a story or make us laugh but to make us see in new ways – in which respect, in its sensuous, dazzlingly inventive integration of music and movement, form and fluidity, *Pas de Deux* is his masterpiece.

Norman McLaren b. 1914 Scotland, d. 1987 Canada. **Pas de Deux** Canada 1967. **Films include** *Boogie Doodle*, 1940; *The Lark*, 1944; *Begone Dull Care*, 1949; *Neighbors, A Phantasy*, 1952; *Blinkity Blank*, 1954; *A Chairy Tale*, 1957; *The Blackbird*, 1958; *Lines Vertical*, 1960; *Canon*, 1964; *Synchromy*, 1971. **See also** LYE, QUAY BROTHERS

The moon, or rather the man in the moon, looks distinctly unhappy about mankind's first visit – unsurprising given that the rocket has plunged into his eye. Méliès is widely regarded as the father of film fantasy, the complementary antithesis to the Lumières and their adherence to documenting actuality. The truth, of course, is less simple: Méliès was not adept at fiction (his storytelling was basic, and he simply placed the camera in front of the flat tableaux he arranged in his studio), but as a magician and magic-lantern showman he delighted in the trickery afforded by the new medium's capacity for playing with time. Stopping, winding back or changing the speed of the film in his camera, he was able to show magically 'impossible' events, even impossible worlds, by means of models, painted sets, cutting, multiple exposure and superimposition. Often, the comic results are merely cinematic conjuring – heads expand or become disembodied, weird vehicles fly through the sky, devils vanish, metamorphose and reappear. But if his interest lay in spectacle rather than story (he also staged tableaux of historic events like Edward VII's coronation, with his studio standing in for Westminster Abbey), his vignettes have an innocent, whimsical charm all of their own. Sadly, he was insufficiently imaginative to proceed beyond anecdotal shorts and his prolific career was brief. His influence is immense, however; not only did he pioneer special effects but his playful vision is often genuinely (if inadvertently) surreal; in Méliès' universe, narrative has the bizarre, haunting logic of a dream.

Georges Méliès b. 1861 France, d. 1938 France. **A Trip to the Moon** France 1902. **Key films include** *The Vanishing Lady*, 1896; *A Swelled Head, The Coronation of Edward VII*, 1902; *The Melomaniac*, 1903; *Wonders of the Deep*, 1903; *An Impossible Voyage*, 1904; *The Merry Frolics of Satan*, 1906; *Tunnelling the English Channel*, 1907; *Conquest of the Pole*, 1912. **See also** GILLIAM, JEUNET AND CARO, LYNCH, QUAY BROTHERS, STAREWICZ, SVANKMAJER

JEAN-PIERRE MELVILLE

A gangster (Lino Ventura) prepares his trademark execution – in a moving car – of a policeman, not to save his skin but because the cop offended his sense of honour by putting it about that he betrayed a partner in crime. In the crime world as envisaged by Americanophile French film-maker Melville, ethics are everything: his cool, laconic heroes – cops and gangsters alike – act out of loyalty, professionalism and a keen sense of how to live (and die) with dignity. Not, maybe, a realistic view of the underworld (though greedy, treacherous and psychotic hoodlums and detectives do figure in his films), but Melville, for all his authentically detailed observations of work methods and social milieu, focused primarily on moral imperatives, paring down characters to their mythic essentials: wearing trench coats and fedoras,

expert with guns, and alert to the ever-present threats of incompetence and betrayal, they are defined by their actions. The stories, too, whether simple and linear (as here or in *Le Samourai*) or tortuous and complex (as in *Le Doulos*), consist of time-honoured elements: not just action set-pieces (he was a master of suspense, as this film's armoured car-robbery shows) but tense meetings in gloomy, seedy rooms and moments of quiet introspection. While he produced superior work in other genres (a version of Cocteau's *Les Enfants Terribles* is especially fine), his crime thrillers represent his most memorable achievement; even *L'Armée des Ombres*, a heartfelt tribute to the Resistance (of which he was a member), is visually and dramatically related to his moody, twilight portraits of the underworld.

Jean-Pierre Melville (Grumbach) b. 1917 France, d. 1973 France. **Le Deuxième Souffle (Second Breath)** France 1966/ w Lino Ventura, Paul Meurisse, Christine Fabrega, Paul Frankeur, Pierre Zimmer. **Key films include** *Le Silence de la Mer*, 1947; *Les Enfants Terribles*, 1949; *Bob le Flambeur*, 1955; *Le Doulos*, 1962; *Le Samourai*, 1967; *L'Armée des Ombres*, 1969; *Le Cercle Rouge*, 1970; *Un Flic*, 1972. **See also** BECKER, BRESSON, GODARD, HAWKS, HILL, HUSTON, KITANO, LEONE, MICHAEL MANN

The mock-shocked expression of a big-breasted radio evangelist surveying a trouserless jock: the outrageous image is immediately recognisable as coming from the wickedly witty, mammary-fixated 'king of the nudies'. Unlike most purveyors of porn, Meyer (who writes, directs, shoots, edits, produces and makes cameo appearances in his films) has cinematic talent; his movies are less erotic (unless one is aroused by cartoon-style capers involving grotesquely over-endowed women and gloriously dumb, insecure studs) than absurdist, irreverent soft-core caricatures of mainstream genres. *Ultravixens* is a manic parody of the smalltown melodrama, with predatory temptresses, morose hicks uncertain of their sexuality, a ludicrous moralising narrator (Meyer) who pops up in the most unlikely situations, and Nazi-in-hiding Martin Boormann (a regular feature of Meyer's swipes at middle-American hypocrisy); *Beyond the Valley of the Dolls*, meanwhile, guyed Hollywood exposés; *Blacksnake* steamy plantation sagas; *Supervixens* road movies. While the stories are slim, repetitive and barely coherent, Meyer derives much comic mileage from the depiction of voracious sexual appetites and absurd coupling positions, revelling in his actresses' pneumatic assets and unsubtle phallic symbolism: *Mondo Topless* intercuts go-go dancers in the desert with San Francisco high-rises while a voiceover pays purple tribute to the thrusting energy of the new West. Meyer's rapid, fluent editing is his forte; as expert as Eisenstein's, it is similarly resonant and inventive in the associative meanings produced – albeit, of course, to cheekier, entirely different ends.

Russ Meyer b. 1922 USA. **Beneath the Valley of the Ultravixens** USA 1979/ w Francesca 'Kitten' Natividad, Anne Marie, Kenn Kerr, June Mack, Russ Meyer. **Films include** *The Immoral Mr Teas*, 1959; *Faster Pussycat! Kill! Kill!*, *Mondo Topless*, 1966; *Vixen*, 1968; *Beyond the Valley of the Dolls*, 1970; *Blacksnake (Slaves)*, 1973; *Supervixens*, 1974; *Up*, 1976. **See also** EISENSTEIN, LYNCH, MAKAVEJEV, SIRK, WATERS

JOHN MILIUS

Three friends walk to meet the challenge of another wave, their easy, confident stride reminiscent of the heroes going to meet their fate at the end of *The Wild Bunch*. Though Milius' film suggests yet another rites-of-passage romp featuring wild parties, courtship rituals and male camaraderie, his personal obsessions – surfing, the socially divisive Vietnam War, man's potential for heroism – lend an otherwise sprawling, anecdotal saga a genuinely epic tone and elegiac depth of feeling. The waves (looking dangerously massive in the rivetingly shot surfing sequences, made even more stirring by Basil Poledouris' rhapsodic score) offer the protagonists a chance to prove their expertise, loyalty, courage and maturity; mutual and self-respect allow them to weather the social upheaval of the darkening 60s. Milius' poetic

notion of surfing prowess as an index of personal growth may be risible, but the film is executed with such style, energy and eloquence that it succeeds as a mythic testament to a lost generation. Likewise, his earlier *Dillinger* and *The Wind and the Lion* (a rousing desert adventure made in tribute to his hero Teddy Roosevelt) are wry but persuasive portraits of virility in action. Sadly, the later *Conan the Barbarian*, *Red Dawn* and *Farewell to the King* were marred by bombast, right-wing hysteria, sentimentality and the simplistic endorsement of macho anarchy. Milius now makes films infrequently. Yet in the 70s his was a very distinctive voice in the American cinema: forceful, even old-fashioned in his adherence to unfashionably 'masculine' ideals, but possessing passion, intelligence and wit.

John Milius b. 1944 USA. **Big Wednesday** USA1978/ w Jan-Michael Vincent, William Katt, Gary Busey, Patti D'Arbanville, Sam Melville, Lee Purcell. **Films include** *Dillinger*, 1973; *The Wind and the Lion*, 1975; *Conan the Barbarian*, 1982; *Red Dawn*, 1984; *Farewell to the King*, 1989; *Flight of the Intruder*, 1991. **See also** COPPOLA, FORD, HAWKS, KUROSAWA, LEAN, MELVILLE, PECKINPAH, SPIELBERG

The muted hues, arty decor and *trompe l'oeil* set, the emblematic costumes of a private eye and *femme fatale*: the Mickey Spillane-inspired ballet sequence from Minnelli's deliciously witty backstage musical typifies his work as one of Hollywood's supreme visual stylists. Best known for his work with producer Arthur Freed's MGM musical unit, Minnelli was influential not only in pioneering the seamless integration of song and dance into the plot, but in his use of imaginative visual design to enhance mood, meaning and characterisation. *The Band Wagon* is partly a comic parody of his own artier pretensions (with Jack Buchanan's producer trying, against Hollywood star Astaire and ballerina Charisse's better judgement, to turn a Broadway show into a high-brow musical *Faust*), but in films like *Meet Me in St Louis*, *The Pirate* and *An American in Paris*, his subtle, sensuous approach to colour, composition and movement held him in good stead, especially in scenes involving humour and dreamlike fantasy. Indeed, many of his finest non-musical films are equally stylised, so that in melodramas like *The Bad and the Beautiful*, *Some Came Running*, and *Two Weeks in Another Town*, a discreetly expressionist use of props, decor, lighting and actions that often seem almost choreographed contributes to the films' emotional energy. Here and in the comedy *Father of the Bride* and the Van Gogh biopic *Lust for Life*, Minnelli delved into darker subject matter; with breakdown, madness, violence and death recurrent elements in his straight dramas, his images – angular, feverish, even lurid – were more evocative of nightmare.

Vincente Minnelli b. 1913 USA, d. 1986 USA. **The Band Wagon** USA 1953/ w Fred Astaire, Cyd Charisse, Jack Buchanan, Oscar Levant, Nanette Farbray. **Films include** *Meet Me in St Louis*, 1942; *The Clock, Yolanda and the Thief*, 1945; *The Pirate*, 1947; *Father of the Bride*, 1950; *An American in Paris,* 1951; *The Bad and the Beautiful,* 1952; *The Cobweb*, 1955; *Lust for Life*, 1956; *Some Came Running*, 1958; *Home from the Hill*, 1960; *Two Weeks in Another Town*, 1963. **See also** DEMY, DONEN AND KELLY, MAMOULIAN, POWELL, SIRK, SCORSESE

In feudal Japan, a young woman (Oharu) is welcomed by a lord who has installed her in his mansion to bear an heir. She, having been advised to marry for love by an admirer who is subsequently executed, is clearly unhappy about the prospect. And rightly so: once the son is born, she will be ejected and drift through years of prostitution into impoverished old age. Mizoguchi repeatedly depicted the plight of women in patriarchal society, questioning its unjust codes and extending an unsentimental sympathy to its powerless victims. Not that his films spiralled into melodrama: the tone was serene, elegiac, with restrained performances providing subtle emotional nuances. Visually, his style was measured: while the compositions are invariably beautiful and immaculately detailed, they are given further resonance by long, sinuous travelling shots charting the physical and spiritual progress of his protagonists (an entire scene might consist of one take). He avoided close-ups, preferring to reveal the characters' relationships to the world around them by means of medium and long-shots. Far from resulting in intellectual detachment, Mizoguchi's reticent, quietly attentive style allows the viewer to identify with the protagonist's predicament, so that the final moments of *Sisters of Gion*, *The Story of the Late Chrysanthemums*, *My Love Has Been Burning*, *Ugetsu Monogatari*, *Sansho the Bailiff* and *The Crucified Lovers* (among others) are emotionally devastating. Sadly, less than half of his films survive, and even those are now infrequently shown. He remains, however, one of cinema's very greatest masters.

Mizoguchi Kenji b. 1898 Japan, d. 1956 Japan. **The Life of Oharu** Japan 1952/ w Tanaka Kinuyo, Matsura Tsuki, Sugai Ichiro, Mifune Toshiro, Konoe Toshiaki, Shimizu Masao. **Films include** *Osaka Elegy, Sisters of Gion*, 1936; *The Story of the Late Chrysanthemums*, 1939; *Five Women Around Utamaro*, 1946; *My Love Has Been Burning*, 1949; *Ugetsu Monogatari*, 1953; *Sansho the Bailiff, The Crucified Lovers*, 1954; *Shin Heike Monogatari, Yang Kwei Fei*, 1955; *Street of Shame*, 1956. **See also** KUROSAWA, MURNAU, OPHÜLS, OZU, RENOIR

NANNI MORETTI

Nanni Moretti, incongruous in sunglasses and crash-helmet, sings on stage with a Rai band. The image, still stranger on film with his stiff demeanour at odds with the sunny, sensuous rhythms, is characteristic of his eccentric take on contemporary culture. In his early films he played an alter ego whose professions – film-maker, teacher, priest, water-polo player – enabled him to guy both the tired conventions of recent Italian cinema and the political, spiritual and emotional confusions of the post-68 generation. But he found international fame by adopting the diary-film format, whose looser narrative allowed him full rein to reflect on and satirise, through subtle exaggeration, his own foibles and those of modern Europe. Here he gently mocks liberal parents indulging their children's endless phone-calls, soap-opera and violent movie obsessives, and the bureaucratic iniquities of the Italian medical establishment, meanwhile paying tribute to suburban Roman architecture and Pasolini (the site of whose murder he visits on his beloved Vespa in a long sequence accompanied only by Keith Jarrett's piano). While Moretti's unadorned style favours long takes and medium or long shots, he mixes realism and poetry, documentary and fiction to present an imaginative distortion of the world, proffering improbably bizarre images (he, in cape and helmet, and his film crew swaying to a dance sequence featuring a Trotskyite pastry chef in a gaudy 50s bakery at the end of *Aprile*). So persuasive is his idiosyncratic vision, so rigorous his absurdist logic that such epiphanies seem oddly normal.

Nanni (Giovanni) Moretti b. 1953 Italy. **Dear Diary (Caro Diario)** Italy 1994/ w Moretti, Renato Carpentieri, Antonio Neiwiller, Jennifer Beals. **Films include** *Io Sono un Autarchico*, 1976; *Ecce Bombo*, 1978; *Sogni d'Oro*, 1981; *Bianca*, 1983; *La Messa e Finita*, 1985; *Palombella Rossa*, 1989; *La Cosa*, 1990; *The Day of the Premiere of Close-Up*, 1996; *Aprile*, 1998. **See also** KIAROSTAMI, MARKER, MORRIS, ROSSELLINI

ERROL MORRIS

A man is interrogated at a police precinct. The blue lighting, exterior view and separate windows, implying communication breakdown, lend an air of unreality seldom associated with documentary. But Morris is no conventional documentarist. His first films – *Gates of Heaven*, about pet cemeteries, and *Vernon, Florida*, about smalltown eccentrics – were wry but never patronising studies in obsession; his genuine curiosity was embodied by a static camera trained at length on subjects speaking directly to camera. With *The Thin Blue Line*, about a man wrongly imprisoned for murder, he combined interviews with similarly oddball witnesses (including the innocent man's sinister 'friend'-turned-betrayer who may, we find, be the guilty party) with stylised, contradictory reconstructions of the crime, and ominous close-ups of objects crucial to the case. The result is both rigorous investigative journalism and a disquisition into the difficulty of defining 'truth'. Philosophical questions are a constant element in Morris' work: *A Brief History of Time* is about Stephen Hawking's theories of the universe, while *Fast, Cheap and Out of Control* is again about eccentrics and how their passions (lion-taming, mole-rats, topiary, robots) constitute an attempt to impose order on life's chaos. Here, he confronts strangeness head-on, using various film stocks, archive footage and weird compositions shot with a constantly moving camera to evoke the interviewees' subjective visions of the world. The style is far from *verité*, but his readiness to listen to, and recreate on film, his subjects' ideas about life, ensures that his work achieves a truth peculiar to itself.

Errol Morris b. 1948 USA. **The Thin Blue Line** USA 1988/ w Randall Adams, David Harris, Edith James, Dennis White, Don Metcalfe. **Films include** *Gates of Heaven*, 1978; *Vernon, Florida*, 1981; *The Thin Blue Line*, 1988; *The Dark Wind*, 1991; *A Brief History of Time*, 1994; *Fast, Cheap and Out of Control*, 1997. **See also** FLAHERTY, HERZOG, MAKAVEJEV, MARKER, MORETTI, PENNEBAKER

It is perhaps more difficult to exemplify Murnau's style with a still than that of any other film-maker, since movement was the essence of his cinema. The exploration of space not only served to express his characters' emotions, but to suggest an entire world in which they lived but which had an independent life of its own. Hence the magnificent studio-built metropolis in *Sunrise*, visited by a farmer and his wife as they try to come to terms with his attempt to murder her at the behest of his flapper-girl lover. The immaculately designed buildings and bustling thoroughfares are no mere decorative backdrop but a dramatic counterpoint to the couple's miserable confusion – the vitality of the city is infectious, enabling them to enjoy each other's company once more, and so revives their mutual love.

(Famously, even the trolley has a precise function in the narrative: a lengthy shot of the couple, absorbed in private thoughts as they travel to the city, shows the landscape behind them change from empty fields to suburbs and crowded streets, so that their voyage is geographical and psychological.) Murnau was a master of cinematic poetry; the subtle artifice of his painterly compositions evokes both the physical world and a deeper reality of the imagination. Accordingly, he was able to alternate between ostensibly 'realist' material (a proud commissionaire reduced to working as a toilet attendant in *The Last Laugh*, Polynesian customs in *Tabu*) and more fantastic fare like *Faust* and *Nosferatu* with great facility, making each a triumphant study of the human spirit and, very often, its need and capacity for love.

Friedrich Wilhelm Murnau b. 1888 Germany, d. 1931 USA. **Sunrise** USA 1927/ w George O'Brien, Janet Gaynor, Margaret Livingston, Bodil Rosing. **Films include** *Nosferatu, A Symphony of Horror*, 1922; *The Last Laugh*, 1924; *Tartüff*, 1925; *Faust*, 1926; *City Girl (Our Daily Bread)*, 1930; *Tabu*, 1931. **See also** ANGELOPOULOS, MIZOGUCHI, OPHÜLS, RENOIR, WELLES

MAX OPHÜLS

Nineteenth-century Vienna: our suave, witty guide (Anton Walbrook) introduces a streetwalker, the first of many characters we'll see involved in a chain of encounters demonstrating the transience and variety of love. What most typifies Ophüls' elegant image is the carousel: mirroring the way the film's characters pass from one liaison to another, it serves as a metaphor for time's inexorable progress and the way that, while lovers may change, love itself remains the same, moving in brief, repetitive circles of pleasure and pain. Ophüls introduced the merry-go-round and the raconteur into his adaptation of Schnitzler's play, just as he transformed it into the stuff of cinema with a fluid camera: the (often circular) tracking and crane shots conjoin style and content, so that the characters seem trapped not only by time and their own desires but by the film itself (Walbrook is even shown splicing it together for our delectation); in *Lola Montès*, the heroine's life literally becomes a spectacle as she sits on a dais in a circus ring, the camera revolving around her in a reflection of our own desire to discover more about her scandalous past. Repeatedly, Ophüls explored the gulf between idealised love and the reality of passion: in *Liebelei*, *Letter from an Unknown Woman*, *Caught* and *Madame De…* (which traces the progress of an adulterous affair through the passing of earrings, a gift of love, from one character to another) disappointment and despair darken the mood, yet the films finally reaffirm love's undying appeal – reflecting, ironically, on the romantic illusions proffered by cinema itself.

Max Ophüls (Oppenheimer) b. 1902 Germany, d. 1957 Germany. **La Ronde** France 1950/ w Anton Walbrook, Simone Signoret, Serge Reggiani, Simone Simon, Daniel Gélin, Danielle Darrieux, Gérard Philippe. **Films include** *Liebelei*, 1932; *La Signora di Tutti*, 1934; *Letter from an Unknown Woman*, 1948; *Caught, The Reckless Moment*, 1949; *Le Plaisir*, 1952; *Madame De…* 1953; *Lola Montès*, 1955.
See also ANGELOPOULOS, MIZOGUCHI, MURNAU, RENOIR, WELLES

The Japanese establishment – a doctor, a politician, a priest and prison officers – gaze down dispassionately at the young Korean they have just hanged; when they discover he's still alive, they are thrown into bureaucratic and moral turmoil. Oshima's sharply analytical, Brechtian political satire uses narrative disruption ('flashbacks' to the Korean's crime in which the authorities find themselves mysteriously involved, scenes of surreal comic fantasy and questions directed at the viewer) not only to interrogate our attitude to capital punishment and the treatment of minorities (as well as Japan's, of course), but to expose its own cinematic artifice. Oshima's films repeatedly confront the way in which Japanese laws, customs and rituals constrain and oppress the individual; from early genre films like *The Catch* and *Violence at Noon*, through experimental works like *Death by Hanging* and *Diary of a Shinjuku Thief* (a collage of fiction, documentary and street theatre), to more straightforward family dramas like *Boy* and *The Ceremony*, he explored the injustices and absurdities of Japanese society, particularly its attempts to quench asocial impulses. His method was always rigorous, the tone provocative, but perhaps his most notorious treatment of this theme was in *Ai No Corrida* (*Empire of the Senses*), a sexually explicit tale of a couple led by their intense passion to withdraw from the world around them. Oshima's recent film-making inactivity is regrettable; his finest work has a moral commitment, a clarity of purpose and an artistic inventiveness and ambition seldom found in contemporary cinema.

Oshima Nagisa b. 1932 Japan. **Death by Hanging** Japan 1968/ w Dun Yun-Do, Sato Kei, Watanabe Fumio, Ishido Toshiro, Adachi Masao. **Films include** *The Catch*, 1961; *Violence at Noon*, 1966; *Diary of a Shinjuku Thief*, 1968; *Boy*, 1969; *The Ceremony*, 1971; *Ai No Corrida*, 1976; *Ai No Borei (Empire of Passion)*, 1978; *Merry Christmas, Mr Lawrence*, 1982; *Max Mon Amour*, 1987. **See also** BUÑUEL, GODARD, KITANO, MAKAVEJEV, TSUKAMOTO

IDRISSA OUÉDRAOGO

A boy's father and aunt argue over his friendship with an ostracised old woman. Though the woman – whom the boy calls 'yaaba' (grandmother) out of respect for her wisdom – will later save his tetanus-afflicted cousin with traditional medicine, the men in the village will still place their faith in the gods and in charlatan witchdoctors pandering to prejudice and superstition. Ouédraogo's stirring rites-of-passage fable is firmly in the humanist-realist tradition; indeed, the boy's relationship with his cousin, the leisurely, often gently comic observation of village life, and 'yaaba's' death all echo Ray's *Pather Panchali* (albeit without the Indian's miniaturist attention to detail and acutely ironic moral nuances). As with Ray, Ouédraogo's visual sense is quietly classical, with characters carefully positioned to reveal the precise nature of their relationship to one another: when the two children, instilled with the men's belief that the old woman is a witch, pass her on their way home, their fear is expressed simply and graphically by the wide berth they give her, even disappearing from the side of the frame. Ouédraogo's films explore the gulf between valuable African tradition and blinkered custom: *Tilaï* concerns the tragic outcome of merely obeying or flouting polygamy laws without recourse to common sense, while *Kini & Adams* depicts how an addiction to modern materialist ideals may erode friendships and families. Though the parable-like simplicity of the stories in his weaker films may make for endings that seem contrived, Ouédraogo's expertise with actors and eye for telling compositions are undeniable.

Idrissa Ouédraogo b. 1954 Burkina Faso. **Yaaba** Burkina Faso/France/Switzerland 1989/ w Datima Sanga, Noufou Ouédraogo, Barry Roukieto, Adama Ouédraogo. **Films include** *Yam Daabo,* 1986; *Tilaï* 1990; *Samba Traore,* 1992; *Gorki,* 1993; *Le Cri du Coeur,* 1994; *Kini & Adams,* 1997. **See also** CHAHINE, CISSÉ, SATYAJIT RAY, SEMBENE

OZU YASUJIRO

A family seated in mourning for a dead woman, shot from slightly below eye-level; the scene is static, introspective, becalmed. No histrionic display of grief is on view; indeed, soon after this scene, when one woman says to another, 'Isn't life disappointing?', the reply ('Yes') is followed by a smile that encapsulates Ozu's resigned acceptance of life's vicissitudes. The quiet composition is also typical of all but Ozu's early films; the low-positioned camera rarely moved from its medium-shot contemplation of faces and figures in a home or work environment (though static long-shots of station platforms, chimneys, roofs and washing lines frequently served as punctuation between scenes). Domestic tales drained of traditional dramatic highs and lows were his forte; whether poignant or gently comic,

Ozu's films focus tenderly on (often misunderstood) communication between ordinary people, in uneventful tales dealing, for example, with a parent's concern that a daughter should marry (*Late Spring, An Autumn Afternoon*), or a battle of wills between parents and faintly rebellious young children (*I Was Born But..., Good Morning*). Repeatedly returning to the same relatively minor domestic crises, Ozu fashioned an amazingly rich series of variations on a handful of themes, paring down his visual and narrative style, and steadily refining his delicately observed studies of emotional dilemmas; though he consistently worked in the commercial mainstream, both his stoic but generous view of human nature and his unassertive, uniquely personal style place him among cinema's very greatest artists.

Ozu Yasujiro b. 1903 Japan, d. 1963 Japan. **Tokyo Story** Japan 1953/ w Ryu Chishu, Hara Setsuko, Higashiyama Chiyeko, Yamamura So, Kagawa Kyoko. **Key films include** *I Was Born But...*, 1932; *A Story of Floating Weeds*, 1934; *The Brothers and Sisters of the Toda Family*, 1941; *The Record of a Tenement Gentleman*, 1947; *Late Spring*, 1949; *The Flavour of Green Tea Over Rice*, 1952; *Early Spring*, 1956; *Equinox Flower*, 1958; *Good Morning*, 1959; *An Autumn Afternoon*, 1962. **See also** Botelho, Bresson, Dreyer, Hou, Jarmusch, Kaurismäki, Kitano, Mizoguchi

G W PABST

A woman seals her destiny by inviting the man who will kill her to her room. The shot is moodily dramatic, and strikingly suggestive of a fateful encounter between two strangers crossing paths and forestalled from going their separate ways by a momentary whim: textbook expressionism. And were it not for Louise Brooks' famously vibrant, sensual, startlingly modern performance as Lulu, whose unashamed, destructive sexuality finally leads to her death at the hands of Jack the Ripper, it's arguable that Pabst's film would simply be a very skilfully shot version of Wedekind's *Lulu* plays rather than a landmark of German cinema. He was a solid technician, adept at creating atmosphere (most notably here, and in *Joyless Street* and *The Threepenny Opera*, he responded especially well to the polarities of squalid hardship and extravagant decadence in city life) through stylish lighting, camerawork and editing, and at eliciting strong, naturalistic performances. Yet for all his ambitions (besides the Brecht and Wedekind adaptations, his most audacious film was *Secrets of a Soul*, an attempt to explore Freud's psychoanalytical theories through a melodrama featuring fantasy sequences), there is something academic about much of his work: certainly, *The Diary of a Lost Girl* looks like a misguided attempt to capitalise again on his 'discovery' of Brooks, while *Westfront 1918* and *Kameradschaft* are well-meaning but unremarkable humanist tracts. At their best, Pabst's silent films display a firm grasp of contemporary social realities, particularly the hypocrisy and corruption of the bourgeoisie; later, however, his lengthy career went into decline.

Georg Wilhelm Pabst b. 1885 Czechoslovakia, d. 1967 Austria. **Pandora's Box** Germany 1928/ w Louise Brooks, Fritz Kortner, Franz Lederer, Carl Goetz, Alice Roberts, Kraft Raschig. **Films include** *Joyless Street*, 1925; *Secrets of a Soul*, 1926; *The Love of Jeanne Ney*, 1927; *The Diary of a Lost Girl,* 1929; *Westfront 1918*, 1930;*The Threepenny Opera, Kameradschaft,* 1931; *L'Atlantide*, 1932. **See also** LANG, MURNAU, SIODMAK, WIENE

A political assassin is cornered on a rooftop high above an American city: the perilous nature of his work could not be more evident. In the early 70s, Pakula made a trio of taut thrillers notable for deft characterisation and a paranoid sense of conspiracy and cover-up. For all the intelligence of their scripts and performances, what distinguished them was their precise deployment of light and space. *Klute*, in which a cop investigating a friend's disappearance starts a hesitant relationship with a hooker who is the killer's intended next victim, is most traditional in its *noir*-like use of shadowy urban interiors to create a claustrophobic mood. More imaginative is the agoraphobic *The Parallax View*, in which Pakula used strange, sometimes almost abstract images of large spaces featuring vertiginous heights – a soaring tower, a dam, a massive arena hosting a political rally shown mostly from its roof girders – to evoke the menace that might arise in seemingly empty or public places. *All the President's Men* turned what might have been a straightforward docudrama about the discovery of the Watergate scandal into a metaphorical thriller by using a diversity of architectural features: a bright newspaper office evocative of the search for truth, meetings with Deep Throat in subterranean car parks at night suggesting the secretive, murky machinations at work, the concentric circles of a library shown by a retreating overhead camera illustrating the reach of the conspiracy under investigation. Sadly, this imaginative conflation of visual style with dramatic meaning declined in Pakula's work as he became a journeyman director.

Alan J Pakula b. 1928 USA, d. 1998 USA. **The Parallax View** USA 1974/ w Warren Beatty, Paula Prentiss, Hume Cronyn, William Daniels, Walter McGinn. **Films include** *Klute*, 1971; *All the President's Men*, 1976; *Comes A Horseman*, 1978; *Rollover*, 1981; *Sophie's Choice*, 1982; *Orphans*, 1987; *Presumed Innocent*, 1990; *The Pelican Brief*, 1993. **See also** ANTONIONI, BOORMAN, LANG, MICHAEL MANN

SERGEI PARADZHANOV

A bizarre tableau: a man in monkish garb, a dumb beast, a woman with a gun, a child tossing a golden ball to an angel over a corpse. But what does it all mean? To be frank, this writer has little idea. The Armenian Paradzhanov's films, wholly personal yet profoundly influenced by Caucasian cinema, art and literature, were a world unto themselves: here, the life of an 18th-century mystic poet, who became an Armenian folk hero after being killed by invading Persians when he refused to renounce Christ, is related in images inspired not only by Armenian history and Sayat Nova's poetry but by the film-maker's own experiences – the woman to the poet's right is his feminine muse/alter ego (Paradzhanov was openly gay). The film consists of separate images, generally shot with a static camera and edited together with no clear narrative connection to one another, in which figures stand in profile or head-on to the camera, surrounded by pagan and Christian symbols; movements are hieratic, motives inscrutable. Yet the film is extraordinarily beautiful; its painterly sensuality can be entrancing. Persecuted by the Kremlin for homosexuality, artistic hermeticism and various trumped-up charges (but actually for political dissidence), Paradzhanov repeatedly drew on folklore and literature to startling effect: *Shadows of Our Forgotten Ancestors* was almost psychedelic in its use of wild colour and camera movement, while *The Legend of the Suram Fortress* and *Ashik Kerib* – further tales of dissidents and artists – continued in the episodic, highly metaphorical vein of *Sayat Nova*. The poetic originality of his work, though difficult for most Westerners to understand, remains undeniable.

Sergei Paradzhanov (Sarkis Paradjanian) b. 1924 Georgia, d. 1990 Armenia. **Sayat Nova (The Colour of Pomegranates)** USSR 1969/ w Sofico Chiaureli, M Aleksanian, V Galstian, G Gegechkori. **Films include** *Shadows of Our Forgotten Ancestors*, 1964; *The Legend of the Suram Fortress*, 1984; *Ashik Kerib*, 1988. **See also** ANGER, DOVZHENKO, MÉLIÈS, PASOLINI, TARKOVSKY

NICK PARK

If Wallace and his dog Gromit were not so conspicuously made of clay, and were the film not in colour, the scene might easily be from one of the determinedly banal 'kitchen sink realism' portraits of British working-class life made in the early 60s. Much of the Oscar-winning appeal of Park's painstakingly perfectionist claymation derives from the ordinariness of his films' settings; *Creature Comforts* simply featured clay zoo animals discussing their homes, their voices those of immigrants pre-recorded in interview. At the same time, it is the juxtaposition of familiar 'everyday life' with the extra-ordinary that defines both his immaculately detailed visual style – the colours of the crockery are just a little too bright for the otherwise authentically drab room – and his stories, which comically transform Wallace and

Gromit's mundane existence into the stuff of genre cinema: *The Wrong Trousers* sees Gromit in conflict with a sinister, possibly murderous new lodger (a penguin posing as a chicken), while *A Close Shave* finds him foiling sheep-rustlers in a parodic scenario which is part *noir* mystery, part action thriller. Like many animators before him, Park – arguably the leading light of the Aardman Animation studio – makes carefully delineated anthropomorphic characterisation the basis of his comedy: though Wallace is an engagingly gullible eccentric, it is the stoic, faintly morose, watchfully perceptive Gromit who is the dramatic and comic hero. Indeed, it is pre-cisely his Protean nature – he somehow simultaneously displays the characteristics of a dog, a human and mere clay – that makes Park's artistry so magically appealing.

Nick Park b. 1958 England. **The Wrong Trousers** GB 1993. **Films include** *War Story*, 1989; *A Grand Day Out*, 1990; *Creature Comforts*, 1991; *A Close Shave*, 1995. **See also** AVERY, DISNEY, HANNA AND BARBERA, JONES, McCAY, STAREWICZ, SVANKMAJER

ALAN PARKER

FBI agents investigating the murder of civil rights activists in the Deep South in 1964 stand before the burning cross of the Ku Klux Klan: facing a cover-up by racists as they try to solve the mystery, northerner Willem Dafoe sticks by the book, while Gene Hackman, a local, believes that to fight scum one must play dirty. Parker's typically hard-hitting thriller opts for clear-cut moral polarities and urgent, emblematic images. A former commercials director, a talented cartoonist and a superior technician, he is a natural storyteller adept at getting messages across by forthright methods: dramatic lighting, vivid characterisation, scenes of violent conflict regularly interrupting sequences of expository dialogue, and an abiding sympathy for the underdog (he is a born liberal with a keen sense of injustice). Though he has a penchant for controversial material (the iniquities of Turkish prisons in *Midnight Express*, the plight of Japanese-Americans during World War Two in *Come See the Paradise*), his preference for working mostly within the bounds of traditional genres and his reliance on intuition rather than intellect ensure that his films have often forsaken complexity for immediate visceral effect. Ironically, it is his smaller, more intimate films – notably *Shoot the Moon*, about a failing marriage, and *The Commitments*, about a Dublin soul band – which are most satisfying: the first marked with genuine insight and anguish, the latter his wittiest, most affectionate movie to date, greatly enhanced by his feel for the music and evident enthusiasm for the working-class characters' ambitions and achievements.

Alan Parker b. 1944 England. **Mississippi Burning** USA 1988/ w Gene Hackman, Willem Dafoe, Frances McDormand, Brad Dourif, R Lee Ermey, Stephen Tobolowsky. **Films include** *Bugsy Malone*, 1976; *Midnight Express*, 1978; *Fame*, 1980; *Shoot the Moon*, 1982; *Birdy*, 1984; *Angel Heart*, 1987; *Come See the Paradise*, 1990; *The Commitments*, 1991; *Evita*, 1996; *Angela's Ashes*, 1999. **See also** COSTA-GAVRAS, DASSIN, FULLER, SCOTT, VIDOR

Though the familiarity of Christian iconography makes it obvious this shot depicts Jesus and his disciples, it differs from other movie representations of Christ both in that there is no kindness in his expression and in the stark simplicity of the grainy composition. Besides being a film-maker, poet and novelist, Pasolini was a committed Marxist and homosexual who sympathised with society's outcasts: his Christ is a rebel idealist driven by anger at injustice. But Pasolini was also profoundly marked by the neo-realist tradition: though the film alluded to religious art and music, it was shot in the arid Calabrian mountains and used non-professional actors chosen for their peasant faces; the imagery was devoid of the pomp and miraculous special effects customary in Biblical epics. Even in allegorical material seemingly ill-suited to a realist approach, like *Theorem* (about a bourgeois family 'possessed' by a seductive stranger), *Pigsty* (a weird, dual-narrative mix of political satire and a poetic fable about primitive cannibalism), or the Greek myths *Oedipus Rex* and *Medea* (in which he made lavish use of exotic costumes and customs), Pasolini's images were as plain and direct as in *Accattone*, his debut about thieves, pimps and prostitutes in the Roman suburbs. Mostly, that aesthetic remained dominant in his versions of *The Decameron*, *The Canterbury Tales* and *The Arabian Nights*, though their bawdiness became increasingly indulgent and uninteresting as the trilogy progressed, and paved the way for the scatological, sado-masochistic, shallow anti-Fascist allegory of *Salò*. He was murdered in mysterious, politically controversial circumstances.

Pier Paolo Pasolini b. 1922 Italy, d. 1975 Italy. **The Gospel According to Matthew** Italy 1964/ w Enrique Irazoqui, Margherita Caruso, Susanna Pasolini, Marcello Morante, Mario Socrate. **Films include** *Accattone*, 1961; *Mamma Roma*, 1962; *Hawks and Sparrows*, 1966; *Oedipus Rex*, 1967; *Theorem*, 1968; *Pigsty, Medea*, 1969; *The Decameron*, 1971; *The Canterbury Tales*, 1972; *The Arabian Nights*, 1974; *Salò, or the 120 Days of Sodom*, 1975. **See also** BERTOLUCCI, GODARD, ROSSELLINI, TAVIANI BROTHERS

SAM PECKINPAH

In Mexico during the Revolution, American outlaws working as mercenaries meet their fate at the hands of an army led by a treacherous general; the odds against them are so overwhelming, the Bunch's decision to fight for their outdated sense of honour is surely a death-wish. The protracted, slow-motion bloodbath climax of Peckinpah's elegiac, controversially violent tale of traditional male virtues – loyalty, energy, enterprise, self-respect, independence – eroded by the compromises and corruption of the twentieth century is typical of his half-celebratory, half-disenchanted attitude to unbridled, anarchic machismo. As Warren Oates jerks in agony at the bullets tearing his flesh, his machine gun whirls wildly, firing at all and sundry: the image is savage yet strangely sexual, with death literally a release. Peckinpah's films were often bitterly ironic, misogynist and brutally visceral; his disdain for modern life could lead to nihilistic, callous endorsements of violence, so that *Straw Dogs* – a western in disguise, set in a ludicrously unreal Cornish countryside – was a reactionary apologia for the triumph of vengeful primal impulse over reason. Yet his finest films show real tenderness -- the friendship of old timers resolved to die honorably in the lyrical *Ride the High Country*, tentative blossoming love in *The Ballad of Cable Hogue*, family loyalty revived in the rodeo saga *Junior Bonner* – and an abiding love for the harsh, poetic beauty of the Western landscape and the sensuality of Mexican life. There is a mournful but robust romanticism to his best work; sadly, his later films are often lazy, crude, chaotic, and verge on self-parody.

Sam Peckinpah b. 1925 USA, d. 1984 USA. **The Wild Bunch** USA 1969/ w William Holden, Ernest Borgnine, Robert Ryan, Warren Oates, Ben Johnson, Emilio Fernandez, Edmond O'Brien. **Films include** *The Deadly Companions*, 1961; *Ride the High Country (Guns in the Afternoon)*, 1962; *Major Dundee*, 1965; *The Ballad of Cable Hogue*, 1970; *Straw Dogs*, 1971; *Junior Bonner*, 1972; *Pat Garrett and Billy the Kid*, 1973; *Bring Me the Head of Alfredo Garcia*, 1974; *Cross of Iron*, 1977; *Convoy*, 1978. **See also** ALDRICH, BOETTICHER, EASTWOOD, FORD, FULLER, LEONE, ANTHONY MANN, SIEGEL, WALSH

The Barrow gang burst from their car, crashed during a police ambush: we know they're guilty of robbery and murder, but want them to escape. Cinema has always glamorised outlaws, but few movies before Penn's amoral saga offered such appealingly childlike, innocent anti-heroes as Faye Dunaway and Warren Beatty (the film's producer), both noticeably better-looking than their real-life counterparts. Though David Newman and Robert Benton's script (originally intended for Truffaut or Godard) was a romantic affair in which jaunty comedy led inexorably to tragedy, Penn's expertise in staging sudden outbursts of explosive, visceral violence and his sympathetic interest in outsiders driven to asocial behaviour by disenchantment with conventional mores made him a fitting director to turn the couple into identifi-cation figures for the late 60s youth audience. 'Straight' society is seen as boring, hypocritical, oppressive; Bonnie and Clyde's acts are fuelled by social and sexual frustration, a desire to mean something (if only to each other and as media celebrities), and resentment at banks making ordinary folk homeless during the Depression. Penn's best films (*The Miracle Worker*, *The Chase*, *Bonnie and Clyde*, *Night Moves* and the uneven *The Missouri Breaks*) focus on rebels unable to articulate their needs, whereas in *Alice's Restaurant* and *Little Big Man* the antagonism between outcast and society is overly schematic, so that the dynamic imagery seems superfluous. Nevertheless, he was a key figure in American cinema of the 60s and 70s; thereafter, his infrequent, minor work betokens a remarkably dramatic decline.

Arthur Penn b. 1922 USA. **Bonnie and Clyde** USA 1967/ w Warren Beatty, Faye Dunaway, Michael J Pollard, Gene Hackman, Estelle Parsons, Denver Pyle. **Films include** *The Left-Handed Gun*, 1958; *The Miracle Worker*, 1962, *Mickey One*, 1965; *The Chase*, 1966; *Alice's Restaurant*, 1969; *Little Big Man*, 1970; *Night Moves*, 1975; *The Missouri Breaks*, 1976; *Four Friends*, 1981; *Target*, 1985, *Dead of Winter*, 1987. **See also** FRANKENHEIMER, LUMET, PECKINPAH, NICHOLAS RAY

D A PENNEBAKER

The amused, relaxed smile of the young Bob Dylan, followed by documentarist Pennebaker during his tour of Britain in 1965, is caught in a grainy, intimate image typical of the Direct Cinema which arose in America in the late 50s and early 60s. Like his peers and occasional collaborators Richard Leacock and Albert and David Maysles, Pennebaker benefited from technical developments (new lightweight, professional-quality cameras, fast film stock and recording equipment) in his efforts to create a less 'staged' and less obtrusive style of documentary film-making. Explanatory narration was largely abandoned, while long takes (in an effort to reflect 'real time') took precedence over montage; ironically, though the aim was 'objective' fly-on-the-wall observation, the regular whip-pans and shifts in focus often meant that the viewer was more aware of the camera's presence than before. (Adherents of Direct Cinema felt the film-making process had no significant effect on their subjects, whereas in the *cinéma verité* of French documentarists like Jean Rouch, the theory was that the camera affected whatever they filmed, and so they should reveal their presence.) Pennebaker himself has concentrated largely on public celebrities, particularly in the field of music (along with *Don't Look Back*, the best instance is the classic concert film *Monterey Pop*), although *Town Bloody Hall*, a lively, very funny record of a debate on feminism between Norman Mailer, Susan Sontag, Germaine Greer and others, is a more illuminating and analytical example of his ability to catch both mood and character on celluloid.

Donn Alan Pennebaker b. 1930 USA. **Don't Look Back** USA 1966/ w Bob Dylan, Joan Baez, Donovan, Alan Price, Allen Ginsberg, Albert Grossman. **Key films include** *Daybreak Express*, 1953; *Primary*, 1960; *The Chair*, 1963; *Monterey Pop*, 1968; *One PM*, 1969; *Ziggy Stardust and the Spiders from Mars*, 1973; *Town Bloody Hall*, 1979. **See also** CASSAVETES, FLAHERTY, MARKER, MORRIS

Slobbish, boozy drifter Gérard Depardieu and bored bourgeoise Isabelle Huppert may love each other, but as this stark image shows, their mismatched relationship will never be easy. Pialat's narratives – straightforward, linear depictions of mundane situations – and his unadorned visual realism are notable for their unsentimental honesty and an awareness that often, the choices we make are more about escape than a sense of purpose: *Passe Ton Bac d'Abord*, about the experiences and ambitions of a group of school-leavers, never pretends that a better adulthood awaits them; *To Our Loves* concerns a 15-year-old whose promiscuity reflects a need to avoid an unhappy home life; *Under Satan's Sun* concerns a priest whose demeanour – seen by some as saintly – derives from suspicions that the Devil, not God,

manipulates mankind. Using a reserved, discreet camera to focus squarely on the actions, gestures and expressions of laconic or inarticulate characters, Pialat simply observes without passing judgement (even in *Police*, about a racist cop obsessed with a female criminal). In his early films, the attentive, lingering gaze was unemphatically tender and compassionate, but as his career has progressed, the constant resort to pessimistic endings has led some to suspect an element of misanthropy at work – certainly, little humour or warmth is displayed on screen, so that the films may make for chastening, even depressing viewing. That said, Pialat is masterful with actors, so that even at its bleakest, his work is characterised by a sense of living, breathing humans simply trying to survive life's disappointments and hardships.

Maurice Pialat b. 1925 France. **Loulou** France 1980/ w Gérard Depardieu, Isabelle Huppert, Guy Marchand, Humbert Balsan, Bernard Tronczyk. **Films include** *L'Enfance Nue*, 1969; *We Will Not Grow Old Together*, 1972; *The Mouth Agape*, 1974; *Passe Ton Bac d'Abord*, 1979; *To Our Loves,* 1983; *Police*, 1985; *Under Satan's Sun*, 1987; *Van Gogh*, 1991; *Le Garçu*, 1997. **See also** CASSAVETES, CLOUZOT, LOACH, ROHMER

ROMAN POLANSKI

Could an image suggest more vividly the vulnerability of a marriage? The wife's smile at a young hitch-hiker invited aboard the couple's yacht for the weekend goes unnoticed by her husband, complacently engrossed in his radio; the claustrophobic intimacy of the situation, with each man aiming to prove his superiority before the increasingly disenchanted woman, is embodied in the cramped composition. Even in his feature debut, which has a cast of three and takes place almost entirely on the small boat, Polanski demonstrated his eye for the telling composition: framing the characters together and apart, making use of a wide variety of angles, close-ups, medium- and long-shots, and alternating static but potentially explosive set-ups with sequences of exhilarating movement, he charted the trio's subtle shifts in allegiance so eloquently that dialogue was rendered virtually redundant. While violence, sexuality, paranoia and moral decay are recurrent elements in films as diverse as *Repulsion*, *Cul-de-Sac*, *Rosemary's Baby*, *Chinatown*, *Bitter Moon* and *Death and the Maiden*, what distinguishes his finest work is an ability not only to depict psychological reality through his expressive use of physical space but to adapt his style to the material: nightmarish surrealism for the psychodramas *Repulsion* and *The Tenant*, brittle, deceptively nostalgic *noir* for *Chinatown*, darkening pastoral romanticism for *Tess*. Uneasy with outright comedy, Polanski excels at exploring the dark recesses of the human mind and the fraught, potentially hostile spaces between people desperate but finally unable to make proper, lasting contact.

Roman Polanski b. 1933 France. **Knife in the Water** Poland 1962/ w Leon Niemczyk, Jolanta Umecka, Zygmunt Malanowicz.
Films include *Repulsion*, 1965; *Cul-de-Sac*, 1966; *Dance of the Vampires*, 1967; *Rosemary's Baby*, 1968; *Macbeth*, 1971; *Chinatown*, 1974; *The Tenant*, 1976; *Tess*, 1979; *Frantic*, 1988; *Bitter Moon*, 1992; *Death and the Maiden*, 1994. **See also** COEN BROTHERS, LYNCH, VON TRIER, WAJDA

GILLO PONTECORVO

Algiers: police and soldiers attempt to contain a riot by the Algerian Liberation Front. Pontecorvo's film is an exemplary political drama, an unsentimental, unsensationalised and (despite been banned in France) unusually fair recreation and analysis of the conflict between colonisers and revolutionaries during the first years of the Algerian War. Mostly using non-professional actors and shooting on locations that played an important part in the actual war, Pontecorvo used grainy, handheld, black-and-white camerawork to give his film the feel of contemporary documentary footage. At the same time, through taut editing and by centring key events on a handful of individuals – including a family of terrorists whose cunning methods are charted in detail – he turned a potentially sprawling, unfocused story of massed

forces into lucid, suspenseful drama. Though Pontecorvo never pulled his punches – the film opens with a man being tortured for information – and it's clear throughout where his sympathies lay, by showing decent, ordinary French colonials alongside less liberal types, and by making the French Colonel an intelligent if ruthlessly effective professional, he avoided the facile distortions of propaganda – a strategy many films influenced by *The Battle of Algiers* have failed to follow. Sadly, his own films are few; only *Queimada!*, about nineteenth-century Portuguese and British imperialism in the Caribbean, has been widely seen, and that, despite its intelligent analysis of power struggles and a fine performance by Brando, is an occasionally clumsy mix of political allegory and heroic adventure.

Gillo Pontecorvo b. 1919 Italy. **The Battle of Algiers** Algeria/Italy 1965/ w Jean Martin, Yacef Saadi, Brahim Haggiag, Tommaso Neri, Samia Kerbash. **Films include** *La Grande Strada Azzurra*, 1957; *Kapo*, 1959; *Queimada! (Burn!)* 1969; *Operazione Ogro*, 1979.
See also COSTA-GAVRAS, EISENSTEIN, ROSI, ROSSELLINI

EDWIN S PORTER

An outlaw raises his gun to fire it directly at the camera (and, of course, at the viewer) – one of the first, and therefore most famous, shots in the history of the cinema to use shock tactics purely for the sake of thrilling the audience. Porter, who joined the Edison Company in 1900, was one of the pioneers of film technique, special effects and narrative. Already, in *The Execution of Czolgosz*, he had juxtaposed a staged recreation of the killing of President McKinley's assassin with documentary footage of the prison in which he was held, while in the more sophisticated *The Life of an American Fireman*, he had used a close-up (of a hand triggering an alarm) and cross-cutting (between the interior of a burning house and firemen travelling to and achieving a succcessful rescue) to heighten suspense. But *The Great Train Robbery* remains his best known film. Though its brief (approximately 12-minute) narrative simply depicts the exploits of a gang of thieves, and their pursuit and eventual defeat by a posse, its sequence of fourteen separate scenes, themselves unedited but put together with a firm grasp of plot development, and filmed mainly in long shot with an occasionally tracking camera, not only consititutes a gripping action movie, but one of the first great screen examples of the archetypal American genre, the Western. This close-up, in fact, was not integrated into the story; cinemas were advised it should be shown either at the start or the end of the film – an early and, as it transpired, prophetic example of cinema's tendency towards gratuitous violence.

Edwin Stanton Porter b. 1869, Italy, Scotland or USA, d. 1941 USA. **The Great Train Robbery** USA 1903/ w George Barnes, Frank Hanaway, G M Anderson, Marie Murray, A C Abadie. **Films include** *The Life of an American Fireman, Uncle Tom's Cabin*, 1903; *The Ex-Convict*, 1904; *The Kleptomaniac*, 1905; *Rescued from an Eagle's Nest*, 1907; *The Eternal City*, 1915. **See also** DWAN, FEUILLADE, GRIFFITH, LUMIÈRE BROTHERS, MÉLIÈS, SENNET

MICHAEL POWELL

A shy photographer kisses his camera, his link to life (his hobby is watching home-movies) and death (he films the terrified faces of women he kills with a blade in its tripod). Powell's masterpiece concerns a gentle murderer who is both compulsive voyeur and victim of voyeurism (his psychosis stems from his having been filmed by his father – played by Powell himself – as research into fear). A disturbing Freudian study of the impulse to watch suffering (it reflects on the unwitting sadism of film-goers), *Peeping Tom* exemplifies Powell's readiness to challenge 'good taste': *A Canterbury Tale* concerns a patriotic magistrate who pours glue into the hair of girls dating American soldiers, while *Black Narcissus* concerns the feverish erotic fantasies of British nuns in the Himalayas. His florid romanticism was at odds with the documentary aesthetic favoured by many of his compatriots: *A Matter of Life and Death* used a fantasy love-story set partly (and comically) in heaven to promote wartime Anglo-American relations, while *The Red Shoes* mixed dance, music and fairy tale into the story of a diabolical Diaghilev figure and his protégée. Mostly working in collaboration with writer/co-producer Emeric Pressburger, Powell brought a quirky, imaginative artiness to unlikely subjects; disdainful of British realism, he favoured lavish Technicolor, outbursts of expressionism, monumental sets, fantasy sequences, irony and extravagant metaphor (*Peeping Tom* is full of brooding reds, films-within-films, in-jokes and phallic symbolism). Inevitably, given his eccentric ambitions, his output was uneven; he was, however, one of Britain's greatest film-makers.

Michael Powell b. 1905 England, d. 1990 England. **Peeping Tom** GB 1960/ w Karl Böhm, Anna Massey, Moira Shearer, Maxine Audley, Esmond Knight, Michael Powell. **Films include** *The Edge of the World*, 1937; *The Thief of Bagdad,* 1940; *The Life and Death of Colonel Blimp*, 1943; *A Canterbury Tale,* 1944; *I Know Where I'm Going,* 1945; *A Matter of Life and Death*, 1946; *Black Narcissus*, 1947; *The Red Shoes, The Small Back Room,* 1948; *Gone to Earth,* 1950; *The Tales of Hoffman,* 1951. **See also** HITCHCOCK, JARMAN, LUHRMANN, MAMOULIAN, OPHÜLS, SCORSESE

OTTO PREMINGER

Who to trust? Scowling soldier Ben Gazzara, accused of murdering a man alleged to have raped his wife Lee Remick? Remick, evidently enjoying her day in court despite the seriousness of the charge? Defence attorney Jimmy Stewart, epitome of the honest American? Preminger's cool, objective camera never lets on: his detached observations of the legal process at work allow that Gazzara may be an insolent brute, Remick a flirt, Stewart's folksy goodness partly a performance for the court – but what has that to do with the truth? We never discover whether Gazzara is guilty (though he is acquitted), but do see that trial by jury is a messy but necessary institution riven with doubt and ambiguity. Preminger's was an uneven career, but at its best, his probing scepticism served to undermine initial prejudices about characters and ethics; no one was without reasons for his behaviour, no issue open-and-shut. Reflecting this refusal to condone easy judgements, his camera style was mostly subtle and discreet, balancing conflicting characters within the frame, observing gestures and glances without emphasis. That said, he took himself very seriously: besides the exploration here of the judicial process, he treated, often at length and portentously, Big Issues like politics (*Advise and Consent*), Zionism (*Exodus*), religion (*The Cardinal*) and war (*In Harm's Way*). Most enjoyable (save this, his masterpiece) were earlier, more modest thrillers like *Laura*, *Whirlpool*, *Where the Sidewalk Ends* and *Angel Face*, and the western *River of No Return*, in which his refusal to take sides paid dividends in terms of characterisation and suspense.

Otto Preminger b. 1906 Austria, d. 1986 USA. **Anatomy of a Murder** USA 1959/ w James Stewart, Lee Remick, Ben Gazzara, Arthur O'Connell, Eve Arden. **Films include** *Laura*, 1944; *Whirlpool*, 1949; *Where the Sidewalk Ends*, 1949; *Angel Face*, 1952; *River of No Return*, 1954; *Bonjour Tristesse*, 1958; *Exodus*, 1960; *Advise and Consent*, 1962; *The Cardinal*, 1963; *In Harm's Way*, 1964; *The Human Factor*, 1979. **See also** COPPOLA, HUSTON, KUBRICK, LANG, STONE

A small boy stares at a strange, sexually suggestive tailor's dummy; he seems lost – though not out of place – in this subterranean world of scratched mirrors and bizarre detritus. The 'plot' of the Quays' enigmatic adaptation of Bruno Schultz's stories simply shows a man exploring derelict rooms while being harrassed by the boy; narrative is less important than mood and image in the twins' painstakingly crafted and shot puppet-animations. Profoundly influenced by expressionism, surrealism and Eastern European culture (notaby Kafka), their films – whether 'documentaries' about Janacek and Svankmajer, a potted 'version' of the *Epic of Gilgamesh* (*This Unnameable Little Broom*), or more abstract studies like *Rehearsals for Extinct Anatomies* or *The Comb* – are dreamlike studies in light, reflection, focus and texture. Puppets, often grotesquely incomplete, wander gloomily sinister settings littered with arcane, archaic paraphernalia. The world is haunting and haunted, with objects as tremulously 'alive' as the protagonists: dust swirls, screws unwind, strings vibrate, surfaces peel of their own volition, while the 'humans' may be dismembered and remodelled. If the exact meaning is often obscure, the tone of paranoia, frustration, despair and claustrophobic entrapment is palpable. Established at the forefront of avant-garde animation, they proceeded to make their first feature, *Institute Benjamenta*, about an innocent, timid pupil at a tyrannical academy for servants. Though it was a live-action film, the actors' stylised gestures, the outlandish sets, the focus on evocative objects and the lyrical monochrome camerawork still successfully suggested a mysterious, magical world.

Steven and Timothy Quay b. 1947 USA. **Street of Crocodiles** GB 1986. **Films include** *Nocturna Artificialia*, 1979; *Ein Brudermord*, 1981; *Intimate Excursions*, 1983; *The Cabinet of Jan Svankmajer*, 1984; *This Unnameable Little Broom*, 1985; *Rehearsals for Extinct Anatomies*, 1988; *Stille Nacht*, 1989; *The Comb*, 1990; *Institute Benjamenta*, 1995. **See also** BOROWCZYK, LYE, LYNCH, MCLAREN, MÉLIÈS, STAREWICZ, SVANKMAJER

NICHOLAS RAY

Frustrated by his father's weak subservience, James Dean hurls him across the room. The symbolic, clashing colours (notably Dean's fiery jacket), the staircase – site of domestic crisis between downstairs/public facade and upstairs/personal needs – and dynamic, turbulent action exemplify Ray's talents as visual storyteller. Whether working in the thriller (*They Live By Night*, *In a Lonely Place*, *On Dangerous Ground*), western (*Johnny Guitar*), war film (*Bitter Victory*), or domestic melodrama (*The Lusty Men*, *Rebel Without a Cause*, *Bigger Than Life*), Ray repeatedly charted the struggles of misfits so unable to cope with a conformist, competitive world they find themselves in bitter conflict with both others and themselves: Dean is no delinquent but an innocent seeking love, guidance, a way to balance his need to belong with a sense of independence – the facade of respectability and success is not enough. Probing the gulfs between violence and vulnerability, individual and society, Ray externalised inner torment through intense performances and vibrant, almost expressionist images: composition, colour, lighting, movement, decor, architecture and landscape all contribute to his elaborate but precise direction. Gradually, his disenchantment extended to conventional genre: films like *Party Girl*, *Wind Across the Everglades* and *The Savage Innocents* became increasingly hard to categorise, and after two (superior) epics, he abandoned commercial film-making for teaching and experimental work. A misfit himself, he was one of American cinema's greatest, most distinctive artists.

Nicholas Ray (**Raymond Nicholas Kienzle**) b. 1911 USA, d. 1979 USA. **Rebel Without a Cause** USA 1955/ w James Dean, Natalie Wood, Sal Mineo, Jim Backus, Ann Doran, Corey Allen, Dennis Hopper. **Films include** *They Live By Night*, 1948; *In a Lonely Place*, 1950; *On Dangerous Ground*, 1951; *The Lusty Men*, 1952; *Johnny Guitar*, 1954; *Bigger Than Life*, 1956; *Bitter Victory*, 1957; *Wind Across the Everglades*, *Party Girl*, 1958; *The Savage Innocents*, 1960; *55 Days at Peking*, 1963; *We Can't Go Home Again* (1973-76); *Lightning Over Water* (1980; with Wenders) **See also** FULLER, GODARD, HOPPER, LOSEY, MINNELLI, SIRK, WENDERS

A small boy, watching. The image is neither cute nor sentimental as it centres on those eyes, wary and intelligent, drinking in the world. Ray's debut, a landmark in Indian cinema and the first film in *The Apu Trilogy*, charts its hero's growth through painful experience from infancy to widowed fatherhood with an episodic, realist account of everyday events – a train's passing, the onset of the monsoon, the death of Apu's aunt and sister – in the lives of a village family. The rounded characterisations, poetic metaphors (the train presages a move to the city in search of an easier life), and classical compositions are profoundly illuminating: small details – a necklace allegedly stolen by his sister, which Apu, to his surprise, finds after her death – gradually take on enormous significance in the boy's spiritual and moral education. (Fittingly, Ray returns repeatedly to close-ups of his silent, watchful gaze.) Often, he was praised as an uncomplicated humanist; learning from his idol Renoir that everyone has his reasons, he extended warm sympathy to his characters, however flawed. But he was also deeply aware of the divisions and shifts in Indian society: *The Music Room* depicts an aristocrat's reluctance and inability to adjust to the modern world, *Days and Nights in the Forest* concerns class snobbery, tensions between Western and Indian lifestyles, and the position of women, while *Distant Thunder* charts the effects of wartime famine and the caste system on individual lives. Ray's miniaturist, slightly old-fashioned sensitivity to psychological, social and moral nuance made him a major film-maker of international importance.

Satyajit Ray b. 1921 India, d. 1992 India. **Pather Panchali** India 1955/ w Subir Bannerjee, Kanu Bannerjee, Karuna Bannerjee, Uma Das Gupta, Chunibala. **Films include** *The Unvanquished*, 1957; *The Music Room*, 1958; *The World of Apu*, 1959; *Devi*, 1960; *Kanchenjunga*, 1962; *Charulata*, 1964; *Days and Nights in the Forest*, 1965; *Company Limited*, 1972; *Distant Thunder*, 1973; *The Middleman*, 1975; *The Home and the World*, 1984. **See also** DE SICA, IVORY, OUÉDRAOGO, RENOIR, ROSSELLINI, VISCONTI

CAROL REED

The Third Man

Racketeer Harry Lime (Orson Welles) takes refuge in the shadows of post-war Vienna – a classic *noir* image, shot on location amid the devastated grandeur of Freud's city. Reed's film of Graham Greene's story is a tough, unsentimental study of loyalty and betrayal (Lime is tracked down by his friend), of the ego and id, of a city divided against itself in war's cynical aftermath. With Robert Krasker's crisp photography, Reed turns city landmarks – a towering ferris wheel from which Lime looks down on the humanity he disdains, the dark maze of sewers through which he is hunted like a rat – into a metaphorical nightmare where ethics are as murky as the subterranean canals. Mirroring the precariousness of civilisation, the images are repeatedly tilted, while characters are dwarfed by their shadow selves; the editing is restless, rapid, creating an air of uncertainty. Mostly, Reed's career was unremarkable, proceeding from modest dramas and thrillers to tepid adaptations and spectaculars where his more extrovert visual flourishes seemed studied and superfluous. Briefly, however, he hit his stride with three films in a row: before *The Third Man*, he made *Odd Man Out*, a moody, intelligent *noir* thriller about a wounded IRA fugitive that becomes steadily more delirious, and *The Fallen Idol* (also by Greene), a quietly perceptive study of friendship between a young boy and a butler who involves him in his adulterous deceits. Again, Reed's use of architecture was telling and atmospheric, but the subtle depiction of innocence betrayed by experience also made it his most touching film.

Carol Reed b. 1906 England, d. 1976 England. **The Third Man** GB 1948/ w Joseph Cotten, Orson Welles, Alida Valli, Trevor Howard, Paul Hoerbiger, Bernard Lee. **Films include** *Bank Holiday*, 1938; *The Stars Look Down*, 1939; *Night Train to Munich*, 1940; *The Way Ahead*, 1944; *Odd Man Out*, 1947; *The Fallen Idol*, 1948; *Outcast of the Islands*, 1951; *Trapeze*, 1956; *Our Man in Havana*, 1960; *The Agony and the Ecstasy*, 1965. **See also** HITCHCOCK, LEAN, PARKER, SCOTT, WELLES

JEAN RENOIR

A poacher caught red-handed argues with an aristocrat landowner and his gamekeepers. The image, though simple, is rich: realistic, yet tinged with theatricality in the poacher's gestures; good-naturedly comic yet authentically depicting class conflict, the rabbit a reminder of poverty, privilege, cruelty and death. Renoir's tragic farce about bourgeoisie and peasantry brought together for a country-house weekend is a landmark of cinema. Funny, tender, satirical and elegiac in its bitter-sweet account of the passing of the old French order, it's notable for its free-wheeling narrative, its sense of life forever threatening to turn into theatre, and a fluent camera that moves from one group of affectionately drawn characters to another with exhilarating ease. Renoir's versatility embraced anarchic comedy (*Boudu Saved from Drowning*), crime (*La Bête Humaine*), war (*La Grande Illusion*), romance (*Une Partie de Campagne*), historical drama (*The Golden Coach*), and uncategorisable films like *The River,* which blends family drama, documentary, mystic fable and lyrical poetry. His signature is discernible in the generous, unsentimental humanity, the assured evocation of milieu, an awareness of the transience of life and love, and a subtle realism whose deceptive simplicity is derived from unobtrusive artifice: deep focus, long takes, complex camera movements, elegant framing, and a wealth of telling incidental detail. Even his experiments with sound, colour and multi-camera shooting techniques were integrated to serve narrative and characterisation. He was unquestionably a master of cinema; the apparent effortlessness of his art only confirms his genius.

Jean Renoir b. 1894 France, d. 1979 USA. **La Règle du Jeu** France 1939/ w Marcel Dalio, Nora Gregor, Roland Toutain, Jean Renoir, Julien Carette, Gaston Modot, Paulette Dubost. **Films include** *Boudu Saved from Drowning*, 1932; *Toni*, 1934; *Le Crime de Monsieur Lange*, 1935; *Une Partie de Campagne*, 1936; *La Grande Illusion*, 1937; *La Marseillaise*, *La Bête Humaine*, 1938; *The Southerner*, 1945; *The River*, 1951; *The Golden Coach*, 1952; *French Can Can*, 1955; *Eléna et les Hommes*, 1956; *The Vanishing Corporal*, 1962. **See also** ALTMAN, BECKER, BUÑUEL, SATYAJIT RAY, MIZOGUCHI, OPHÜLS, ROSSELLINI, TRUFFAUT, VIGO

ALAIN RESNAIS

Rich, elegant couples are dancing in a grand spa hotel. Or are they? All, even the central couple – a woman and a man who insists they met, or may have met, a year earlier, when she promised to run away with him the following year (though she claims to recall no such meeting) – look strangely unreal: stiff, joyless, distracted, even ghostly. Resnais' film, written by *nouveau roman* writer Alain Robbe-Grillet, is one of the few avant-garde features to have reached a wide audience. The characters are subordinate to the theme of time, memory and imagination (the non-chronological 'plot', charting the man's efforts to convince the woman of their real, non-existent or future affair, comprises repeated sequences which vary mainly in terms of her response). The camera mirrors the labyrinthine narrative with long, gliding takes down endless corridors, coming across figures posed hieratically in geometric groups (notably in a formal garden where they cast shadows but the topiary doesn't). In film after film, Resnais intercuts and merges past, present and future, reality and fantasy; from the harrowing exhortation to remember the death camps in *Night and Fog*, to portraits of lives haunted by war in *Hiroshima Mon Amour* and *Muriel*, a study of a writer confusing art and life in *Providence*, and *On Connaît la Chanson*, an atypically light-hearted romance whose participants express feelings by miming to popular songs. A determined modernist seemingly more interested in form than content, Resnais can be genuinely inventive or infuriatingly obscure; but his films' emotional reticence suggest that behind the stylish facade, there may be less than meets the eye.

Alain Resnais b. 1922 France. **L'Année Dernière à Marienbad** France1961/ w Delphine Seyrig, Giorgio Albertazzi, Sacha Pitoeff, Françoise Bertin, Luce Garcia-Ville. **Films include** *Night and Fog*, 1955; *Hiroshima Mon Amour*, 1959; *Muriel*, 1963; *La Guerre est Finie*, 1966; *Je t'Aime, Je t'Aime*, 1968; *Stavisky*, 1974; *Providence*, 1977; *My Oncle d'Amerique*, 1980; *Mélo*, 1986; *Smoking/No Smoking*, 1993; *On Connaît la Chanson*, 1998. **See also** Cocteau, Feuillade, Greenaway, Marker, Roeg, Ruiz

The glistening naked beauty of an Aryan girl involved, almost ecstatically, in healthy physical activity: the image is characteristic of former art student, dancer and film star Riefenstahl, (in)famous as the Third Reich's sanctioned film-maker. After directing and acting in *The Blue Light* – a massive hit in the German 'mountain film' genre – she was invited to film the Nazis' 1934 rally. Responding with dramatically lit, geometrically-framed tableaux of huge crowds surrounded by Nazi insignia, uniformly enthralled by Hitler (first seen in a plane making a Godlike entrance through swirling clouds), she created *Triumph of the Will*, the ultimate in Fascist propaganda. *Olympia*, a documentary account of the 1936 Olympic Games, is marginally less oppressive since less explicitly propagandistic (it even shows black American Jesse Owens' remarkable victories), but still a rhapsodic hymn to the Aryan ideals of athleticism and physical beauty. Besides the sporting events themselves – for which Riefenstahl employed a range of techniques, including rapid montage, slow-motion (notably for the high-diving), tracking and dolly shots, close-ups and long shots of the competitors dwarfed by the stadium – the film features a prologue tracing the Olympic flame's progress from Athens to Berlin (with shots of temples and statuary implying a spiritual link between the ancient deities and the Third Reich), and scenes of contestants at play in the Olympic village. One need not decry Riefenstahl's virtuosity, nor indeed her epic vision, to feel unease at the relentless objectification of human individuals and celebration of heroic power, ambition and achievement.

Leni (Helene) Riefenstahl b. 1902 Germany. **Olympia** Germany 1938. **Films include** *The Blue Light*, 1932; *Sieg der Glaubens* (*Victory of Faith*), 1933; *Triumph of the Will*, 1936; *Tiefland*, 1954; *Schwarze Fracht* (*Black Cargo*; unfinished), 1956. **See also** BERKELEY, EISENSTEIN, FLAHERTY, KUBRICK, VERTOV

JACQUES RIVETTE

Céline and Julie Go Boating

A child's head beneath a pillow, her nurse, her widowed father, a beautiful aunt who may be plotting the girl's death in order to marry him: the faintly sinister scene is reminiscent of Hollywood melodrama, yet the graininess, flat lighting and 'ordinary' decor are evocative of a home-movie. Rivette's films are like no others: long (*Out One* ran almost 13 hours), discursive, often largely improvised around the theme of 'real life' interacting and merging with theatre, art (as in his late masterpiece *La Belle Noiseuse*) or a fiction suggestive of conspiracy. In the unusually light-hearted *Céline and Julie*, a librarian and a magician make friends and, by eating mysterious, possibly hallucinogenic sweets, witness and finally participate in the intrigue depicted above: as they, like us, piece together the slowly unravelling story, their wacky naturalism is juxtaposed with the stilted, swooning demeanour of the sophisticates they 'visit'. Since his cheaply made debut, *Paris Nous Appartient*, where a girl on the fringes of a group rehearsing Shakespeare's *Pericles* comes to suspect they may be murderers, Rivette has obsessively explored the thin line between reality and artifice, shifting between them until it's hard to tell where 'performance' begins and ends. The unexplained coincidences and mystificatory hints of arcane ritual, while echoing our need to make sense of life's chaos, may seem frustratingly obscure or portentous. Nevertheless, the long, meandering, often unresolved narratives – comprising casually composed shots elliptically and ingeniously edited to create an air of magic and mystery – can make for thought-provoking, hypnotically compelling cinema.

Jacques Rivette b. 1928 France. **Céline and Julie Go Boating** France 1974/ w Juliet Berto, Dominique Labourier, Bulle Ogier, Marie-France Pisier, Barbet Schroeder. **Films include** *Paris Nous Appartient*, 1960; *La Religieuse*, 1966; *L'Amour Fou*, 1968; *Out One*, 1971; *Out One: Spectre*, 1972; *Le Pont du Nord*, 1981; *Love on the Ground*, 1984; *La Belle Noiseuse*, 1991; *Joan of Arc*, 1994. **See also** CUKOR, FEUILLADE, GODARD, KIAROSTAMI, LANG, MAKHMALBAF, RENOIR, WARHOL

A woman stands with friends (one a blind clairvoyant) on a funeral barge mourning her husband. The elegant composition is itself unremarkable; what's significant is that it represents the viewpoint of the husband, forewarned of his own demise. Roeg's densely allusive supernatural thriller, about a couple recuperating in Venice after their daughter's death, concerns the tangled threads linking grief, memory, hope and fear: centred on the emotional/mental states of the husband and wife, who respectively look to the future and live in the past, it conflates time through montage, each moment echoing others. Visually, Roeg, a former cameraman, mirrors this 'synchronicity' with rhymed compositions and colours: memorably, the couple keep seeing and following a figure in a blood-red raincoat, reminiscent of their child but really a deranged dwarf who turns out to be the husband's killer. From his directing debut *Performance* (made with Donald Cammell) onwards, Roeg deployed a fragmented, associative editing style to shift between reality and fantasy, fear and desire, past, present and future in diverse genres: anthropological allegory (*Walkabout*), sci-fi (*The Man Who Fell to Earth*), melodrama (*Bad Timing*). Excepting *Walkabout* and *Don't Look Now*, the results, while intriguing, have often lacked coherence; the narrative complexity and bold, baroque images can seem a gloss imposed on conventional stories; those two films succeed because the cross-cutting is wholly appropriate to studies of culture clash and psychic prescience. As time passed, Roeg applied his idiosyncratic mannerisms to increasingly banal material, and his once fertile imagination appears to have run dry.

Nicolas Roeg b. 1928 England. **Don't Look Now** GB 1973/ w Julie Christie, Donald Sutherland, Hilary Mason, Clelia Matania, Massimo Serrato. **Films include** *Performance*, 1970; *Walkabout*, 1971; *The Man Who Fell to Earth*, 1976; *Bad Timing*, 1980; *Eureka*, 1982; *Insignificance*, 1985; *Castaway*, 1986; *Track 29*, 1988; *The Witches*, 1989; *Cold Heaven*, 1992; *Two Deaths*, 1994. **See also** BOORMAN, LESTER, MARKER, MAKHMALBAF, RESNAIS

ERIC ROHMER

An engineer, forced by snow to sleep over at the flat of a divorcee he's just met, tries to keep his distance from her naked body. Intent on marrying a stranger he's seen at church, he finds his belief in Pascal's wager (it pays to believe in God because if right, you win eternity; if wrong, you lose nothing) undermined not only by his host's advocacy of free will but by her easy sensuality. The interweaving of physical and metaphysical dilemmas is typical of Rohmer, the most thematically and stylistically consistent investigator of human desire in cinema history. While the illuminating psychological precision of his witty, erudite dialogue (his characters endlessly discuss love, beauty, ethics, etc) indicates a literary sensibility, Rohmer's ability to elicit superb naturalistic performances from his (often young and

unknown) actors, his attention to exact details of time and place, and his fascination with how characters relate through gestures, glances and spatial proximity to one another make him a master of 'intimist' cinema. The engineer's absurdly awkward efforts to resist temptation in cramped quarters are both comically suggestive of emotional and moral indecision and an incisive test of the philosophical rigidity informing his life. Subtly revealing discrepancies between word and deed, rationality and impulse, Rohmer exposes the frailty of intention and the erroneous vanity of self-image. Yet the warmth of his gently comic stories, the refusal to mock aspirations, and the insistence that everyone, however misguided, deserves respectful observation confirm him as one of cinema's most sympathetic humanists.

Eric Rohmer (Jean-Marie Maurice Scherer) b. 1920 France. My Night with Maud France 1969/ w Jean-Louis Trintignant, Françoise Fabian, Marie-Christine Barrault, Antoine Vitez. Films include *The Sign of Leo*, 1959; *Claire's Knee*, 1970; *The Marquise Von O...*, 1976; *The Aviator's Wife*, 1980; *The Green Ray*, 1986; *Four Adventures of Reinette and Mirabelle*, 1987; *A Winter's Tale*, 1992; *The Tree, the Mayor and the Mediatheque*, 1993; *An Autumn Tale*, 1998. See also BECKER, MANKIEWICZ, PIALAT, RENOIR, STILLMAN

A man battles to keep flesh-eating zombies out of the house in which he and a few others have taken refuge. Romero's seminal low-budget horror movie differed from most of its predecessors not only by making the carnage graphically explicit but also in its unrelentingly grim, pessimistic tone. The besieged fall prey both to the cannibals (who by killing the living increase their own number, so that one young victim starts feeding on her own mother), and to hysterical in-fighting; the nominal 'heroine', traumatised by her brother's death in the opening scene, never recovers, while the hero devises sensible defence strategies to no avail and is finally killed by cops, mistaken for a vigilante. Romero's grainy black-and-white images lend an urgent, visceral immediacy reminiscent of newsreel, even as the zombies – recognisably human but possessed of no fear, only the primal impulse to eat – take the film into the realm of nightmare. His finest work is located within a clearly defined social milieu: *The Crazies*, about homicidal maniacs produced by a deadly government-invented virus, shows the dangers of social collapse and martial law; *Martin*, about a modern teenage vampire, implies that his bloodlust derives from sexual and psychological insecurity and an oppressive dysfunctional family background; while *Zombies – Dawn of the Dead* satirises consumerism as the corpses head once more to shopping malls, where the besieged fight over luxury goods redundant in an apocalyptic world. Subsequently, Romero has repeated himself or produced more slickly conventional horror fare, but the generic influence of his early films remains substantial.

George Andrew Romero b. 1940 USA. **Night of the Living Dead** USA 1968/ w Duane Jones, Judith O'Dea, Karl Hardman, Keith Wayne, Judith Ridley. **Films include** *Jack's Wife (Season of the Witch)*, *The Crazies*, 1973; *Martin*, 1978; *Zombies – Dawn of the Dead*, 1979; *Knightriders*, 1981; *Creepshow*, 1982; *Day of the Dead*, 1985; *Monkey Shines*, 1988; *The Dark Half*, 1993. **See also** ARNOLD, BAVA, BROWNING, CARPENTER, CRONENBERG, WHALE

FRANCESCO ROSI

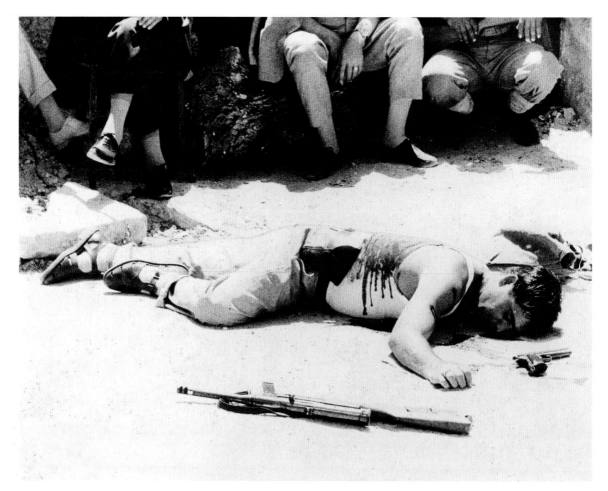

The legendary Sicilian bandit Giuliano Salvatore lies dead, his long evasion of retribution for his crimes finally ended. Rosi's stark political docudrama takes this as the starting point for a complex analysis not of the man himself, who remains something of a mystery, but of Sicilian society – the various roles played in the bandit's crimes by peasants, police, politicians and the Mafia. Profoundly influenced by neo-realism, Rosi used historical facts (and, often, non-professional actors) in his cool, probing speculative dramas exploring the social, political and economic forces of influence and corruption in modern Italy. Flashbacks trace cause and effect, while the camerawork often suggests that what we are watching is documentary footage rather than fiction or a staged reconstruction. In later films, however, such as

The Mattei Affair, Lucky Luciano and *Illustrious Corpses*, Rosi often borrowed iconography and narrative conventions from the American crime thriller to create a palpable atmosphere of conspiracy and paranoia; the result was simultaneously stylish, suspenseful and thought-provoking. Thereafter he moved with variable results into less politically contentious, more conventional art-movie fare, with literary adaptations like *Christ Stopped at Eboli, Carmen, Chronicle of a Death Foretold* and *The Truce*. For all their visual elegance and meticulous attention to historical detail, these films were rather self-consciously worthy, ponderous and lacking in the raw power that characterised his best work. His decline is sadly symptomatic of the staleness of much contemporary Italian cinema.

Francesco Rosi b. 1922 Italy. **Salvatore Giuliano** Italy 1961/ w Frank Wolff, Salvo Randone, Federico Zardi, Pietro Cammarata, Fernando Cicero. **Films include** *Hands Across the City*, 1963; *The Mattei Affair,* 1972; *Lucky Luciano, Illustrious Corpses*, 1973; *Christ Stopped at Eboli,* 1979; *Three Brothers*, 1981; *Carmen*, 1964; *Chronicle of a Death Foretold*, 1987; *The Truce*, 1997. **See also** COSTA-GAVRAS, GUNEY, PONTECORVO, SAURA

Pompeii – a middle-class English couple have just witnessed an excavation of lovers encased in lava; the sight of their eternal union has driven the already troubled Joyces to the brink of divorce. First acclaimed for his documentary-style accounts of the ravages of war in *Rome, Open City*, *Paisà* and *Germany, Year Zero*, Rossellini went on to transcend neo-realism's rather sentimental preoccupation with working-class heroes in a series of psychological dramas starring his then wife Ingrid Bergman. Fictional but partly (auto-)biographical portraits of problematic marriages, they mix dedramatised narratives with a sense of people relating to social milieu and landscape. Hence, there's little 'plot' in *Viaggio in Italia*: the couple voice resentment and boredom, the emotionally reticent man briefly considers the possibility of infidelity,

and the woman, sightseeing in Naples, is made aware of the physical aridity of her life by the sight of pregnant women, naked statues and the dead lovers. Rossellini's visual style is discreet but telling: seemingly off-hand shots of the couple together reveal the growing distance between them, while montage sequences, juxtaposing vibrant Italian life with the characters' reactions to it, show their remoteness they are from the world. Rossellini's simple observational methods endured as he progressed to educational TV docudramas about figures like Garibaldi, Louis XIV and Pascal. His calm, understated direction was also often aligned to a Catholic fascination with faith: finally, the Joyces are miraculously and movingly reunited by a recognition of their unspoken mutual need while witnessing a procession involving the Madonna.

Roberto Rossellini b. 1906 Italy, d. 1977 Italy. **Viaggio in Italia** Italy 1953/ w Ingrid Bergman, George Sanders, Maria Mauban, Paul Muller, Leslie Daniels, Natalia Ray. **Films include** *Rome, Open City*, 1945; *Paisà*, 1946; *Germany, Year Zero*, 1947; *L'Amore*, 1948; *Stromboli*, 1949; *Francis, God's Jester*, 1950; *Fear*, 1954; *Era Notte a Roma*, 1960; *Viva l'Italia*, 1960; *The Rise to Power of Louis XIV*, 1966; *Blaise Pascal*, 1972; *The Age of Cosimo de Medici*, 1973. **See also** ANTONIONI, DE SICA, GODARD, KIAROSTAMI, MORETTI, PASOLINI, TAVIANI BROTHERS

ALAN RUDOLPH

A rich patroness extols her appreciation of the arts, but what does she love most – the paintings, prestige or her power over artists and collectors? Certainly she's not above seducing an obscure, talented painter into forgery. The erratic Rudolph's long-planned portrait of creativity and commerce in conflict in 1920s Paris is a sumptuously colourful, gently ironic tribute to the heady spirit of artistic endeavour that produced some of the finest masterpieces of modern times. The mix of romanticism, artiness, scepticism and whimsy is typical of Rudolph, whose finest work – *Remember My Name*, *Choose Me*, *The Moderns* and parts of *Mrs Parker and the Vicious Circle* – is characterised by his creation of credibly off-kilter worlds rooted in reality yet imbued with a dream-like, fairy-tale strangeness: here, fictional characters rub shoulders with Hemingway and Stein, while the questionable authenticity of both the artworks and the various characters' motives enhances the air of unreality. Elsewhere, his work has often been let down either by an evident lack of commitment to the material (several of his earlier films were directorial chores) or by a rather precious, self-conscious eccentricity: for all their quirky characterisations and avoidance of cliché, *Trouble in Mind*, *Love At Large*, *Equinox* and even the relatively subdued *Afterglow* simply seem incoherent, inconsequential or pretentious. Still, like his former mentor Altman, Rudolph is skilful with colour, costume, camera movement and the wide screen: though he seldom penetrates beyond the pictorial surface to probe deeper meanings, few of his films are anything but elegant.

Alan Rudolph b. 1943 USA. **The Moderns** USA 1988/ w Keith Carradine, Linda Fiorentino, John Lone, Geraldine Chaplin, Wallace Shawn, Geneviève Bujold, Kevin O'Connor. **Films include** *Welcome to LA*, 1977; *Remember My Name*, 1979; *Choose Me*, 1984; *Trouble in Mind*, 1985; *Made in Heaven*, 1987; *Love at Large*, 1990; *Mortal Thoughts*, 1991; *Equinox*, 1993; *Mrs Parker and the Vicious Circle*, 1994; *Afterglow*, 1997. **See also** ALTMAN, DEMY, LUBITSCH, OPHÜLS

In a grey-lit mansion, people are positioned in a *tableau vivant* to imitate the hieratic gestures of one of a series of paintings, the arcane significance of which an art historian explains as he leads us from room to room; not only are his convoluted theories contradicted by an unseen narrator, but the key to the mystery is a painting now lost and forgotten. The eccentric, experimental and erudite films of prolific Chilean-in-exile Ruiz are marked by off-centre, labyrinthine narratives and copious references to art, literature and film. Cheaply made yet visually rich, they explore philosophical questions of identity, representation and the line between reality and fantasy: the imagery, though often verging on the minimalist, tends to the dreamlike and surreal. Borges, Calderón and Kafka are among his literary forebears; visually, his influences are many, though Magritte, Welles and American B-movies figure strongly. Here, the camera prowls slowly among carefully lit tableaux to investigate mysterious objects, inexplicable glances and the spatial relationship between human figures. In *Three Crowns of the Sailor* the film progresses from murky sepia to dazzling ornate colour, mirroring a fabulist's increasingly tall stories within stories. *Shattered Image* intercuts and overemphasises generic iconography to imply that its tacky psychological thriller plot may all be a crazed dream. Though style and content in Ruiz's films are often so baroque and allusive as to be indecipherable, much intellectual enjoyment may be had from trying to unravel the densely tangled strands of his imaginatively fecund fictions.

Raúl (Raoul) Ruiz b. 1941 Chile. **The Hypothesis of the Stolen Painting** France 1978/ w Jean Rougeul, Gabriel Gascon, Chantal Paley, Jean Reno. **Films include** *Three Sad Tigers*, 1965; *The Penal Colony*, 1970; *On Top of the Whale*, 1981; *Three Crowns of the Sailor*, 1982; *City of Pirates*, 1983; *Treasure Island*, *Life Is a Dream*, 1986; *Three Lives and One Death*, 1996; *Genealogies of a Crime*, 1997; *Shattered Image*, 1998; *Le Temps Retrouvé*, 1999. **See also** Botelho, Corman, Godard, Greenaway, Resnais, Welles

KEN RUSSELL

Tchaikovsky conducts his 1812 Overture, festooned with triumphal ribbons, clearly on the verge of ecstasy. To Russell, it matters not that the composer never conducted from windy rooftops, nor that he is unlikely to have imagined cannonfire decapitating his wife and brother (both images occur in this scene): for British cinema's self-appointed *enfant terrible* it's enough that the music impels him to flights of surreal Freudian fantasy. One cannot deny his ability to create vividly grotesque, excessive images – all lurid colours, spectacular sets, swirling camera movements and wild gestures – nor that his disdain for genteel realism might have led to a refreshingly impressionistic brand of psychodrama. Sadly, however, after a relatively subdued, even lyrical adaptation of Lawrence's *Women in Love,* he let his feverish imagination run riot. Tchaikovsky's music simplistically became a product of homosexual guilt and torment at being forced to marry a nymphomaniac; worse, *Mahler* and the ludicrous *Lisztomania* flirted in kitsch fashion with Nazi insignia and ideology. In making films about artists (he also dealt with Henri Gaudier-Brzeska, Valentino, Byron and the Shelleys, and Wilde), Russell adhered, perhaps self-aggrandisingly, to romantic clichés of rebellious, misfit geniuses at odds with philistine, repressive society (inevitably, sex looms large). His own work too seems aimed to shock and offend, but his gloating, misanthropic sensationalism is so overemphatic, beyond even caricature, that his stabs at satire and social comment are too remote from reality to hit home. Indeed, his more recent films look like hapless self-parody.

Ken Russell b. 1927 England. **The Music Lovers** GB 1970/ w Richard Chamberlain, Glenda Jackson, Max Adrian, Kenneth Colley, Christopher Gable. **Films include** *Women in Love*, 1969; *The Devils*, 1971; *Savage Messiah*, 1972; *Mahler*, 1974; *Tommy, Lisztomania*, 1975; *Valentino*, 1977; *Crimes of Passion*, 1980; *Gothic*, 1986; *Salome's Last Dance, The Rainbow*, 1989; *Whore*, 1991. **See also** FELLINI, JARMAN, KUSTURICA, POWELL, ROEG

Amid the dismally uniform houses of an industrial new town in the Brazilian hinterland, a world-weary ex-teacher's feelings of friendship and responsibility are reawakened by a boy she's reluctantly helping in his search for his absent father. Salles' film is a landmark in the renaissance of Brazilian cinema, long after the 60s heyday of *cinema novo* directors like Glauber Rocha and Ruy Guerra. Cleverly, he avoids sentimental cliché: here, the harsh sunlight, the drab setting and the symmetrical composition invest what might otherwise have been conventional 'realism' with a stylised formality. In this and two fine features co-directed with Daniela Thomas – *Foreign Land* and *Midnight* – the former documentarist used genre (*film noir*, the road-movie, the prison escape thriller crossed with a love story) to create popular entertainment that reflects sharply on the social, moral, economic and political plight of modern Brazil. Here, the odd couple's wanderings take them from the Rio slums to tawdry truckstops and dying shantytowns populated by displaced exiles; the teacher represents self-centred expediency, the boy hope for the future. Salles is a dazzling visual stylist, his pacy narratives packed with striking images: the high-contrast black and white of *Foreign Land* evokes the delirious paranoia of being lost in a strange country, while *Central Station* moves from muted colours, cramped close-ups and shallow depth of field to brighter tones and more panoramic perspectives, not to mention integrated religious imagery, to reflect its heroine's regeneration with a subtle inventiveness that confirm Salles as a film-maker of considerable promise.

Walter Salles b.1955 Brazil. **Central Station** Brazil 1998/ w Fernanda Motenegro, Vinicius de Oliveira, Marilia Pêra, Sôia Lira. **Films include** *High Art (The Knife)*, 1991; *Foreign Land*, 1995; *Somewhere Else (Socorro Nobre)*, 1996; *Midnight*, 1998. **See also** CARNÉ, NICHOLAS RAY, SAYLES, SCHRADER, SCORSESE

CARLOS SAURA

Carmen

A rehearsal for a flamenco version of Merimée's classic: Carmen and her rival in love square up to each other with fiery passion. Saura's exquisitely mounted film, made in collaboration with dancer-choreographer Antonio Gades, is typical of his dance movies (*Blood Wedding, El Amor Brujo, Sevillanas, Tango*) in several respects: mainly depicting rehearsals, it highlights the vibrant folk tradition of flamenco music and dance, as opposed to Bizet's popular but decidedly un-Spanish opera; and the events of Merimée's story are somewhat simplistically mirrored in the backstage romantic intrigues of the dancers. Saura has always been fascinated by tradition, history and the way fantasy and artifice intersect with reality. His early films, made under Franco, are dark allegorical dramas (and occasionally comedies) which explore how the repressive dictatorship had a baneful effect on all areas of life: in *La Caza*, friends on a hunting trip (at the site of a Civil War battle) fall out as guilt and recrimination rise to the surface; in *Cría Cuervos*, a young girl's refusal to accept that her parents are dead symbolises the way the past hangs heavily over the future. The need to evade censorship made for dramatic subtlety, delicacy and psychological resonance; after Franco's death, Saura's work became more direct and, surprisingly, less political. While his recent work has invariably been visually polished, making attractive use of carefully composed colours, reflections, shadows, and proud, passionate gestures, it has also tended towards the decorative – he now often seems to endorse, rather than question, stereo-typically romantic notions of Spain, its culture and history.

Carlos Saura b. 1932 Spain. **Carmen** Spain 1983/ w Antonio Gades, Laura del Sol, Christina Hoyos, Paco de Lucia, Juan Antonio Jimenez. **Films include** *Los Golfos*, 1960; *La Caza*, 1966; *Peppermint Frappé*, 1967; *Ana and the Wolves*, 1973; *Cría Cuervos*, 1976; *Deprisa, Deprisa*, 1980; *Blood Wedding*, 1981; *El Amor Brujo*, 1986; *El Dorado*, 1988; *Ay! Carmela*, 1990; *Sevillanas*, 1992; *Tango*, 1998. **See also** ALMODÓVAR, BUÑUEL, ERICE, MINNELLI, ROSI

194

Soap star Mary McDonell, bitterly reclusive since an accident left her half-paralysed, chats with live-in nurse Alfre Woodard: a classically simple image of friendship. In context, it's far richer than that: a variation on the disease-exploiting melodramas which made the actress famous, the film eschews cliché to focus on her psychological trauma and on how her resentment is finally soothed by the realisation that Woodard, a recovering crack addict whose daughter is in care, has her own problems. Without overly stressing the feminist and racial aspects of his story, Sayles precisely delineates the social, cultural and economic parameters of the pair's faltering progress towards a new perspective on their options (fittingly, McDonell's regeneration coincides with a renewed interest in photography and a magically shot trip to the bayoux, away from her imprisoning mansion). Repeatedly subverting traditional genres – teen romance (*Baby It's You*), sci-fi (*The Brother from Another Planet*), the Western (*Matewan*), the sports saga (*Eight Men Out*), the detective mystery (*Lone Star*) – his abiding fascination with America's political and historical fabric ensures that his characters' personal experiences illuminate social divisions of race, gender, class and money. A very talented writer, expert with sharp, witty dialogue and complex narrative structures involving large groups of interrelated characters, he has become increasingly assured visually, using long, sinuous camera movements to link characters in chains of cause and effect, and generic iconography to lend an epic or mythical dimension to his heroes' struggles against injustice.

John Sayles b. 1950 USA. **Passion Fish** USA 1993/ w Mary McDonell, Alfre Woodard, Vondie Curtis-Hall, David Strathairn, Angela Bassett.
Films include *Return of the Secaucus Seven*, 1979; *Lianna*, 1982; *Baby It's You*, 1983; *The Brother from Another Planet*, 1984; *Matewan*, 1987; *Eight Men Out*, 1988; *City of Hope*, 1991; *The Secret of Roan Inish*, 1994; *Lone Star*, 1995; *Men with Guns*, 1997; *Limbo*, 1999.
See also ALTMAN, HAYNES, LEE, LOACH, PENN, STONE

A king in New York: the giant ape, dragged from his jungle home and put on display by a none too eco-friendly film crew, escapes to the world's tallest building to fend off fighter planes, driven by his love for relatively diminutive Fay Wray. If only for this final, mythic scene from the daddy of all monster-movies, Schoedsack and Cooper deserve acclaim. The former cameraman and explorer-turned-producer first collaborated on the ethnographic documentaries *Grass* and *Chang* (respectively about Persian nomads and Siamese tribesmen), before making a version of the imperialist yarn *The Four Feathers*. Adventure and exploration were dear to their hearts, for *Kong*'s turgid early scenes depict the crew's foolhardy expedition to a mysterious primeval island: only when the ape and various murderously argumentative dinosaurs appear does the film take off, thanks to Willis O'Brien's impressively expressive stop-motion model work. During the ape's brief domination of the quintessential twentieth-century city, pathos kicks in: the notion of a noble savage laid low by man's short-sighted opportunism and his own barely comprehended sexual longing for a pint-sized blonde ('It was Beauty killed the Beast') is poetic and poignant enough to overcome misgivings about his occasionally faltering, jerky movements, sudden changes in scale, and the wooden acting of his human counterparts. Cooper went on to produce for Ford; Schoedsack, who had already made the disturbingly sadistic fable *The Most Dangerous Game*, tried to repeat his success with *Son of Kong* and *Mighty Joe Young*; neither, however, would again scale the lofty heights of *King Kong*.

Ernest B Schoedsack b. 1893 USA, d. 1979 USA. **Merian C Cooper** b. 1893 USA, d. 1973 USA. **King Kong** USA 1933/ w Fay Wray, Robert Armstrong, Bruce Cabot, Frank Reicher, Sam Hardy, Noble Johnson. **Films include** *Grass*, 1926; *Chang*, 1927; *The Four Feathers*, 1929; *Rango* (Schoedsack), 1931; *The Most Dangerous Game (The Hounds of Zaroff)* (Schoedsack/ Irving Pichel)1932; *Song of Kong* (Schoedsack), 1933; *Dr Cyclops* (Schoedsack), 1940; *Mighty Joe Young* (Schoedsack), 1949. **See also** ARNOLD, FLAHERTY, WOOD

Gigolo Richard Gere indulges in a moment of self-contemplation. The split reflection, suggesting a personality riven by dilemmas and contradictions, is reworked to sharply stylish yet faintly austere effect in Schrader's fable about an innocent man accused of murder, whose cool professional expertise in the ways of the flesh has distanced him from love. Only by finally confessing his feelings for a married woman who provides an alibi will he achieve self-knowledge and grace. Former critic and screenwriter Schrader has made some of the most personal American movies of recent decades. Raised a Calvinist, fascinated by sensual abandon, he has repeatedly returned to the theme of sin and redemption as experienced by anguished, solitary, self-destructive men. While allusions to other movies are common, a frequent motif has been the descent into hell; red recurs in much of his work, along with images of reflection, alienation and entrapment. Often, it's as if the very films have a split personality as they alternate between carnality and introspection, dazzlingly stylised decor, lighting and camerawork and compositions bordering on ascetic minimalism. *Hardcore* juxtaposed rural religious puritanism with the urban sex-industry, *Mishima* intercut between monochrome and colour, documentary-style footage and expressionist studio artifice, while much of *Patty Hearst* takes place in a dark, claustrophobic closet, the rest in sunlit exteriors. An intellectual and aesthete, Schrader has striven to turn his doubts and desires, fear and confusion into thought-provoking, adult entertainment; often, he has succeeded.

Paul Schrader b. 1946 USA. **American Gigolo** USA 1980/ w Richard Gere, Lauren Hutton, Hector Elizondo, Nina Van Pallandt, Bill Duke. **Films include** *Blue Collar*, 1977; *Hardcore*, 1978; *Cat People*, 1981; *Mishima*, 1985; *Light of Day*, 1987; *Patty Hearst*, 1988; *The Comfort of Strangers*, 1991; *Light Sleeper*, 1992; *Affliction*, 1997. **See also** BERTOLUCCI, BRESSON, DREYER, OZU, SALLES, SCORSESE

MARTIN SCORSESE

'You talkin' to me?' In his lonely room, cabbie Robert De Niro practises his techniques for clearing human filth from the streets of New York. His nakedness suggests the ascetic saintliness of his deranged self-image; the mirror reflects both his split character (he's a moral crusader and a killer) and his solipsistic vision of the world. Scorsese, arguably the most cinematically eloquent American director of modern times, is best characterised as an expressionist and cinephile; for all his fascination with the vividly profane street life of New York, he's no social realist. His exhilaratingly long, complex camera movements, his often staccato editing, and his carefully controlled use of colour, props, decor and music are all designed not only to take us inside the minds of his often paranoid, volatile or disturbed protagonists, but to pay tribute, in passing, to movies he loves. While sexual insecurity, misogyny, an obsessive need for respect, and a capacity for violence are common characteristics of his 'heroes', his Catholicism insists that their very humanity – their energy, ambition, torment and confusion – renders them open to redemption. Indeed, on the few occasions when he has focused on 'good' protagonists (notably Christ and the Dalai Lama), the films seem to lack a proper dramatic centre. Occasionally, as in *The Color of Money*, *Casino* and *Cape Fear*, Scorsese has let his bravura style get the better of him; but in his best work (*Taxi Driver*, *New York, New York*, *Raging Bull*, *The King of Comedy, The Age of Innocence*), form and content are imaginatively combined to make the world on screen a precise topography of the protagonist's tortured soul.

Martin Scorsese b. 1942 USA. **Taxi Driver** USA 1976/ w Robert De Niro, Cybill Shepherd, Jodie Foster, Harvey Keitel, Peter Boyle, Albert Brooks. **Films include** *Mean Streets*, 1972; *Alice Doesn't Live Here Anymore*, 1974; *New York, New York*, 1977; *Raging Bull*, 1980; *The King of Comedy*, 1983; *After Hours*, 1985; *The Last Temptation of Christ*, 1988; *GoodFellas*, 1990; *The Age of Innocence*, 1993; *Casino*, 1995; *Kundun*, 1997. **See also** CASSAVETES, DE PALMA, FULLER, GODARD, KAZAN, LEE, MINNELLI, POWELL, SCHRADER

Los Angeles, 2019 AD: cop Harrison Ford pursues an android 'replicant', a fugitive mutineer from a space colony, through dark, neon-lit streets full of punks, priests and men carrying illuminated umbrellas to fend off the continuous rain. Though Scott's adaptation of Philip K Dick's *Do Androids Dream of Electric Sheep* is sci-fi *film noir* centred on a world-weary hero, the real protagonist is the evocative dystopian metropolis of towering architectural canyons and frighteningly overcrowded thoroughfares. The former set-designer and commercials-director revels in striking, grandiose visuals, from *Alien*'s huge dark space ship and grotesque monsters to the modern architecture of Tokyo in *Black Rain* and the ancient mesas of Monument Valley in *Thelma and Louise*. Too often, he has shown little interest in fleshing out human characters (*Blade Runner*'s hapless replicants are among his most sympathetic creations) or in making narrative coherent or plausible. His talents are essentially decorative, favouring huge vistas, monumental sets, back lighting, and the dramatically atmospheric use of sun, rain, mist and shadow to highlight scenes of ominous, frequently violent encounters and vigorous action. In the more modest, intimate *noir* thriller *Someone to Watch Over Me*, the ultra-stylish Manhattan apartment that was its central setting at least reflected the social and economic gulf between the socialite heroine and her Brooklyn cop lover, raising the film a few notches above Scott's customarily attractive, enjoyable but needlessly overblown hokum. More recently, however, *White Squall* and *GI Jane* effectively failed to deliver even on that lowly level.

Ridley Scott b. 1937 England. **Blade Runner** USA 1982/ w Harrison Ford, Rutger Hauer, Sean Young, Edward James Olmos, Darryl Hannah, M Emmet Walsh. **Films include** *The Duellists*, 1977; *Alien*, 1979; *Legend*, 1986; *Someone to Watch Over Me*, 1987; *Black Rain*, 1989; *Thelma and Louise*, 1991; *1492: Conquest of Paradise*, 1992; *White Squall*, 1996; *GI Jane*, 1997. **See also** BESSON, BIGELOW, CAMERON, CIMINO, PARKER

OUSMANE SEMBENE

A Dakar businessman argues with one of his wives; afflicted with impotence since the night of his third marriage, he finds his domestic, social and economic standing in jeopardy. The image is realistic, yet subtly and wittily indicative of bourgeois pretensions inherited from years of French rule: the clothes and the wife's wigs show how they have abandoned African traditions, even though the confused husband still turns to witchdoctors to cure his 'curse'. Former novelist Sembene, widely regarded as the father of sub-Saharan cinema, is committed to exploring, dramatically and comically, the legacy of European colonialism in a nation unsure of its political and cultural identity. In *Ceddo* (eighteenth-century villagers attempt to resist conversion to Islam and Christianity) and *Camp Thiaroye* (about cultural trans-

formations and tragedy suffered by Africans conscripted to fight for France in World War II), his analyses of how Europe has created and exploited divisions in African society are influenced both by neo-realism and traditional *griot* storytelling. In *The Money Order* (a satire on bureaucracy), *Emitai* (about a village's disorganised wartime efforts to prevent itself being exploited by the white authorities), and *The Curse*, Sembene's seriousness of purpose is made still more effective by the addition of comedy, at the expense both of the elite's hyopcritical emulation of their former rulers' corrupt ways, and of the traditionalists' refusal to fight their oppressors on their own modern, ruthlessly efficient terms. Sembene's images are sharp, simple, to the point; his wit is astute and telling, and never descends into facile caricature.

Ousmane Sembene b. 1923 Senegal. **The Curse (Xala)** Senegal 1974/ w Thienro Leye, Seun Samb, Younousse Seye, Dieynaba Dieng.
Films include *Borom Sarret*, 1963; *Niaye*, 1964; *Black Girl*, 1966; *The Money Order*, 1968; *Taaw*, 1971; *Emitai (God of Thunder)*, 1972; *Ceddo (The People)*, 1976; *Camp Thiaroye*, 1988; *Guelwaar: An African Legend for the 21st Century*, 1992. **See also** BUÑUEL, CHAHINE, CISSÉ, DE SICA, OUÉDRAOGO

Chaos invades the serene, sunny suburbs of early twentieth-century Los Angeles: cops dangle from wires and sit dazed among car wreckage, a driver is on his tram's roof, a dotty old sailor stares at the camera – and a light reflector is visible in frame. This is a publicity still, and there is no one film entitled *The Keystone Cops*. No matter: Sennett's comedies were remarkably uniform, and the image is symptomatic of his wildly anarchic slapstick. A former vaudevillian and actor (he worked for Griffith and headed the Biograph comedy unit before setting up his own Keystone company), he cared little for story, visual style or meaning: his shorts, shot on location and churned out at conveyor-belt speed, were virtually improvised, moving inexorably from a single, simple idea to a crazily destructive, pell-mell chase involving colliding vehicles, bumbling fogies, cross-eyed imbeciles, nubile beauties and the invariably incompetent constables. Although, as director and/or producer, he worked with such talents as Mabel Normand, Fatty Arbuckle, Harold Lloyd, Harry Langdon, Gloria Swanson and Charlie Chaplin, he seldom bothered with anything more sophisticated than comic-strip caricature and the straightforward recording of pranks and pratfalls with a static or tracking camera: impeccably timed, rapidly edited action was everything. Inevitably, this limited attitude left the pioneer ill-equipped to face the onset of sound; even by the mid-20s he'd been left far behind by the likes of Keaton, Chaplin and Lloyd. His films, however, remain enjoyable both for their delirious energy and for the charming background views of Hollywood in its infancy.

Mack Sennett (Mikall Sinnott) b. 1880 Canada, d. 1960 USA. **Films include** *When the Fire Bells Rang, Mabel's Lovers*, 1912; *The Bangville Police, The New Conductor, Mabel's Awful Mistake, The Speed Queen, The Speed Kings,* 1913; *Mabel at the Wheel, A Bathing Beauty, Mabel's Strange Predicament, Tillie's Punctured Romance*, 1914. **See also** CHAPLIN, GRIFFITH, KEATON, MÉLIÈS, PORTER, TATI

DON SIEGEL

Arizona cop Clint Eastwood, in New York to hunt down an escaped prisoner, comes into conflict with local police chief Lee J Cobb. While Siegel's rogue-cop movie finds humour in a cowboy incongruously stalking his prey down the concrete canyons of an Eastern city, it's typical in portraying an outsider so sure of himself he finds himself in a battle of wits against the world around him: not only the fugitive killer but society at large (here, New York is to Eastwood a haven of decadent sexuality, indolent hippies, and condescending hostility), including his by-the-book NYPD counterparts. Siegel himself was something of a Hollywood misfit. Having worked for years on low-budget B-movies like *The Big Steal*, *Riot in Cell Block 11*, *Baby Face Nelson* and *The Line-Up*, he never seemed entirely comfortable with the larger resources that accompanied success and, even as he won a degree of creative independence, he preferred to stick to old-fashioned action movies like the Eastwood films, *Charley Varrick* and *The Shootist*. His style changed little: his classically composed and edited images were as clean, uncluttered and direct as his storylines; his disenchanted but professional (anti-)heroes tended to express frustration through violent action rather than words; the world they fought against was depicted with broad, vivid strokes. Still, Siegel's films could be subtle: *Invasion of the Body Snatchers* is unsettling allegorical sci-fi about conformism and complacency, *Dirty Harry* a provocatively ambiguous study of righteous bigotry, *Escape from Alcatraz* an austere account of resilient determination, *The Shootist* a lyrical tribute to John Wayne and the western tradition.

Don Siegel b. 1912 USA, d. 1991 USA. **Coogan's Bluff** USA 1968/ w Clint Eastwood, Lee J Cobb, Susan Clark, Tisha Sterling, Don Stroud, Betty Field. **Films include** *Riot in Cell Block 11*, 1954; *Invasion of the Body Snatchers*, 1956; *Baby Face Nelson*, 1957; *The Line-Up*, 1958; *Hell is for Heroes*, 1962; *The Killers*, 1964; *The Beguiled*, 1970; *Dirty Harry*, 1971; *Charley Varrick*, 1972; *The Shootist*, 1976; *Escape from Alcatraz*, 1979. **See also** ALDRICH, EASTWOOD, FULLER, PECKINPAH, WALSH

Secretary Ella Raines, disguised as a tart, flirts with a jazz drummer she suspects can help her in her search for a killer; soon his sexual arousal will become clear as, playing a solo to impress her, he builds to an orgasmic crescendo, while the expressionist images of the band – all tilted angles, sweaty close-ups and raised phallic horns, edited together in feverishly rapid fashion – break down into near-abstraction. One of the greatest stylists of *film noir*, German emigré Siodmak used shadows, isolated pools of light and off-kilter perspectives not to convey, like Lang, a fatalistic vision of the world, but to probe his characters' fraught or delirious mental states. In this way, a rare generosity imbues many of his thrillers; for all their taut narrative suspense, *The Suspect, Uncle Harry, The Killers, Criss Cross* and *The File on Thelma Jordon* are sympathetic studies of decent, ordinary men lured into crime by foolishly obsessive romantic infatuation, while *Phantom Lady, The Spiral Staircase* and *The Dark Mirror* feature murderers who kill not from greed or malice but because of schizophrenia and a pathological dissatisfaction with the world's imperfections. Even in *Cry of the City*, a location-shot thriller, Siodmak uses the respectively black and white coats of a cop and his now criminal childhood friend to imply that they are simply different sides of the same coin. *Noir*, emphatically, was his forte. Though he worked with wit and intelligence in other styles and genres (notably in the gloriously exuberant swashbuckler *The Crimson Pirate*), only in his expressionist crime films of the 40s did form and content come so harmoniously together.

Robert Siodmak b. 1900 USA, d. 1973 Switzerland. **Phantom Lady** USA 1944/ w Ella Raines, Franchot Tone, Alan Curtis, Thomas Gomez, Elisha Cook Jr, Fay Helm. **Films include** *Menschen am Sontag (People on Sunday)*, 1929; *Son of Dracula*, 1943; *Christmas Holiday*, 1944; *The Suspect, Uncle Harry, The Spiral Staircase*, 1945; *The Killers, The Dark Mirror*, 1946; *Cry of the City, Criss Cross*, 1948; *The File on Thelma Jordon*, 1949; *The Crimson Pirate*, 1952. **See also** HITCHCOCK, LANG, LEWIS, MICHAEL MANN, TOURNEUR

An African-American girl who passes for white talks happily to a suitor while her adoring, self-sacrificing but resented mother (maid to a kind but workaholic actress who unwittingly neglects her own daughter) watches from the shadows. Sirk's final 'weepie' may highlight the heartbreaks of mother-love, but its real theme is how racism and material ambition drive people to lead 'imitations' of life, distanced from loved ones and their true selves. Though the erudite Sirk worked in the intellectually disreputable realm of melodrama, his alertness to the injustices underlying the American Dream and his commitment to underdog characters made for heart-rending, thought-provoking cinema. To sugar the pill of his pessimistic critiques of contemporary mores, he made his films glossily seductive, casting glamorous stars, pointing up the tragic twists and ironies of his stories, and shooting in heightened colours to underline the dramatic artifice which thinly conceals his films' real meaning. Frames within frames, reflections and decorative objects (here, the blind behind which the duplicitous daughter stands) suggest double-lives, flagrant symbolism hidden motives. In *Written on the Wind*, the impotence that makes the 'bad' protagonist turn drunkenly against his wife and his upright friend is evoked by a boy frantically rocking on a toy horse (as if masturbating) outside a doctor's surgery, while his sister's self-destructive promiscuity is 'explained' when she hugs a phallic model of one of her father's oil derricks. Sirk's genius, finally, lay not in working against melodramatic conventions, but in refining, exceeding and transcending them.

Douglas Sirk (Hans Detlef Sierck) b. 1900 Germany, d. 1987 Switzerland. **Imitation of Life** USA 1958/ w Lana Turner, John Gavin, Susan Kohner, Juanita Moore, Sandra Dee, Troy Donahue, Mahalia Jackson. **Films include** *Schlussakkord*, 1936; *To New Shores*, 1937; *Meet Me at the Fair,* 1952; *Take Me to Town, All I Desire*, 1953; *Magnificent Obsession*, 1954; *All That Heaven Allows*, 1955; *Written on the Wind*, 1956; *The Tarnished Angels*, 1957; *A Time to Love and a Time to Die*, 1958. **See also** ALMODÓVAR, BORZAGE, FASSBINDER, LEISEN, MINNELLI, NICHOLAS RAY

Genteel, virginal Easterner Lillian Gish, visiting family in the Midwest, is made to feel unwelcome as her cowboy cousin's wife sharpens a knife to skin a carcass. Sjöström was adept at conveying psychological unease and torment through a seamless mix of underplayed melodrama, unforced symbolism and full-blown expressionism. In his masterpiece *The Wind*, Gish's romantic illusions are steadily eroded not only by the harsh physical realities of pioneer life but by the desert itself: only after she kills, in self-defence, a rapist, and sees (or feverishly imagines) a raging storm peel away the sands from his corpse where she buried it, does she come to accept a tender husband she hitherto despised. Sjöström's evocative, poetic use of Nature – landscape, light, weather, seasons – to reflect his characters' vulnerability, isolation and inner turmoil was a defining aspect of the films he made in his native Sweden (*Terje Vigen*, *The Outlaw and His Wife* and *The Phantom Carriage* are the finest), but a Hollywood sojourn saw no decline or compromise. Indeed, the way *The Wind* shifts subtly from a deftly observed comedy of manners to epic tragedy (with Gish's mounting hysteria, rooted in sexual repression, depicted by dreamlike shots of a stallion careering amid storm-tossed clouds) is wonderfully impressive. Desire, guilt and redemption were recurrent themes, whether in pastoral dramas like *The Outlaw and His Wife* and *The Scarlet Letter* or in the remarkably sophisticated portrait of a masochistic circus clown, *He Who Gets Slapped*. Sadly, much of his work is now lost; what survives reveals a master of the silent cinema.

Victor Sjöström b. 1879 Sweden, d. 1960 Sweden. **The Wind** USA 1928/ w Lillian Gish, Lars Hanson, Montague Love, Dorothy Cumming, Edward Earle, William Orlamond. **Films include** *Ingeborg Holm*, 1913; *Terje Vigen*, 1917; *The Outlaw and His Wife*, 1918; *The Ingmarssons*, 1919; *The Monastery of Sendomir, Mästerman*, 1920; *The Phantom Carriage*, 1921; *Love's Crucible*, 1922; *He Who Gets Slapped*, 1924; *The Scarlet Letter*, 1926; *Under the Red Robe*, 1937. **See also** BERGMAN, DREYER, GRIFFITH, KAURISMÄKI, LANG, MURNAU, VON STROHEIM

A plain schoolgirl ponders the horrors of puberty as she stares sulkily into the bathroom mirror. The kitschy day-glo colours, like the tutu constantly worn by her spoilt sister, betray her middle-class family's forlorn aspirations to unity and contentment and ironically counterpoint her misery. Known so far only for this second feature and its even more corrosive follow-up, *Happiness*, Solondz looks likely to establish himself as a distinctive chronicler of the American Nightmare. His characters are lost, isolated, dissatisfied with their lot, caught in a constant, vain struggle against life's injustices. Here, ignored and bullied by family and classmates, the girl desperately seeks consolation with a delinquent who threatens to 'rape' her (neither knows the word's real meaning), only to find his life is worse than hers. Solondz's unsettling blend of

tragedy, dark comic satire and semi-ironic soap-style coincidence deploys a discreet deadpan, visual style: the usually static camera stares dispassionately at visibly unhappy characters as they try to show a brave face, conscious of their social, sexual and psychological torments but unable to articulate their feelings properly to others. *Happiness* opens with almost grotesque close-ups of a couple grimacing as they search for words that might ease their break-up; inevitably, recriminatory cruelty wins the day. Yet Solondz insists his flawed creations merit sympathetic understanding: in *Happiness*, a paedophile's long, painful confessions to his confused teenage son are written, performed and shot with such unhysterical calm that we comprehend his agony and feel compassion for his genuinely concerned love for the boy.

Todd Solondz b. 1960 USA. **Welcome to the Dollhouse** USA 1995/ w Heather Matarazzo, Brendan Sexton Jr, Daria Kalininia, Matthew Faber. **Films include** *Fear, Anxiety and Depression*, 1989; *Happiness*, 1999. **See also** ALLEN, HARTLEY, HAYNES, KAURISMÄKI, LEIGH, LYNCH, WILDER

Scientists – and, crucially, a small boy – witness the first arrival of aliens on earth. The monumental size and brilliant lights of the 'mother ship' testify to Spielberg's abiding fascination with gadgetry and spectacle; no other film-maker has so profitably raised once lowly genre fare – sci-fi, monster movies, adventure serials – to blockbuster status. But it is the assembly's awestruck response that best typifies his work: whether dealing with manifestations of the Other (a driverless truck, a shark, an ugly but benevolent alien, dinosaurs) in cinematic roller-coasters like *Duel*, *Jaws*, *ET* and *Jurassic Park*, or with unfathomable heroism, as in the atypically solemn *Schindler's List* and *Saving Private Ryan*, Spielberg is entranced by the Unknown erupting into a familiar world. Visually, he endeavours to render audiences similarly awestruck and childlike by accentuating the sheer scale of his dramatically lit compositions: gigantic creatures and machines, vast landscapes and milling crowds dwarf the emphatically 'ordinary' characters with whom we are encouraged sentimentally to identify; dynamic scenes of expertly choreographed movement alternate with moments of repose which are either a suspenseful lull before the storm or an opportunity for us (and the characters) to take in and marvel at the spectacle just seen. Often, such wonder precludes deeper emotional or intellectual response: despite his technical facility and commercial acumen, only in the films up to and including *Close Encounters* and in his three World War Two movies has Spielberg successfully explored a recognisably complex, adult world of experience.

Steven Spielberg b. 1947 USA. **Close Encounters of the Third Kind** USA 1977/ w Richard Dreyfuss, François Truffaut, Teri Garr, Melinda Dillon, Bob Balaban. **Films include** *Duel*, 1971; *The Sugarland Express*, 1974; *Jaws*, 1975; *Raiders of the Lost Ark*, 1981; *ET The Extra-Terrestrial*, 1982; *Empire of the Sun*, 1984; *The Color Purple*, 1985; *Hook*, 1991; *Jurassic Park, Schindler's List,* 1993; *Amistad*, 1997; *Saving Private Ryan*, 1998. **See also** ARNOLD, DANTE, DISNEY, HITCHCOCK, LEAN, LUCAS, ZEMECKIS

WLADISLAW STAREWICZ

In heroic silhouette, soldier ants carry one of their wounded across a ravaged landscape; if their props and actions recall the human world, they undeniably remain ants. Entomologist-turned-animator Starewicz was a superb technician – his realistically modelled insects, animals, birds, buildings and landscapes are masterpieces of miniaturist detail – and an eccentric artist with a surreal, satirically sharp vision of the world. His characters, though humanised in their actions, ambitions, anxieties and, often, meticulously designed clothes, were seldom sentimentalised. In *The Cameraman's Revenge*, adultery between beetles and grasshoppers is exposed when a voyeur's footage of multi-limbed embraces in a honeymoon hotel is shown at a cinema, while in the allegorical *Frogland*, the amphibians' gullible trust in any leader sees them kowtow to a plank of wood and a stork that devours them. His stories were fables of lust, greed and violence: *Town Rat, Country Rat* detailed the latter's disastrous flirtation with boozy city decadence, while the amazingly ornate feature *The Tale of the Fox*, with its hundreds of immaculately designed characters often exquisitely animated within a single frame, charted the conflict between a cunning fox and a proud lion king. Even in *The Mascot*, which mixed animation with live-action as a sickly child's cuddly toy dog finds himself lost in Paris, sentimentality was held at bay by the mutt's nightmarish initiation into a black mass involving weirdly grotesque monsters. The secret of Starewicz's artistry was his ability to create an imagined world with its own skewed but persuasively coherent logic: the mark of a true visionary.

Wladislaw Starewicz b. 1892 Poland, d. 1965 France. **The Queen of the Butterflies** France 1920. **Films include** *The Beautiful Leukanida, The Grasshopper and the Ant, The Cameraman's Revenge*, 1911; *In the Claws of the Spider*, 1920; *Frogland*, 1922; *Love in Black and White*, 1923; *Town Rat, Country Rat*, 1927; *The Magic Clock*, 1928, *The Tale of the Fox*, 1930, *The Mascot*, 1933. **See also** AVERY, JONES, HANNA AND BARBERA, MCKAY, MÉLIÈS, QUAY BROTHERS, SVANKMAJER

In an early 80s New York nightclub, would-be sophisticates gossip bitchily: the girl is tactlessly pronouncing that her friend, having refused an alcoholic drink, must be taking medication for a venereal disease. Stillman is an oddity in modern American film: his sharp but wryly affectionate comedies of tribal manners revolve around brilliantly written dialogue (rather than the customary caricature and slapstick) while focusing on comfortably-off, educated, young professionals. In this and his low-key narratives, his films more closely resemble Rohmer's conversation pieces than films by his compatriots (excepting Woody Allen, though Stillman is less concerned with one-liners than with the exploration of the gulf between self-image and reality, word and action, intention and achievement). Though some see him as a wordsmith who pays scant attention to visual style, he is adept at creating mood through precise evocations of time and place – the fairy-tale hotels and salons inhabited by Manhattan débutantes and their escorts in *Metropolitan*, the seedy student-style garrets contrasted with the glitzy nightclubs frequented by yuppies starting in their first jobs in *Disco* – and at deflating his characters' pretensions with images verging on the incongruous or surreal: here, the clubbers' emphatic modishness is undercut by one of their number's ludicrous fancy-dress costume, while in *Barcelona* one particularly earnest character becomes engrossed in reading the Bible while dancing, absent-mindedly and alone in his apartment, to Glenn Miller. Stillman's classically shot anthropological studies prove that visual style need not trumpet its existence to be effective.

Whit Stillman b. 1952 USA. **The Last Days of Disco** USA 1998/ w Kate Beckinsale, Chloe Sevigny, Mackenzie Astin, Matt Keeslar, Chris Eigeman. **Films include** *Metropolitan*, 1990; *Barcelona*, 1994. **See also** Allen, Cukor, Lewin, Mankiewicz, Rohmer, Wilder

A murderer displays his contempt for the world with a gun. The cartoon backdrop is just one of the expressionistic devices – film and video, black-and-white and colour, back and front-projection, TV soap parody, tilted angles, ultra-rapid cutting – used by Stone to indict the way the amoral, scoop-hungry media demonise, romanticise and finally aid and abet rebellious young lovers on a reckless killing spree. The redundant visual bombast and provocative but facile moralising typify Stone's work after *Salvador* and *Platoon*, both of which offered intelligent and comparatively restrained accounts of America's military involvement in Central America and Vietnam. He repeatedly tackles Big Issues – war, the corrupting influence of greed and power in the worlds of finance and politics, the demise of 60s idealism – but a fondness for simplistically polarised characters and attitudes, his equation of serious, in-depth analysis with overlong running-times, and his cynical tendency to see conspiracy, cover-up and corruption everywhere make for turgid, unconvincing narratives. Stylistically and dramatically, his later work is characterised by overload: wary of simplicity, he prefers collage, so that his chronologically fragmented storylines frequently merge a melodramatic form of 'realism' with hyperbolic caricature, fantasy, mystic metaphor and outbursts of proselytising didacticism. Indeed, perhaps Stone's greatest weakness is his humourless sense of his films' importance; even a modest pastiche thriller like *U Turn* is marred by grandiloquent visual trickery, absurd overstatement, and the impression that he feels intellectually superior to the routine material.

Oliver Stone b. 1946 USA. **Natural Born Killers** USA 1994/ w Woody Harrelson, Juliette Lewis, Robert Downey Jr, Tommy Lee Jones, Tom Sizemore. **Films include** *Salvador*, *Platoon*, 1986; *Wall Street*, 1987; *Talk Radio*, 1988; *Born on the Fourth of July*, 1991; T*he Doors*, *JFK*, 1991; *Heaven and Earth*, 1993; *Nixon*, 1995; *U Turn*, 1997. **See also** ALDRICH, CAMERON, COSTA-GAVRAS, FULLER, PARKER

Bach's music is played in a church. The shot is static, devoid of dramatic spectacle and, typically of the minimalist Straub and his wife/collaborator Danièle Huillet, held for a long time; while the instruments are of Bach's era, the (real) musicians, despite wigs and finery, look modern. With its commentary largely assembled from various texts and letters and spoken in barely inflected tones, its non-professional actors (including harpsichordist Gustav Leonhardt 'as' Bach) filmed on locations known to the composer, and its long unedited takes of live-recorded musical performance, the film is emphatically no conventional biopic. Though Bach's second wife is the nominal subject, we learn little of her feelings, and their love is suggested not by any actorly displays of emotion but by the music itself; indeed, what 'story' there

is stems mainly from her comments on the hardships Bach suffered in his dealings with patrons. In this last respect, the film is political, just as Straub's minimalism is a radical aesthetic intended to provoke contemplation. In *History Lessons*, adapted from Brecht, a banker, lawyer, writer and former soldier, dressed in togas but in a modern setting (the film repeatedly cuts away to long tracking shots of a car driving through Rome's teeming streets), discuss the harsh economic and political realities neglected by conventional histories of Caesar's Empire. Likewise, versions of Corneille's *Othon* and Schoenberg's *Moses and Aaron* are unadorned except by the particular circumstances of their live-recorded performance; in short, Straub's demanding but intellectually rewarding cinema rigorously rejects the illusionism favoured by mainstream cinema.

Jean-Marie Straub b. 1933 France. **Chronicle of Anna Magdalena Bach** W Germany/Italy 1968/ w Gustav Leonhardt, Christiane Lang, Paolo Carlini, Ernst Castelli. **Films include** *Not Reconciled*, 1965; *Othon*, 1971; *History Lessons*, 1972; *Moses and Aaron*, 1975; *Fortini/Cani*, 1976; *From the Cloud to the Resistance*, 1979; *Class Relations*, 1984; *The Death of Empedocles*, 1986; *Schwarze Sunde*, *Cézanne*, 1989; *Sicilia!*, 1999. **See also** BRESSON, FASSBINDER, GODARD, HANEKE, KIAROSTAMI, WARHOL

PRESTON STURGES

Inventor Joel McCrea is clearly peeved at estranged wife Claudette Colbert (posing as his sister to wheedle money from millionaire suitor Rudy Vallee) getting on so well with the latter's promiscuous sister Mary Astor (a princess keen to lure McCrea into marriage); Vallee, meanwhile, is just befuddled. As might we be: Sturges, scatty specialist in screwball comedy, revelled in absurdly complicated tales of deceitful shenanigans and mistaken identities, featuring cunning women, slow-witted men and rich eccentrics at play. He himself was from a wealthy Bohemian family and invented bizarre contraptions, but he was firstly a writer who served up amoral plots (over)populated with larger-than-life characters. (*The Palm Beach Story* includes a ludicrously gruff, deaf sausage mogul, a mysteriously foreign gigolo whose non-existent English means he never understands Astor's brush-offs, and a host of childishly irresponsible, drunken, gun-crazy millionaires.) So concerned was Sturges with colourfully unlikely dialogue, madcap antics and spiralling chaos that, visually, his style rarely strayed beyond frantic slapstick, saucy innuendo and the straightforward recording of conversations between characters lined before the camera as if on stage. *The Great McGinty, Sullivan's Travels* and *Unfaithfully Yours* dabbled with shadowy Expressionism, but mostly he confined himself to escapist opulent settings, as here and in *The Lady Eve*, or to caricatured working-class Americana (*Hail the Conquering Hero, The Beautiful Blonde from Bashful Bend*). His films are dazzlingly, raucously energetic, so inventive that it was hardly surprising his creativity had burned out by the 50s.

Preston Sturges (Edmund P Biden) b. 1898 USA, d. 1959 USA. **The Palm Beach Story** USA 1942/ w Claudette Colbert, Joel McCrea, Rudy Vallee, Mary Astor, Sig Arno, William Demarest. **Films include** *The Great McGinty, Christmas in July,* 1940; *The Lady Eve, Sullivan's Travels,* 1941; *The Miracle of Morgan's Creek, Hail the Conquering Hero,* 1944; *The Sin of Harold Dibbledock,* 1946; *Unfaithfully Yours,* 1948; *The Beautiful Blonde from Bashful Bend,* 1949. **See also** COEN BROTHERS, HAWKS, LEISEN, TASHLIN, WILDER

SUZUKI SEIJUN

A yakuza arranges a deal with a rival gang, while his boss and a secretary – both will betray him – listen in: standard fare for gangster films which thrive on double-cross; less so the bizarre painting in the background and the hero's impossibly immaculate, cool blue suit. Suzuki churned out production-line crime films and erotic melodramas for Nikkatsu Studios for years, until success, confidence and boredom led him to play with the generic rules: introducing absurd comedy, rhetorical excess (*Gate of Flesh*, set in a post-war brothel, mixes observations about poverty and machismo with lurid, expressionist scenes of violence and sado-masochism), garish coded colours, and narrative fragmentation. Alongside the brazenly illogical *Branded to Kill*, *Tokyo Drifter* is his masterpiece, a riotous embellishment of yakuza thriller conventions:

frantic action scenes are left 'unfinished' by elliptical editing that refuses to clarify plot development or character motivation; 'serious' moments are disrupted by gags; a slapstick brawl in a cowboy-bar involving characters wholly irrelevant to the story breaks out to no dramatic purpose; the moody hero's existential solitude is confirmed when he breaks into the pop song of the film's title. Equally extraordinary is Suzuki's visual bravura, employing inexplicable changes in the weather, obvious backdrops, bleached or clashing colours, frames within frames and surreally stylised pop-art design: memorably, the climax takes place in a ravishing white nightclub containing only a black piano and a weirdly lit sculpture resembling a giant doughnut on a pole. Amazingly, Suzuki's best work succeeds both as inventive parody and as thrilling entertainment.

Suzuki Seijun b. 1923 Japan. **Tokyo Drifter** Japan 1966/ w Watari Tetsuya, Matsubara Chieko, Nitani Hideaki, Kita Ryuji, Yoshida Tsuyoshi. **Films include** *Youth of the Beast*, *The Bastard*, *Kanto Wanderer*, 1963; *Gate of Flesh*, 1964; *Story of a Prostitute*, 1965; *Fighting Elegy*, 1966; *Branded to Kill*, 1967; *Zigeunerweisen*, 1980; *Heat-Haze Theatre*, 1981; *Yumeji*, 1991. **See also** CORMAN, FULLER, GODARD, KITANO, LEONE, MEYER, SIRK

Communication breakdown: in Svankmajer's macabre satirical masterpiece, two clay heads – suspiciously politician-like – engage in a grotesque variation on the scissors/paper/stone game, misunderstanding each other, before haplessly 'agreeing' (matching shoe with shoe, knife with knife) so strenuously that they collapse, tongues lolling from cracked, panting heads. Svankmajer is a true surrealist, juxtaposing familiar objects and images to witty, nightmarish effect: the first part of this triptych sees human heads made up of fruit, vegetables and utensils (as in Arcimboldo's symbolic paintings) repeatedly swallow and regurgitate each other until the blended elements resemble flesh tones; in *Virile Games*, a satire on hero worship, footballers commit outrageous 'fouls' by dismemberment, hammering one another into the pitch,

and driving trains into each other's mouths, before taking the match into a fan's apartment as he obliviously watches it on TV. Svankmajer's rapid, Eisensteinian montage links immaculately framed compositions of clay models, puppets, artifacts, cut-outs, graphics and live-action; the result is startlingly dreamlike yet familiarly 'real', reflecting his interest in Freud, ritual and the Czech tradition of alchemical transformation. While most of his painstakingly assembled films are shorts, he has made inventive feature-length adaptations of Lewis Carroll's *Alice* and Goethe's *Faust* and a bizarre, hilarious study of obsessive sexual fantasy, *Conspirators of Pleasure*. His astonishingly imaginative work succeeds both intellectually and viscerally; profoundly original, and morally and politically subtly subversive, he is one of modern cinema's rare geniuses.

Jan Svankmajer b. 1934 Czechoslovakia. **Dimensions of Dialogue** Czechoslovakia 1982. **Films include** *The Last Trick*, 1964; *Historia Naturae*, 1967; *The Flat*, 1968; *The Ossuary*, 1970; *Jabberwocky*, 1971; *The Pendulum, the Pit and Hope*, 1983; *Alice*, 1988; *Virile Games*, 1988; *The Death of Stalinism in Bohemia*, 1990; *Faust*, 1992; *Conspirators of Pleasure*, 1996. **See also** BOROWCZYK, BUÑUEL, EISENSTEIN, MÉLIÈS, QUAY BROTHERS, STAREWICZ

Bavaria's eccentric, lonely monarch sits dreamily amid soldiers, politicians, burghers and a nude courtesan; behind is a clearly artificial back-projection of romantic grandeur. The extravagant, studio-shot tableaux of Syberberg's disquisition into German history and culture offer a heady, baroque mix of camp theatricality, epic drama (in the Brechtian sense) and Méliès-like fantasy. Symphonic in its sweep and use of symbolic and musical leitmotifs (Wagner features on the soundtrack and as a character), his essay on the blend of Romanticism and rationality that led from Ludwig's aesthetic idealism to Hitler's patriotic fervour assembles a bizarre array of ideas, characters and images (Hitler dancing a rumba, Bismarck riding a motorcycle, back-projected shots of modern tourists visiting one of Ludwig's fairy-tale castles) to chart a topography of the German soul that is psychological, political and historical, ironic yet poetic. The camera rarely moves, shots may seem interminable (memorably Ludwig dozing off to *Tristan and Isolde* while artificial snow falls around him), but the fecundity of allusions and the multi-layered images make for exhilarating didactic cinema. Ludwig was the first film in a 'German Trilogy' that continued with a portrait of the popular novelist Karl May and the even more grandiose and complex *Hitler*. Syberberg's fascination with mythology and ideology also marked the monumental documentary *The Confessions of Winifred Wagner* and his studio-set but wholly cinematic opera-film *Parsifal*. Sadly, his ambitious conception of cinema proved too demanding for many, and his later theatrically-based work has seldom been shown.

Hans-Jurgen Syberberg b. 1935 Germany. **Ludwig – Requiem for a Virgin King** w Germany 1972/ w Harry Baer, Balthasar Thomas, Peter Kern, Ingrid Caven, Peter Moland. **Films include** *Scarabea*, 1968; *Ludwig's Cook*, 1972; *Karl May*, 1974; *The Confessions of Winifred Wagner,* 1975; *Hitler, A Film From Germany*, 1977; *Parsifal*, 1982; *Die Nacht*, 1984; *Ein Traum, Was Sonst*, 1990. **See also** EISENSTEIN, FASSBINDER, GODARD, HERZOG, MÉLIÈS, STRAUB, WARHOL, WELLES

QUENTIN TARANTINO

In an empty warehouse – a thieves' meeting-place after a robbery gone disastrously wrong – Mr Pink and Mr White, each believing the other might have betrayed the gang to the cops, draw guns at point-blank in a 'Mexican stand-off'. The scene is both archetypal and excessive: movie-fanatic Tarantino rose rapidly to fame with *Reservoir Dogs* and *Pulp Fiction*, graphically bloody, amoral, semi-comic variations on traditional crime themes: loyalty, betrayal, professionalism, the need for mutual respect. Much was made of his expertise in staging dynamic scenes of violent conflict and writing colourfully profane dialogue, which frequently alluded, wittily and incongruously, to popular culture (*Reservoir Dogs* opens with the gang relaxing before the heist – audaciously never shown – by discussing Madonna's lyrics and

tipping). Rather more rewarding, however, than his robust, slightly unreal use of conversation, colour, costumes and sets to turn his crime thrillers into semi-ironic pastiche (the gang's colour-coded names turn them into generic ciphers) is his idiosyncratic approach to narrative structure. By using flashbacks within flashbacks and disrupting linear chronology, Tarantino both foregrounds the mechanics of storytelling and allows us to see and interpret events from different points of view. *Pulp Fiction*'s relentless emphasis on verbal and visual style occasionally smacked of self-indulgent gimmickry; *Jackie Brown*, however, developed the dishonour-among-thieves theme of his debut with impressive maturity, making for a more quietly affecting, at times almost classically elegiac study of ageing loners and desperate last-chance ambitions.

Quentin Tarantino b. 1963 USA. **Reservoir Dogs** USA 1991/ w Harvey Keitel, Tim Roth, Steve Buscemi, Michael Madsen, Chris Penn, Lawrence Tierney. **Films include** *Pulp Fiction*, 1994; *The Man from Hollywood* episode from *Four Rooms*, 1995; *Jackie Brown*, 1997. **See also** DE PALMA, GODARD, HAWKS, KITANO, MELVILLE, PECKINPAH, SCORSESE, WOO

ANDREI TARKOVSKY

The haunted face of a man crossing a forbidden 'Zone' to reach a 'Room' where prayers are answered: the crown of thorns and gloomy atmosphere typify Tarkovsky's bleakly 'spiritual' art. His epic fables tended towards allegory – here, Stalker, Writer and Professor (the absence of names reflects their metaphorical status) travel a police state in search of meaning and redemption – and focused on sketchily drawn artists, intellectuals and mystics oppressed by life's random cruelty. In *Ivan's Childhood* (his best film, about a boy whose heroism in war ends in death) and *Andrei Roublev* (about a medieval monk driven by despair to give up icon-painting), the sense of a troubled universe is convincingly conveyed by lyrically foreboding landscape photography, while the characters are recognisably individualised. From *Solaris* on, however, Tarkovsky's pessimism and aloof mysticism led to increasingly portentous, turgid, even obscure narratives with woolly philosophising couched in laboured dialogue, meticulous compositions featuring a hackneyed use of conventional symbolism, and long, often wordless scenes shot with an almost imperceptibly slow-moving camera; the sparse, glum, painstakingly composed 'beauty' often seemed hollow, hinting at deeper metaphysical meanings than story, characters or dialogue could convey. While he was widely praised as a great visionary, Tarkovsky's cinema demanded faith (both religious, and in the film-maker himself) from the audience, nowhere more so than in his final *The Sacrifice*, in which a man makes a pact with God to save the world from nuclear holocaust and, unconvincingly, perhaps succeeds.

Andrei Tarkovsky b. 1932 USSR, d. 1986 France. **Stalker** USSR 1979/ w Aleksandr Kaidanovsky, Anatoly Solonitsin, Nikolai Grinko, Alisa Freindlikh. **Films include** *The Steamroller and the Violin*, 1960; *Ivan's Childhood,* 1960; *Andrei Roublev*, 1966; *Solaris*, 1972; *The Mirror,* 1975; *Nostalghia*, 1983; *The Sacrifice*, 1985. **See also** BERGMAN, BRESSON, DOVZHENKO, DREYER, KIESLOWSKI, PARADZHANOV

FRANK TASHLIN

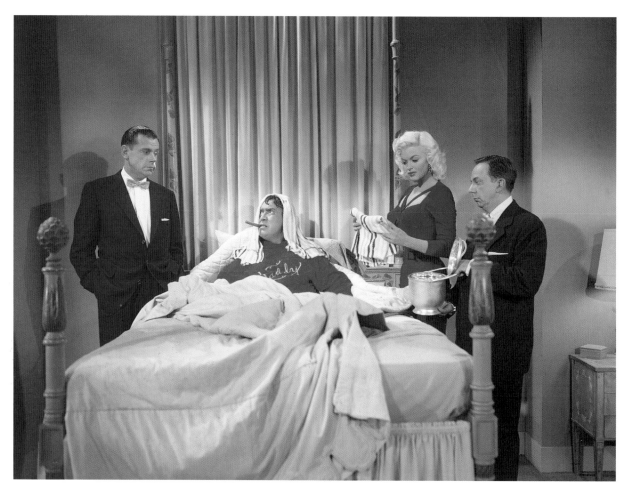

There is something cheerfully, unashamedly vulgar and brash about the scene: the irascible, bullying gangster (Edmond O'Brien) made to look pathetically ridiculous in front of his pneumatic, dumb-blonde moll (Jayne Mansfield) and the has-been press agent (Tom Ewell) he's hired to further her career in the music business. But it's not just the broad satirising of a crass entertainment industry (allowing for appearances by a host of then popular rock'n'roll acts) that is characteristic of Tashlin's style; it's also the lurid colours and outrageous visual gags (one notorious example links Mansfield's breasts with a milkman's bottles boiling over at the sight of her) which betray his origins as an animator in the Avery mould. So knowing was Tashlin's inventive trashing of 50s pop culture that he even, for the film's prologue, had Ewell transform the image into Fox's trademark CinemaScope and De Luxe Colour, while *Will Success Spoil Rock Hunter?*, a satire on the American obsession with advertising, sex and television, opened with multiple images of Tony Randall playing the Fox fanfare on various instruments before the screen shrank to the size of a black and white TV. His characters were cartoon-like grotesques (frequently played by the likes of Bob Hope or Jerry Lewis), and his stories basically ragbag strings of gags rooted in slapstick and sexist innuendo, but there is a genuinely frenetic energy and anarchic, even surreal irreverence in his best films; sadly, his later work was increasingly marred by Lewis' penchant for maudlin sentimentality, and in the 60s he seemed simply to lose his way.

Frank Tashlin b. 1913 USA, d. 1972 USA. **The Girl Can't Help It** USA 1956/ w Tom Ewell, Jayne Mansfield, Edmond O'Brien, Little Richard, Eddie Cochran, Gene Vincent. **Films include** *Son of Paleface*, 1952; *Artists and Models*, 1955; *Hollywood or Bust*, 1956; *Will Success Spoil Rock Hunter?*, 1957; *The Geisha Boy*, 1958; *Cinderfella*, 1960; *Who's Minding the Store?*, 1963; *The Disorderly Orderly*, 1965. **See also** AVERY, DANTE, HANNA AND BARBERA, JONES, MEYER, STURGES

Absent-minded, angular, affable Hulot (writer-director Tati) stumbles along a beach, oblivious to the near-naked girl in a cabin doorway. Hulot was something of a misfit, his bashful, old-fashioned innocence tangential to the modern world; as such, he was a classic comic creation, and the legacy was underlined by the fact that Tati's movies, while not silent (they included music and sound effects), were essentially filmed mime; just as he mostly eschewed close-ups: so dialogue was either absent, barely audible or garbled and incomprehensible. The gentle, miniaturist humour was based on precisely timed, often complex strings of visual gags involving Hulot's gangly gait and clumsy, off-kilter dealings with people, props and architecture. Even in his first feature, *Jour de Fête,* Tati's unease at technology and its effects on the quality of life was apparent in the tale of a traditional rural postman competing with a mechanised mail system. After *Monsieur Hulot's Holiday*, his films became more heavy-handedly 'serious' and simplistic in their contrasting of Hulot's bumbling, eccentric charm with the almost robotic behaviour of city-dwellers obsessed with and subtly dehumanised by gimmicky gadgetry designed to make life more comfortable and efficient. While Tati's satirical targets became more socially 'relevant', Hulot himself became less vividly characterised as an individual and slid towards the sidelines of his more meandering, episodic narratives, so that in the innovative *Playtime* he is mainly a passive witness to mankind's folly, a small, often almost invisible figure on the margins of the teeming, choreographed chaos shown in long-shot.

Jacques Tati (Tatischeff) b. 1908 France, d. 1982 France. **Monsieur Hulot's Holiday (Les Vacances de M Hulot)** France 1953/ w Tati, Nathalie Pascaud, Michèle Rolla, Louis Perrault, André Dubois. **Films include** *L'Ecole de Facteurs*, 1947; *Jour de Fête,* 1949; *Mon Oncle,* 1958; *Playtime,* 1967; *Traffic,* 1970; *Parade,* 1974. **See also** ANTONIONI, CHAPLIN, CLAIR, KEATON, SENNETT

VITTORIO AND PAOLO TAVIANI

Men watch the burning of an elephant built by two of them – Italian brothers from a family of stonemasons – for the Babylonian set of *Intolerance*. The image is realistic, surreal, and suggestive of ancient ritual; the statue itself is real (it is a statue), illusory (it isn't a real elephant) and symbolic of traditional craftsmanship, cinema (Griffith's monumental set is one of film's most famous images) and memory. While the Tavianis' early documentaries and features were marked by neo-realism, their later work is more richly poetic and resonant. Repeatedly they have turned to historical subjects involving a collective or individual revolutionary quest for a kind of Utopia (here the brothers emigrate to America to work in a new collaborative art-form which, the film implies, is a modern equivalent to medieval church-building).

Inevitably, the quest fails (the set is destroyed, the brothers die in the Great War), but the process of following a dream is valuable and essential. Blending history, political parable, literature, music and myth, the Tavianis create intimate epics of timeless relevance. While their fluent images are richly allusive and often verge on the fantastic (*Padre Padrone*'s 'realist' Oedipal story of a downtrodden Sicilian peasant advancing himself through literacy was memorably disrupted by bizarre, comic shots suggestive of his indulging in bestiality), they are also direct and lucid; characters are positioned symmetrically or mid-frame, clearly defined against landscape or architecture. The key to the Tavianis' work is its subtly deceptive simplicity; at its best, it has the magical power and dreamlike charm of a fable.

Vittorio Taviani b. 1929 Italy. **Paolo Taviani** b. 1931 Italy. **Good Morning Babylon** Italy/France/USA 1986/ w Vincent Spano, Joaquim De Almeida, Greta Scacchi, Omero Antonutti, Charles Dance. **Films include** *Subversives*, 1967; *Under the Sign of Scorpio*, 1969; *Allonsanfan*, 1975; *Padre Padrone*, 1977; *The Meadow*, 1979; *The Night of San Lorenzo*, 1981; *Kaos*, 1984; *Night Sun*, 1990; *Fiorile*, 1993; *Elective Affinities*, 1996; *Tu Ridi*, 1998. **See also** ANGELOPOULOS, DOVZHENKO, JANCSO, PASOLINI, ROSSELLINI

A nurse, in the Caribbean to tend to a woman suffering from mental paralysis, wakes to find herself watched over by a mute, undead sentry. Hokum, perhaps, but Tourneur's impressively atmospheric horror-movie is an imaginative, sensitive transposition of *Jane Eyre* to a dark, dreamlike realm of superstition and voodoo. Directing this and the likewise metaphorical mysteries *Cat People* and *The Leopard Man* for producer Val Lewton, B-movie stylist Tourneur displayed a talent not only for creating a fear of the unseen and unknown through a subtle use of shadows and off-screen sound, but for turning potentially lowly material into pulp poetry: *Zombie* uses elegant compositions, graceful camera movements and painterly lighting in magical but nightmarish images of sinister giants and vulnerable beauties sharing a strange, misty, moonlit domaine suggestive of a fevered imagination. Not surprisingly, Tourneur directed fine *noir* thrillers: *Experiment Perilous*, *Berlin Express*, *Nightfall* and, most memorable, *Out of the Past*, a classic variation on the theme of a private eye infatuated with a *femme fatale*, which makes superb use both of studio artifice (the exotically romantic moonlit Mexican beach where Robert Mitchum and Jane Greer keep a tryst among fishing nets) and empty landscapes where there is no refuge from sudden danger. In later years, Tourneur mostly worked with less fruitful material (though *The Flame and the Arrow* is a witty, colourful swashbuckler, *Night of the Demon* a largely successful return to psychological horror); at his peak, however, his visual inventiveness regularly raised his films above their low-budget origins.

Jacques Tourneur b. France 1904, d. France 1977. **I Walked with a Zombie** USA 1943/ w Frances Dee, Tom Conway, James Ellison, Christine Gordon, Darby Jones. **Films include** *Cat People, The Leopard Man*, 1943; *Experiment Perilous*, 1944; *Out of the Past*, 1947; *Berlin Express*, 1948; *Easy Living*, 1948; *The Flame and the Arrow*, 1950; *Great Day in the Morning, Nightfall*, 1956; *Night of the Demon*, 1957; *The Comedy of Terrors*, 1963. **See also** CURTIZ, LAUGHTON, LEWIS, SIODMAK, ULMER

FRANÇOIS TRUFFAUT

A film director (Truffaut) comforts a *grande dame* anxious about her fading talent and looks. Though the preceding scenes have hilariously shown her forgetting lines, it's typical of Truffaut that the comedy arouses tender sympathy for the woman. The critic-turned-*nouvelle vague* director lived for cinema, and *Day for Night* is a personal, bitter-sweet account of the fraught relationship between life and illusion and the off-screen emotional upheavals and intrigues between cast and crew. From his outstanding, sensitive tale of a lonely, painful childhood, *Les Quatre Cents Coups*, onwards, nearly all his work deals with the search for love, the need to belong, loneliness and the gulf between hope and reality. In his lesser films, he tended to rely too flagrantly on sentimental charm, melodramatic contrivance and romantic whimsy,

and an insistent fascination with the mystery of women. Except for his debut, his semi-autobiographical Antoine Doinel films, with Jean-Pierre Léaud as his alter ego, are overly indulgent of the immature, womanising protagonist. His finest work, however – *Shoot the Pianist, Jules et Jim, La Peau Douce, Mississippi Mermaid, L'Enfant Sauvage, Les Deux Anglaises et le Continent*, and *The Green Room* – is precariously but deftly balanced between sympathetic involvement with his characters' doubts, frustration and confusion, and gently ironic detachment; accordingly, he favoured the medium close-up and medium-shot, linear but subtly elliptical narratives and, occasionally, voiceover narration, literary in tone. Here lyricism and restraint, emotional realism and cinematic artifice combine to achieve genuine poignancy.

François Truffaut b. 1932 France, d. 1984 France. **Day for Night (La Nuit Américaine)** France 1973/ w Truffaut, Jacqueline Bisset, Jean-Pierre Léaud, Valentina Cortese, Jean-Pierre Aumont. **Films include** *Les Quatre Cents Coups*, 1959; *Shoot the Pianist*, 1960; *Jules et Jim*, 1961; *La Peau Douce*, 1964; *Mississippi Mermaid, L'Enfant Sauvage*, 1969; *Les Deux Anglaises et le Continent*, 1971; *The Story of Adèle H*, 1975; *The Green Room*, 1978; *The Last Metro*, 1981; *Finally Sunday!*, 1983. **See also** BECKER, GODARD, OPHÜLS, RENOIR, VIGO

Enraged at thugs who have shot him with a rivet gun and murdered his son, a mild-mannered salaryman sprouts weapons from his chest and kills his tormentors. A remake/ sequel to his earlier low-budget *Tetsuo*, in which a man's guilt, desire and anguish take anatomical shape as his body transmutes into seething metallic matter, Tsukamoto's film largely divests itself of its predecessor's faintly misogynistic phallic imagery (the aroused protagonist's penis became a massive power drill). But it retains his trademark fascination with flesh painfully and inexplicably transformed into metal as a manifestation of volatile sado-masochistic emotions. Narrative logic is not Tsukamoto's strong point – his impressionistic, fragmented stories shift between 'reality' and fantasy to often bewildering effect – but the metaphor (recalling not only Otomo Katsuhiro's *animé Akira* but the films of Cronenberg and writings of J G Ballard) survives intact thanks to the visceral, convulsive intensity of his images. Shooting in steely greys, blues, blacks and occasional flashes of blood-red with a reeling camera, he creates a nightmarishly apocalyptic world in which the dividing lines between mind and body, self and other, organic and inorganic, are simpy erased: the frantic kinetic whirl acknowledges no spatial limits. Writing, designing, shooting, directing, editing and acting in his films, Tsukamoto is a maverick with a recognisably extreme surreal/expressionist vision: though *Tokyo Fist* and *Bullet Ballet* abandon sci-fi for boxing, body-piercing and guns, his sense of human fear and desire as an unremittingly violent arena of crazed, physically and emotionally agonising conflict remains distinctive.

Tsukamoto Shinya b. 1960 Japan. **Tetsuo II: Bodyhammer** Japan 1991/ w Taguchi Tomoroh, Kanaoka Nobu, Tsukamoto, Tomioka Keinosuke, Kim Sujin. **Films include** *The Adventures of Denchu-kozo*, 1987; *Tetsuo (Tetsuo: The Iron Man)*, 1989; *Hiruko the Goblin*, 1990; *Tokyo Fist*, 1995; *Bullet Ballet*, 1998. **See also** AVERY, BOROWCZYK, CRONENBERG, GILLIAM, JEUNET AND CARO, LYNCH, SVANKMAJER

A couple playing cards: the man miserable, distracted, the woman hard as nails (note her hand includes the ace of spades): in yielding to desire and greed, and taking up with *femme fatale* Ann Savage, drifter Tom Neal is gambling with death. A familiar theme in *film noir*, but the fact that Ulmer, who mostly worked for Poverty Row studios, was forced to shoot *Detour* in just six days, using a small, unglamorous, unprestigious cast, sparse decor and obvious back-projection for the scenes of the couple in their car, proved perversely fruitful in providing the film's seedy ambience and nightmarish air of fatalism. Ulmer was used to making the most of very little: though he began promisingly, assisting Murnau and collaborating with Siodmak, Wilder and Zinnemann on the classic *People on Sunday*, his move to Hollywood soon confined him to the industry's lower depths, often making ultra-cheap programme-fillers for ethnic minorities. But somehow he contrived to direct a number of genuinely impressive films, notable for their taut narratives, broodingly intense mood, and an expressive visual style in which he made imaginative use of long, fluid camera movements, looming shadows and – when the budget allowed – evocative sets (he'd worked as a designer in Germany). *The Black Cat* is a masterfully macabre study in evil, with its sadistic villain installed in a Bauhaus mansion built on the site of a wartime death camp; *Bluebeard* an atmospheric study of the murderer; *Ruthless*, about unbridled ambition, a poor-man's *Citizen Kane*; *The Naked Dawn* an expressionist western. Seldom has cinematic invention succcessfully transcended such impoverished resources.

Edgar Georg Ulmer b. 1900, Austria, d. 1978 France. **Detour** USA 1945/ w Tom Neal, Ann Savage, Claudia Drake, Edmund MacDonald, Tim Ryan. **Films include** *People on Sunday*, 1929; *The Black Cat*, 1934; *Isle of Forgotten Sins*, 1943; *Bluebeard*, 1944; *Club Havana, Strange Illusion*, 1945; *The Strange Woman*, 1946; *Ruthless*, 1948; *The Man from Planet X*, 1951; *The Naked Dawn*, 1955; *Beyond the Time Barrier*, 1960. **See also** ARNOLD, CORMAN, CURTIZ, LEWIS, SIODMAK, TOURNEUR, WOOD

Moscow crowds are recorded in all their ordinariness by the camera; at the same time, split-screen editing turns them into a kaleidoscopic pattern. Of the directors involved in Soviet propaganda after the 1917 Revolution, Vertov was the most devoted to documentary – his Kino-Eye group travelled the Union, taking newsreels to, and documenting the lives of, the masses – yet he was profoundly influenced by Constructivism: using experimental montage and camera techniques, he explored and celebrated the film medium itself. His masterpiece *Man with a Movie Camera* is both a fragmented, impressionistic study of a day in the life of a city, lyrically recording the masses at work and play, and an avant-garde, self-reflexive essay on the relationship between film-maker, camera, and subject. Reality is transformed by subliminally rapid cutting, slow-, fast- and reverse-motion, superimposition, juxtaposition, graphics and animation (his anti-capitalist satire *Soviet Toys* was Russia's first cartoon short). And we are repeatedly reminded that we are seeing a distillation of that reality by inserted scenes of the film-making process: the cameraman and editor at work, a cinema audience watching shots from the film we have been watching, and – again through animation – the camera coming alive and moving around on its tripod. This exhilaratingly imaginative, witty blend of actuality and artifice, later abandoned in keeping with Stalin's preference for sober 'social realism', anticipated both *cinéma verité* and the essay-films of Godard and Marker. He was a pioneer of documentary and modernism, yet his lively inventiveness remains enthralling to this day.

Dziga Vertov (Denis Arkadievitch Kaufman) b. 1896 Poland, d. 1954 USSR. **Man with a Movie Camera** USSR 1929.
Films include *Kino-Weekly* (newsreels), 1918-19; *Soviet Toys*, 1924; *Kino-Pravda* (newsreels), 1922-25; *A Sixth of the World*, 1926; *Symphony of the Dom Basin*, 1930; *Three Songs of Lenin*, 1934; *Lullaby*, 1937. **See also** EISENSTEIN, GODARD, KEATON, MARKER, MORRIS, PENNEBAKER, VIGO

KING VIDOR

A man alone, alienated and dwarfed by the gleaming architecture of a massive, modern office building. Vidor's fable about an ordinary Joe, ambitious to stand out in the world but doomed to remain one of the mob, is typically a study of the individual's struggle against larger forces – war, poverty, conformist society, nature, even his own inner demons. Though there was often a strong moralising or metaphysical aspect to Vidor's straightforward, even crudely simplistic stories, they were distinguished by a muscular visual style. In *The Crowd*, the hero is frequently shown at his desk, surrounded by endless rows of near-identical workers at similar desks, or in teeming streets, while its predecessor *The Big Parade*, about patriotism muted by the reality of war, moves from shots of proudly regimented troops and light-hearted camaraderie to the murky, muddy trenches. Though Vidor was a versatile director whose finest films include sophisticated Hollywood comedy (*Show People*) and poignant melodrama (*Stella Dallas*), his most typical work is notable for an emotional and visual boldness, later often bordering on bombast: an adaptation of Ayn Rand's *The Fountainhead* equates creative independence and sexual drive through robust imagery full of thrusting, phallic architecture, the western *Duel in the Sun*'s shimmering desert scenery mirrors its (often risibly) feverish tale of primeval *amour fou*, while *Ruby Gentry* located a similar tale of uncontrollable, neurotic, forbidden passion in the swamps of the Deep South. Though Vidor's work was seldom subtle, the vigour and scale of his storytelling and imagery make for enjoyably forthright entertainment.

King Vidor b. 1894 USA, d. 1982 USA. **The Crowd** USA 1927/ w James Murray, Eleanor Boardman, Bert Roach, Estelle Clark, Daniel G Tomlinson. **Films include** *The Big Parade*, 1925; *Show People*, 1928; *Hallelujah*, 1929; *The Champ*, 1931; *Our Daily Bread*, 1934; *Stella Dallas,* 1937; *Northwest Passage*, 1940; *Duel in the Sun*, 1946; *The Fountainhead,* 1949; *Ruby Gentry,* 1952; *War and Peace*, 1956. **See also** FULLER, MEYER, MILIUS, PARKER, SIRK, STONE

A bride at the tiller of her husband's barge: her face shows trepidation (it's her wedding night), a little unhappiness at leaving home…and strength of will. Most striking is the wedding gown, luminous in the dusk against an ominous black backdrop of industrial architecture (her workaholic husband will neglect her need for adventure). An anarchist's son, Vigo was one of cinema's finest poets, able to transcend mundane reality with his unique blend of lyricism, wit, sensuality and surrealism. His distaste for authority, injustice and inequality (evident in the ironic documentary *A Propos de Nice* and the featurette *Zéro de Conduite*, which celebrates a boarding-school rebellion against hypocritical, mean-spirited teachers) was balanced by a love of individuality, innocence and independence. *L'Atalante*, the most honest, unsentimental yet profoundly moving of love stories, recognises that marriage is demandingly difficult – only if we respect our partners' very different needs can true, lasting union be achieved. Vigo's imagery could be fantastic (*Zéro*'s school dignitaries are literally dummies); experimental (slow-motion and music played in reverse turn the pupils' pillow fight into a magical, snowy tribal ritual); grotesquely funny (the barge's eccentric bosun shows the fascinated bride his rude tattoos and collection of bizarre bric-à-brac, including, among other things, severed hands); or dreamily erotic (the captain's underwater vision of his runaway wife). It was, however, always imaginative and rapturous, imbued with a passion for film. Tragically, he died at 29, having made only one full-length feature; nevertheless, he remains one of cinema's greatest, most influential masters.

Jean Vigo b. 1905 France, d. 1934 France. **L'Atalante** France 1934/ w Dita Parlo, Jean Dasté, Michel Simon, Gilles Margaritis, Louis Lefebvre. **Films include** *A Propos de Nice*, 1929; *Taris*, 1931; *Zéro de Conduite*, 1933. **See also** ANDERSON, BERTOLUCCI, BUÑUEL, COCTEAU, GODARD, RENOIR, TRUFFAUT, VERTOV

At a grand ball, a Sicilian aristocrat deigns to dance with his daughter-in-law; since this is the time of Garibaldi's *risorgimento*, and she's of bourgeois stock, the waltz symbolises an epochal shift in society, transformation and compromise. Visconti's fascination with the elegance of the swirling, bejewelled assembly and lush, palatial decor reveals a lofty nostalgia for the old order; though his early *Ossessione* and *La Terra Trema* dabbled with neo-realism, he proceeded to a lavishly ornate, even vulgar aestheticism. He repeatedly treated prestigious historical and literary subjects, but his penchant for stately camera movements, exquisite finery and characters locked in melancholy reverie increasingly made for lifeless drama devoid of narrative drive, psychological nuance and – for all the pretensions to political significance in *Senso*,

The Damned and *Ludwig* – genuine commitment or analysis. The best of his early films (*Ossessione* and *Rocco and His Brothers*) succeed as melodrama, and there's no denying the pictorial beauty of *The Leopard*; but *The Stranger* was a hollow, overblown travesty of Camus, while *The Damned* slid into camp histrionics wholly inadequate for an account of the rise of Nazism. *Death in Venice* was perhaps the nadir of his decadent decorative style: applying a funereal pace to Thomas Mann's slim storyline, repeatedly resorting to Mahler's music and dreamily picturesque shots of Venice to underline emotions unexplored by dialogue and performance, he turned a meditation on beauty into an overextended, bathetic tale of unrequited passion. Thereafter, his work remained sumptuous, shallow and turgid.

Count Don Luchino Visconti di Morone b. 1906 Italy, d. 1976 Italy. **The Leopard** Italy 1963/ w Burt Lancaster, Alain Delon, Claudia Cardinale, Paolo Stoppa, Serge Reggiani. **Films include** *Ossessione*, 1942; *La Terra Trema*, 1948; *Senso*, 1954; *White Nights*, 1957; *Rocco and His Brothers*, 1960; *The Stranger*, 1967; *The Damned*, 1969; *Death in Venice*, 1970; *Ludwig*, 1972; *Conversation Piece*, 1974; *The Innocent*, 1976. **See also** ANTONIONI, CIMINO, COPPOLA, IVORY, LEAN

Before her ladies-in-waiting, Catherine the Great, assured of her control of Russia, treats a former lover with contempt. The penultimate of Von Sternberg's seven films with Marlene Dietrich typically celebrates female eroticism, determination and empowerment: as Catherine turns from innocent pawn to manipulative, promiscuous Empress, she abandons frilly frocks for masculine garb and suppresses girlish romanticism to exploit entranced suitors. Heady expressionism charts her rise to power, deploying to extravagant effect costumes, decor (the Imperial Palace's oppressive religious statuary and the lacy bedroom netting behind which she keeps secret trysts), light, shadows and symbolism: Catherine's final triumph sees her ride through the palace on a white stallion, wickedly hinting at rumours of her scandalous demise. For Von Sternberg, story increasingly became an excuse to indulge in spectacular, often camp visual artifice, so that his films became more abstract: from the relatively low-key realism of *The Salvation Hunters, Underworld* and *The Last Command* (all still notable for their visual elegance), he progressed through absurdly exotic Dietrich vehicles like *The Blue Angel, Morocco, Shanghai Express* and *The Devil Is a Woman* to *The Shanghai Gesture* and *The Saga of Anatahan*, wildly stylised melodramas about the relationship of power to sexual desire and despair. Increasingly, his taste for excess alienated producers and public alike, and many later projects were beset by problems. Nevertheless, his cruel, ironic wit, ravishing sense of design and luminous camerawork remain compelling to this day.

Josef Von Sternberg (Jonas Sternberg) b. 1894 Austria, d. 1969 USA. **The Scarlet Empress** USA 1934/ w Marlene Dietrich, John Lodge, Louise Dresser, Sam Jaffe, C Aubrey Smith. **Films include** *The Salvation Hunters*, 1925; *Underworld*, 1927; *The Last Command*, 1928; *The Blue Angel, Morocco*, 1930; *Dishonored*, 1931; *Shanghai Express, Blonde Venus*, 1932; *The Devil Is a Woman*, 1935; *The Shanghai Gesture*, 1941; *The Saga of Anatahan*, 1953. **See also** BORZAGE, DEMY, EISENSTEIN, FASSBINDER, MINNELLI, OPHÜLS, POWELL, SIRK

Two old friends, rivals not over a girl they love but over the lottery fortune she won, confront each other in Death Valley; when the vengeful deputy kills the husband, he'll find he's handcufffed to the corpse, and doomed himself. Von Stroheim's ravaged masterpiece (cut by the studio from ten hours to two) atypically focuses on working-class Americans as opposed to European aristocrats and sophisticates (*Blind Husbands*, *Foolish Wives*, *The Wedding March* and *Queen Kelly*). Yet it is characteristic not only in its acerbically cynical examination of love and friendship being eroded by envy, avarice and deceit, but in its naturalistic yet poetically resonant imagery. In *Greed*, a marriage's future is foreshadowed when he intercuts a funeral procession outside the wedding ceremony; in *The Wedding March*, the destructive influences on another romance are evoked when the lovers' tryst in an orchard glowing with blossom is counterpointed by sordid orgy scenes in a brothel. Von Stroheim, whose acting roles as a cruel, predatory Prussian popularised him as 'the man you love to hate', was obsessive about authenticity, insisting every costume, prop and set be accurate to the tiniest (even invisible) detail, and eliciting performances unusually subtle and exact in expression and gesture. Though producers disliked such perfectionism, so that his brief directing career was littered with unfinished or re-edited projects, his achievements were remarkable. Few film-makers have so masterfully combined realism with ironic metaphor, miniaturist social and psychological observation with epic narrative, romanticism with moral rigour.

Erich Von Stroheim (Erich Oswald Stroheim) b. 1885 Austria, d. 1957 France. **Greed** USA 1923/ w Gibson Gowland, Jean Hersholt, Za Su Pitts, Tempe Piggott, Frank Hayes, Dale Fuller. **Films include** *Blind Husbands*, 1918; *Foolish Wives*, 1921; *The Merry Widow*, 1925; *The Wedding March*, *Queen Kelly*, 1928; *Walking Down Broadway (Hello Sister)*, 1933. **See also** GRIFFITH, LUBITSCH, RENOIR, VON STERNBERG, WELLES

An innocent bride, her husband and a stern priest in a Scottish village in the 70s: the grainy, bleached image has the look of 'realism', accentuated in the film by a continually mobile hand-held camera. It's an aesthetic seldom associated with the expanses of the 'Scope frame, let alone a story that demands we believe in saintly goodness and a miracle. After her husband's accident, and at his suggestion (he wants her not to be lonely), the girl has sex with other men in the hope of saving his life – sacrificing her own, she succeeds. Von Trier is an eccentric, provocative film-maker with a penchant for extreme stylistic strategies: *The Element of Crime*, an obscure, brooding *noir* thriller, was shot in sulphurous yellows; *Europa*, a dreamlike drama set in postwar Germany, mixed black-and-white and colour,

live action and obvious backdrops to virtuoso but flashy effect; the TV series *The Kingdom* was a hospital soap imbued with supernatural horror, thumping satire and surreal illogic. His early films are overblown attempts to create a dazzlingly strange, sinister world, but in the more recent *Breaking the Waves* and *The Idiots* (a funny if painful study of a group of friends pretending to be handicapped, which highlights hypocritical responses to 'abnormality' and unravels links between performance and emotional manipulation), simpler narratives and closer attention to individual characters suggest there is perhaps a major film-maker behind the emphatic irony (here, the final miracle is conveyed by a kitschy shot of heavenly bells) and insistent, bludgeoning technique. With conviction, he may achieve greatness.

Lars Von Trier b. 1956 Denmark. **Breaking the Waves** Denmark 1996/ w Emily Watson, Stellan Skarsgård, Katrin Cartlidge, Jean-Marc Barr, Adrian Rawlins, Udo Kier. **Films include** *The Element of Crime*, 1984; *Epidemic*, 1987; *Europa (Zentropa)*, 1991; *The Kingdom*, 1994; *The Kingdom II*, 1997; *The Idiots*, 1998. **See also** CASSAVETES, DREYER, FASSBINDER, LANG, LYNCH

ANDRZEJ WAJDA

The 1944 Warsaw Uprising: a wounded resistance fighter and his guide (who, unbeknown to him, loves him) flee the Nazis through the sewers. The image, rooted in many Poles' wartime experiences, suggests both documentary realism and a more baroque vein of film-making. Charting the doomed flight of a crippled platoon through the stinking labyrinth, Wajda transforms recent history into an allegorical vision of hell (a character quotes Dante's *Inferno*): as the fugitives struggle to survive the Germans' gunfire, gas and booby-traps, and succumb to fatigue, fever and fear, the imagery shifts from a relatively conventional depiction of a ruined Warsaw (filmed with long, complex tracking shots) to grotesque, nightmarish scenes featuring bubbling sewerage, floating corpses, and lost souls wandering demented through the carnage and darkness. Wajda has repeatedly used defining moments in Polish history – his trilogy of *A Generation, Kanal* and *Ashes and Diamonds* concerned the Nazi occupation and its immediate aftermath – to question traditional notions of national heroism, identity and ideology, while his style has steadily become more poetic, even to the point of excess: he takes a metaphor and runs with it, so that *Ashes and Diamonds* is as notable for its visual flourishes and celebration of its existentialist hero as for its portrait of Poland newly facing Communism. Later, in *Man of Marble, Man of Iron* and *Danton*, while still using analogy to reflect on his country's politics, he successfully adopted a rather less flamboyant style; more recently, however, this shift has often resulted in worthy, dull predictability.

Andrzej Wajda b. 1927 Poland. **Kanal** Poland 1956/ w Wienczslaw Glinski, Tadeusz Janczar, Teresa Izewska, Emil Karewicz, Vladek Sheybal.
Films include *A Generation*, 1954; *Ashes and Diamonds*, 1958; *Siberian Lady Macbeth*, 1962; *Everything for Sale*, 1968; *Landscape After Battle*, 1970; *The Wedding*, 1972; *Man of Marble*, 1976; *Man of Iron, The Conductor*, 1980; *A Love in Germany, Danton*, 1983; *Korczak*, 1990.
See also KIESLOWSKI, LOSEY, POLANSKI

'Made it, Ma – to the top of the world!' Cornered by cops, mother-fixated gangster Cagney embraces destiny by firing into a gas cylinder and blowing himself to oblivion. The image, evocative of uncontrollable psychopathic energy, typifies Walsh's unpretentious expertise in the action picture. Pacy, classically shot, and making imaginative metaphorical use of locations (Cagney's gangster in *The Roaring Twenties* expires on the steps of a church; Bogart's lonely, embattled, ageing desperado in *High Sierra* dies on the bleak, scarred cliffs of the film's title), his finest films are notable for a robust physicality (his first major hit was *The Thief of Bagdad*, starring Douglas Fairbanks). Bogart, Errol Flynn, Gary Cooper, Robert Mitchum were all effective Walsh heroes, though it was Cagney's jerkily dynamic dancer's movements that were most memorably used, particularly in *White Heat* when, learning of his mother's death and stricken by a blinding migraine, he staggers wildy around a prison canteen, trashing it like a human tornado. Walsh was prolific and versatile – black comedy distinguished *The Bowery*; nostalgia for small-town Americana *The Strawberry Blonde* – but he was at his best with muscular westerns, war, crime and adventure movies. Though *The Roaring Twenties* situated its rise-and-fall-of-a-mobster story within a clearly delineated socio-economic and historical context, and the *noir* western *Pursued* included Freudian elements, Walsh never let subtlety overwhelm a good yarn and vivid characterisation built on expressive physical action. Though he seldom ventured beyond genre conventions, sheer vitality makes his films superior popular entertainment.

Raoul Walsh b. 1887 USA, d. 1980 USA. **White Heat** USA 1949/ w James Cagney, Edmond O'Brien, Virginia Mayo, Margaret Wycherly, Steve Cochran. **Films include** *The Thief of Bagdad*, 1924; *What Price Glory?*, 1926; *The Bowery*, 1933; *The Roaring Twenties*, 1939; *They Drive By Night*, 1940; *The Strawberry Blonde, High Sierra*, 1941; *Gentleman Jim*, 1942; *Objective, Burma!*, 1945; *Pursued*, 1947; *A Distant Trumpet*, 1963. **See also** Dwan, Hawks, Anthony Mann, Peckinpah, Siegel, Wellman

ANDY WARHOL

Gay hustler 'Paul America' completes his toilet in a Fire Island bathroom; little happens as admirers drop by to chat inanely about sex, shaving and so on. The shot, filmed with a static camera for an entire, unedited reel, matches the film's desultory first half, which pans between the stud sunning himself on the beach and three friends bitching on a patio. Influenced by Hollywood (he saw his garrulous Factory friends as iconic 'superstars'), porn (sex is endlessly discussed, though sexual activity is seldom very explicit: *Blow Job* focuses throughout on a man's face as he's fellated), and underground cinema, Warhol returned to basics, treating his minimalist films as moving paintings: *Sleep* shows a man in bed over six hours, *Empire* is a static, eight-hour shot of the Empire State Building, *Couch* observes people sitting, eating and

indulging in sex on a sofa. With the addition of sound, dialogue (improvised, meandering, often off-screen and unintelligible) contributed a modicum of camp humour, even drama, though until the twin-screen *The Chelsea Girls*, an epic series of confessional vignettes shot in colour and monochrome, Warhol mostly eschewed cutting and camera movement. The performers' narcissistic exhibitionism and the impassive stare of the camera raises questions about role-playing, voyeurism and the director's role (his authorial interference was minimal). After *The Chelsea Girls*, this conceptual rigour dissipated as Warhol handed over direction to Paul Morrissey, who exploited the fashionably banal posing of the studs, drag queens and supertars in increasingly narrative-driven, sexually graphic, parodic melodramas like *Flesh, Trash* and *Heat*.

Andy Warhol b. 1928 USA, d. 1987 USA. **My Hustler** USA 1965/ w Paul America, Ed Hood, Joe Campbell, Geneviève Charbon.
Films include *Kiss, Blow Job, Eat, Sleep*, 1963; *Couch, Empire, Harlot*, 1964; *Beauty # 2, Kitchen, Vinyl*, 1965; *The Velvet Undergound and Nico*, 1966; *Bike Boy, Nude Restaurant*, 1967; *Blue Movie, Lonesome Cowboys*, 1968; *L'Amour*, 1972. **See also** ANGER, FASSBINDER, GODARD, LUMIÈRE, STRAUB, SYBERBERG, WATERS

Which is more repellent – the pig's head, or the grotesquely made-up face of 300lb transvestite Divine? And will (s)he eat it? Fending off challengers to her claim to be 'the filthiest person alive', she finally triumphs by eating, on camera, dog-shit. Waters' deliberately offensive black comedy for the midnight-movie crowd aimed to compensate for visibly low-budget production values with bad-taste gags strung together seemingly at random to suggest a semblance of plot. With Baltimore friends like Divine and Edie 'The Egg Lady' Massey (an obese slob whose gluttony inspires repeated shots of her half-dressed body spattered with half-eaten food) hamming it up with histrionic gestures and laughably melodramatic dialogue, Waters set about outraging bourgeois sensibilities with trashy comedies depicting repulsive, dysfunctional families in scenarios – involving rape, baby-trading, transsexuality, sadism, murder, and all things scatological – deemed unsuitable for mainstream comedy. The camerawork was rudimentary, the characterisation cartoon-thin, the only evident attempt at *mise-en-scène* the garish design of costumes and decor. Nevertheless, he rapidly achieved cult success, enabling him to move closer to the mainstream with *Polyester*, in which the visual gags were toned down and the novelty element refocused on 'Odorama', a scratch-card of smells handed to audiences. In later films (which even feature proper stars), Waters steadily abandoned his (admittedly trivial) more iconoclastic excesses for simple kitsch, hyperbolic parody and black comedy; though plotting, dialogue and camerawork are more polished, the comedy is no less hit-and-miss.

John Waters b. 1946 USA. **Pink Flamingos** USA 1972/ w Divine, David Lochary, Mary Vivian Pearce, Mink Stole, Edith Massey, Danny Mills. **Films include** *Mondo Trasho*, 1970; *Female Trouble*, 1975; *Desperate Living*, 1977, *Polyester*, 1981; *Hairspray*, 1988; *Cry-Baby*, 1990; *Serial Mom*, 1994; *Pecker*, 1998. **See also** ALMODÓVAR, LYNCH, MEYER, SOLONDZ, WARHOL, WOOD

PETER WEIR

A man alone in an airplane, empty and blindingly bright, after a devastating crash: is he dead, reborn as a fearless visionary, or trapped in an imaginary world, traumatised by guilt and grief? Weir's ambitious film about the psychological aftermath of a near-death experience is, like much of his work, littered with mysterious, almost mystical imagery. Save for a few relatively anonymous movies (*Dead Poets Society, Green Card*) notable mainly for their hackneyed liberal sentiments, he has repeatedly examined the irruption of the extraordinary and irrational into everyday life. *Picnic at Hanging Rock* and *The Last Wave* dealt respectively with repressed schoolgirls and a strait-laced lawyer influenced by the supernatural power of the primeval Australian landscape; *Witness* and *The Mosquito Coast* concerned modern Westerners transformed by traditional Amish religion and jungle madness; *The Truman Show* a suburban Everyman who finds his life is programmed by the Godlike creator of a TV docusoap. Through strange lighting effects, sinuous camera movements, striking music and dramatic shots of architecture and landscape, Weir implies the presence of unseen forces; sadly, he seldom follows these implications through to satisfactory narrative closure, and intriguing premises yield to conventional plot development (*Witness* and *Fearless* slide into mundane romance and soft-centred humanism) or strained ambiguity. That said, few of his films are without intelligence or visual felicities, and his early *The Cars That Ate Paris*, a modest but ingenious comic horror-movie about a remote community cannibalising passing cars for its economy, is genuinely witty, surreal and unsettling.

Peter Weir b. 1944 Australia. **Fearless** USA 1993/ w Jeff Bridges, Isabella Rossellini, Rosie Perez, Tom Hulce, John Turturro, Benicio Del Toro. **Films include** *The Cars That Ate Paris*, 1974; *Picnic at Hanging Rock*, 1975; *The Last Wave*, 1977; *Gallipoli*, 1981; *The Year of Living Dangerously*, 1983; *Witness*, 1985; *The Mosquito Coast*, 1986; *Dead Poets Society*, 1989; *Green Card*, 1990; *The Truman Show*, 1998. **See also** KIESLOWSKI, PARKER, SCOTT, SPIELBERG

A vast, echoing mansion: a widow looks lovingly but despairingly at her spoilt son, who is discouraging her automobile-engineer suitor – the beau of her youth – whom he foolishly deems unworthy of their good name. Welles' magnificent, elegiac portrait of America on the brink of industrialisation (tragically hacked by RKO) is full of strikingly dramatic but precisely telling images: the extreme, deep-focus perspective, sombre lighting and monumental set embody the gulf between the desires of self-effacing mother and bullying son, and the imminent demise of the Ambersons' hollow grandeur. Even in his debut *Citizen Kane* – a stylistically adventurous, philosophically profound study of a lonely tycoon so riven by contradictions that even as he dies he barely understands himself – Welles put his narrative flair and technical expertise to sophisticated dramatic use: expressionist lighting, compositions and sound, complex camera movements, overlapping dialogue, an eclectic array of editing techniques and memorably vivid performances from his Mercury Theatre group not only revealed his unbridled enthusiasm for the film medium but his intention of exploring and expanding its expressive boundaries. Though his plans were repeatedly frustrated by a cautious film-making establishment few directors made so many exhilaratingly audacious, imaginative movies: *The Lady from Shanghai, Othello, Touch of Evil, The Trial, Chimes at Midnight* and *F for Fake* – all investigations into truth and falsehood, character and destiny, ambition and failure – are triumphs of invention over stunted resources. He remains that rarity – an undeniable genius of the cinema.

(George) Orson Welles b. 1916 USA, d. 1985 USA. **The Magnificent Ambersons** USA 1942/ w Joseph Cotten, Tim Holt, Dolores Costello, Agnes Moorehead, Anne Baxter, Ray Collins. **Films include** *Citizen Kane*, 1941; *The Lady from Shanghai, Macbeth*, 1946; *Othello*, 1952; *Mr Arkadin (Confidential Report)*, 1955; *Touch of Evil*, 1958; *The Trial*, 1963; *Chimes at Midnight*, 1966; *The Immortal Story*, 1968; *F for Fake*, 1973. **See also** ANGELOPOULOS, FORD, GRIFFITH, KIESLOWSKI, MURNAU, OPHÜLS, POWELL, RENOIR, VIGO

An alcoholic Hollywood star (Fredric March), whose decline counterpoints his wife's meteoric rise from waitress to America's sweetheart, is so irritated by a press agent's cruel contempt that he is on the verge of violence. Wellman's classical compositions favour medium-shots, background details softened to focus attention on the protagonists, and naturalistic colour (though note how the rich Technicolor tones have faded – Hollywood, seeing itself as purveying entertainment, not art, has seldom taken posterity seriously). Wellman was an efficient, erratic journeyman, as good as his material. Though praised for his handling of vigorous masculine action in war movies (*Wings, The Story of GI Joe*), thrillers (*The Public Enemy*), westerns and outdoor adventures (*Beggars of Life, Wild Boys of the Road*), he was at his best with dark satire and melodrama, where his cynicism about modern mores enhanced sparkling scripts by Dorothy Parker (*A Star Is Born*), Ben Hecht (*Nothing Sacred*, a scabrous satire on a scoop-crazy press pandering to a public devoted to bogus sentiment), and Nunnally Johnson (*Roxie Hart*). Even then, his characters expressed themselves most eloquently through physical action: March's low-point comes when he drunkenly and accidently hits his wife at an Oscar ceremony: while the leads in *Nothing Sacred* reveal their mutual love in a violent brawl. Occasionally, as in the nocturnal studio-shot western *The Ox-Bow Incident* and the thriller *Track of the Cat* (which made symbolic use of muted colours), Wellman flirted with expressionism; mostly, however, his lighting, compositions and pacy editing are simple, forthright and to the point.

William Wellman b. 1896 USA, d. 1975 USA. **A Star Is Born** USA 1937/ w Janet Gaynor, Fredric March, Adolphe Menjou, Lionel Stander, May Robson. **Films include** *Beggars of Life*, 1928; *Wings*, 1929; *The Public Enemy, Night Nurse*, 1931; *Wild Boys of the Road*, 1933; *Nothing Sacred*, 1937; *Roxie Hart*, 1942; *The Ox-Bow Incident*, 1943; *The Story of GI Joe*, 1945; *Across the Wide Missouri*, 1951; *Track of the Cat*, 1954. **See also** CURTIZ, HAWKS, HUSTON, LUPINO, WALSH

A man climbs derelict machinery to inspect the landscape he's travelling through with a cinema engineer. The act is without direction, the vista empty; the camera simply observes him, as cool, detached and seemingly purposeless as his gaze. Wenders' early films (*The Goalkeeper's Fear of the Penalty, Alice in the Cities*) are subtle geographical/emotional odysseys in which quiet, lonely men, beset by rootlessness, make hesitant attempts at friendship and ponder the ambivalent influence on post-war Germany of American culture (to which the films' cinematic, musical and literary references repeatedly allude). They explore identity crisis: in the characters, Germany, and Wenders himself, who constantly veers between philosophical contemplation and generic narrative (though 'thrillers', *The American Friend* and *Hammett* were more concerned with inner doubts and mood than with mystery or suspense) just as the aimless *Kings of the Road* meander along the East German border. Wenders' camerawork is crisp, lyrical, leisurely and suitably mobile, with long takes following characters, as they travel or sink into lassitude, at a slight distance; landscapes mirror states of mind. More recently, as if aware he might be repeating himself, Wenders has invested his slim, slow, picaresque stories with more emphatic meaning: rapturously in *Wings of Desire*, a poetic meditation on life, love and death as witnessed by angels in modern Berlin; portentously in his later films (including the visually gorgeous but relatively conventional conspiracy thriller *The End of Violence*), in which narrative and characterisation are subordinate to anxieties about the potentially malign influence of contemporary cinema itself.

Wim Wenders b. 1945 Germany. **Kings of the Road (Im Lauf der Zeit)** W Germany 1976/ w Hans Zischler, Rudiger Vogler, Liza Kreuzer, Rudolph Schündler. **Films include** *The Goalkeeper's Fear of the Penalty*, 1971; *Alice in the Cities*, 1974; *The American Friend*, 1977; *The State of Things*, 1982; *Hammett*, 1983; *Paris, Texas*, 1984; *Wings of Desire*, 1987; *Until the End of the World*, 1991; *Faraway, So Close!*, 1993; *Lisbon Story*, 1995; *The End of Violence*, 1998. **See also** ANTONIONI, FORD, GODARD, HAWKS, JARMUSCH, OZU, NICHOLAS RAY

The monster tenderly takes the hand of his newly created mate, who responds with shock and contempt. The gloomy laboratory, Elsa Lanchester's white gown, Karloff's grotesque make-up and the faintly expressionist lighting betoken the horror film, but Lanchester's ludicrously electric hair and bizarre, bird-like expression, Karloff's smile and the air of pastiche typify the English gallows humour Whale brought to the four fantasies that made him famous. The first, *Frankenstein*, combined meticulous monumental sets, looming shadows, and scenes more poetic and poignant than horrific (Karloff unwittingly killing a child by tossing her, just as she taught him to throw flowers, into a river) to depict the monster as an unusually sympathetic victim of mankind's folly. *The Old Dark House* and *The Invisible Man* revelled in absurd English stereotypes, superb chiaroscuro and special effects, ironic verbal wit and visual gags to parody Gothic movie conventions even as they developed them. *Bride of Frankenstein* was Whale's masterpiece, a flight of fancy inspired by Mary Shelley's novel (with pleasing irony Lanchester plays the writer and the Bride), in which his penchant for macabre comedy, vividly eccentric characters (including an incredibly unflappable scientist proudly exhibiting his miniaturised humans) and striking visuals was given free rein. Not that he limited himself to horror; the war drama *Journey's End*, the sophisticated mystery *Remember Last Night?* and a version of *Show Boat* were also impressive. Sadly, his later work was relatively minor, and he retired to concentrate on painting, before being found dead, mysteriously, in his swimming pool.

James Whale b. 1889 England, d. 1957 USA. **Bride of Frankenstein** USA 1935/ w Boris Karloff, Colin Clive, Elsa Lanchester, Ernest Thesiger, Valerie Hobson. **Films include** *Journey's End*, 1930; *Frankenstein*, 1931; *The Old Dark House*, 1932; *The Invisible Man*, *By Candlelight*, 1933; *Remember Last Night?*, 1935; *Show Boat*, 1936; *The Great Garrick*, 1937; *Port of Seven Seas*, 1938; *The Man in the Iron Mask*, 1939. **See also** BAVA, BROOKS, BROWNING, FISHER, HITCHCOCK, MAMOULIAN

Cesare, a somnambulist killer controlled by hypnotist Caligari, prepares to abduct a young woman: a moment reminiscent of classic beauty-and-the-beast fairy-tales. Yet with its histrionically posed actors in emphatic make-up and distorted, angular architecture very evidently painted on 'flats', the image is also insistently from an 'art-movie'. There has been much argument over the authorship of cinema's most famous (albeit not very influential) foray into German expressionism: the story of madness, murder and malign authority was by Carl Mayer and Hans Janowitz, while the trademark sets, by Hermann Warm, Walter Reimann and Walter Röhrig, were in the tradition of contemporary art and theatrical design, notably Alfred Kubin's chiaroscuro paintings of Prague's cramped medieval streets. Wiene – now remembered for

only a few movies, including the likewise expressionist *Genuine*, *Raskolnikov* and *The Hands of Orlac* – is widely considered of minor significance, yet it was he, after all, who orchestrated the film's diverse elements to create a coherent, original whole. Crucially, it seems he was chiefly responsible for the framing scenes at the film's beginning and end, which reveal that the main story has been told by a man kept in a mental asylum; accordingly, the crazed, extravagantly unreal look of the film reflects his paranoid vision of the world. Nor is the visual strangeness confined to the intersecting diagonals, forced perspectives and sharp black and white tones of the sets, since Wiene successfully deployed the weird, automaton-like gestures of Werner Krauss' grotesque Caligari and Conrad Veidt's Cesare to authentically nightmarish effect.

Robert Wiene b. 1881 Germany, d. 1938 France. **The Cabinet of Dr Caligari** Germany 1920/ w Werner Krauss, Conrad Veidt, Lil Dagover, Friedrich Feyer. **Films include** *Genuine*, 1920; *INRI, Raskolnikov*, 1923; *The Hands of Orlac*, 1924; *Der Rosenkavalier*, 1925.
See also CRONENBERG, LANG, LYNCH, PABST, SIODMAK, TSUKAMOTO

A has-been Hollywood star, arrested for murdering her screenwriter-gigolo lover, imagines cops and photographers celebrating her long-awaited comeback. Ending a bitterly satirical tale of exploitation, humiliation and failed dreams, the image, like the moment, is cleverly ironic and gleefully grotesque: her tatty glamour and histrionic demeanour (playing on Gloria Swanson's own faded glory) divest her of dignity. Wilder's most famous films (*Double Indemnity, The Lost Weekend, Some Like It Hot, The Apartment*) are renowned for their misanthropic cynicism. Yet often that attitude seems a conceit, a revelling in man's vain foibles for the sake of melodramatic effect or strings of heartless verbal gags. As his characters can become mere mouthpieces for Wilder's facility with memorable wisecracks, rather than rounded individuals, so the writer

in him may overshadow the director. While his early films, this included, are efficiently if conventionally *noir*, much of his later work seems unconcerned with cinema's potential to explore motivation, mood and meaning through imagery, and what visual 'style' there is occurs in pastiche and overstatement: the recreation of the roaring 20s in *Some Like It Hot* is as broad and unsubtle as Jack Lemmon's performance in drag. For all its wittiness, Wilder's hard-boiled scepticism was regularly undercut by sentimentality, and only in the utterly cynical *Ace in the Hole* and the wholly romantic *The Private Life of Sherlock Holmes* was his tone consistent and truly persuasive – films in which, respectively, a grimly unglamorous mid-Western landscape and the splendour of the Scottish Highlands mirrored the protagonists' inner torments.

Billy (Samuel) Wilder b. 1906 Austria. **Sunset Boulevard** USA 1950/ w Gloria Swanson, William Holden, Erich Von Stroheim, Nancy Olsen, Fred Clark. **Films include** *Double Indemnity*, 1944; *The Lost Weekend*, 1945; *Ace in the Hole*, 1951; *Sabrina*, 1954; *The Seven Year Itch*, 1955; *Some Like It Hot*, 1959; *The Apartment*, 1960; *Kiss Me, Stupid*, 1964; *The Private Life of Sherlock Holmes*, 1960; *Avanti!*, 1972; *Fedora*, 1978. **See also** CUKOR, CLOUZOT, LEISEN, LUBITSCH, MANKIEWICZ, STILLMAN, STURGES

WONG KAR-WAI

A glamorous mystery woman (in a blonde wig recalling gangster's moll Gena Rowlands in Cassavetes' *Gloria*) suddenly turns violent in the neon-lit nightworld of Hong Kong's bustling Chungking Mansions; the tight, shallow focus, lurid colours and blurred action of Chris Doyle's virtuoso, largely hand-held camerawork embody Hong Kong writer-director Wong's abiding fascination with time's fleeting transience, the allure of romance in a fast, materialistic, urban world, and doomed obsessions with unsuitable or unresponsive love-objects. Here, in the first of *Chungking Express'* two loosely rhyming (but, finally, cleverly contrasted) stories, Brigitte Lin plays a woman with whom a young cop, already mourning the demise of one affair, falls in love soon after they pass each other in a crowded thoroughfare; sadly, he's unaware that, by nature and profession, she's a loner – a dangerous heroin-smuggler. Wong's extraordinarily kinetic visual style, using a variety of film-speeds, jump-cuts, extreme angles, distorted perspectives and pixillation (which recur even in the generic martial-arts epic *Ashes of Time*), can resemble an action-painting brought to life, lending a dynamic vitality, playfulness and often very funny sense of irony to his otherwise melancholy meditations (expressed in moody, resigned voiceover) on the cruelty of love. Few modern directors display as much ambition and promise, and none is as thrillingly alert to the enduring poignancy of the passing moment or to the ever-fresh resonance of memory and unrequited desire.

Wong Kar-wai b. 1958 China. **Chungking Express** Hong Kong 1994/ w Brigitte Lin, Kinashiro Takeshi, Tony Leung, Faye Wang.
Key films include *Days of Being Wild*, 1990; *Ashes of Time*, 1994; *Fallen Angels*, 1995; *Happy Together*, 1997. **See also** CARAX, GODARD, KIESLOWSKI, SCORSESE, SIRK

A cop and his hired-assassin prey join forces, partly to defend themselves against hitmen sent by the latter's client, partly because, having got to know one another, they recognise their shared interest in honour, professionalism and courage. A virtuoso of the modern action film, Woo is not only notable for hyperbolic set-pieces involving massive explosions, implausible body-counts and seemingly inexhaustible arsenals of firepower; he is also fascinated by male bonding, loyalty and treachery, and a relativist view of crime and punishment. His baroque, technically adept direction can seem excessive and hysterical: his films alternate between brief soul-searching scenes of almost cloying sentimentality (often verging on the homoerotic) and lengthy sequences in which the antagonists' dynamically violent antics are staged with lurid colours, super-loud sound effects, and an array of editing devices such as slow-motion, dissolves and freeze-frame (a recurrent image is of a gunman, surrounded by detritus, fireballs and carnage, leaping sideways while shooting two guns at once). This rhetoric – most evident in the ambitious, uneven epic *Bullet in the Head* – is often accompanied by knowing, ironic humour: the final shoot-out of *Hard-Boiled*, an expertly choreographed three-minute take set in a maternity ward, has a cop cradle a baby in his arms as he shoots his way out of a hospital, while *Face/Off*, best of his American films to date, derives much comedy from John Travolta and Nicolas Cage's mimicry of each other's mannerisms. Woo is undeniably a supremely talented stylist: it would be interesting to see him work with more substantial material.

John Woo (Wu Yusen) b. 1948 China. **The Killer** Hong Kong 1989/ w Chow Yun-Fat, Danny Lee, Sally Yeh, Chu Kong, Kenneth Tsang. **Films include** *Last Hurrah for Chivalry*, 1979; *A Better Tomorrow*, 1986; *Bullet in the Head*, 1990; *Once a Thief*, 1991; *Hard-Boiled,* 1992; *Hard Target*, 1994; *Broken Arrow*, 1996; *Face/Off*, 1997. **See also** HAWKS, HILL, KITANO, MELVILLE, PECKINPAH, SCORSESE, TARANTINO

Who is this man? In his threadbare armchair, surrounded by bizarre bric-à-brac, a heavy tome in his lap, has-been Bela Lugosi (by then a morphine addict in real life) is clearly meant to be an expert on transvestism and transsexualism (the autobiographical subject of Wood's feature début) and, quite possibly, God: how else to explain ominous ravings like 'Pull the strings!' and 'Bevare the big green dragon that sits on your doorstep!'? Not that Wood, the most cherishably inept *auteur* to arise from Hollywood's lowest depths, cared much for explanation; it was enough that he had 'actors' (in the loosest sense of the word), whatever few props came to hand, and a semblance of plot to commit to film for posterity. Working in sci-fi, horror, porn and the delinquent-teen genre, Wood seldom moved his camera or framed elegantly; favouring single takes, he was content to let conspicuously cardboard tombstones wobble at a zombie's passing (*Plan 9 From Outer Space*), disregard continuity by mixing day and night shots, let his casts (friends, psychics, ex-wrestlers and other losers) fluff the nonsensical dialogue, and stage decidedly unspecial effects (tin-foil plates as flying saucers, an unaccommodatingly immobile model octopus in *Bride of the Monster*). His editing verged on the radical: *Glen or Glenda?* not only made startlingly inappropriate use of stock war footage, but cut away from a cop reading a transvestite's suicide note to a brief, altogether irrelevant shot of a radiator. No other Hollywood *auteur*'s work is so impoverished, naive or imaginatively wayward – immediately recognisable qualities which perversely ensure its deathless charm.

Edward D Wood Jr b. 1924 USA, d. 1978 USA. **Glen or Glenda? (I Led Two Lives/I Changed My Sex)** USA 1953/ w Bela Lugosi, Wood, Dolores Fuller, Tim Farrell, Lyle Talbot. **Films include** *Jailbait*, 1954; *Bride of the Monster*, 1955; *Plan 9 from Outer Space*, 1956; *Night of the Ghouls*, 1958; *The Sinister Urge*, 1960; *Take It Out in Trade*, 1970; *Necromania*, 1971. **See also** ARNOLD, CORMAN, LEWIS, MEYER, ULMER, WARHOL

WILLIAM WYLER

A smalltown American family, reunited by the father's return from war – an ordinary enough scene, but what one notices is the tangle of looks: though the 'action' is clearly the conversation between father and daughter, the attentive reactions of mother and son are equally important. With cameraman Gregg Toland, Wyler developed a visual style centred on long takes and 'deep focus', with background details as dramatically relevant as foreground events. The result 'democratised' the image (close-ups were generally avoided), though the overall fastidiousness often made the films seem rather academic; while there's no denying Wyler's expertise with actors or his ability to make the most out of a scene's topography in terms of the characters' emotional and psychological proximity to or distance from

one another, his work could seem passionless and schematic. *The Best Years of Our Lives* saw him at the peak of his powers, his cool, even slightly aloof reticence serving to avoid the sentimental pitfalls of a typically liberal tale of returning war veterans. Ironically, his other artistic highpoint was *The Letter*, an adaptation of Maugham's play about adultery and murder in the Tropics in which, atypically, he allowed Tony Gaudio's lustrous camerawork to point up, rather than downplay, the emotional dynamics. Elsewhere, whether working in historical or domestic drama, crime films or westerns, Wyler simply set about telling a story elegantly and sensitively, though in later epics like *The Big Country* and *Ben-Hur*, not to mention the musical *Funny Girl*, his solemnity merely seemed stolid and overblown.

William Wyler b. 1902 Germany, d. 1981 USA. **The Best Years of Our Lives** USA 1946/ w Fredric March, Myrna Loy, Teresa Wright, Dana Andrews, Harold Russell, Hoagy Carmichael. **Films include** *Dodsworth*, 1936; *Dead End*, 1937; *Jezebel*, 1938; *Wuthering Heights*, 1939; *The Letter*, 1940; *The Little Foxes*, 1941; *Mrs Miniver*, 1942; *The Heiress*, 1949; *Detective Story*, 1951; *Carrie*, 1952; *The Big Country*, 1958; *Ben-Hur*, 1959; *Funny Girl*, 1968. **See also** IVORY, KAZAN, LEAN, PREMINGER, VISCONTI, ZINNEMANN

A 14-year-old girl confronts a suitor with a knife he planned to use on a rival in love; in a moment, depressed and confused, he'll stab her instead. The fatal outcome to Yang's epic account of life in Taipei in 1960 might have been a conventional dramatic climax to a teen melodrama, were it not for his jigsaw narrative structure, understated style and abiding fascination with the relationship of individuals to society. The gang-members in *A Brighter Summer Day* are disenchanted, directionless products of the way their parents – refugees from mainland China – suffered a loss of cultural and political identity in exile; the protagonist is troubled both by his romanticism, which fails to understand the girl's more pragmatic attitude to relationships, and by ill-founded rumours that his idealist father is a Communist spy. Such uncertainties

are eloquently mirrored by Yang's oblique, elliptical narrative, which carefully traces the consequences of seemingly undramatic actions as a wide range of characters make and break allegiances, and by his crisp, discreet imagery. Largely eschewing close-ups, Yang prefers medium and long shots (usually from a fixed standpoint) to relate characters to one another and to the world around them; lighting and colour evoke mood (this film is largely nocturnal, reflecting its protagonist's growing despondency), while decor and costume deftly delineate class, background and aspiration. Even when inflected by trappings of the crime genre (*The Terroriser*) or comedy (*A Confucian Confusion*), Yang's films are distinctly his own, painting in subtle but clear lines social panoramas remarkable for their historical precision and emotional authenticity.

Edward Yang (Yang Dechang) b. 1947 China. **A Brighter Summer Day** Taiwan 1991/ w Zhang Zhen, Lisa Yang, Zhang Guozhu, Elaine Jin, Wang Qizan, Tan Zhigang. **Films include** *That Day on the Beach*, 1983; *Taipei Story*, 1985; *The Terroriser*, 1986; *A Confucian Confusion*, 1994; *Mahjong*, 1996. **See also** CHEN, HOU, MIZOGUCHI, OZU, ZHANG

ROBERT ZEMECKIS

Private eye Bob Hoskins is astonished by the sight of Toon torch-singer Jessica Rabbit, not only because of her upfront *femme fatale* sexiness, but because he hadn't imagined the wife of pain-in-the-neck Hollywood stunt-Toon Roger could be so, well, human. ('I'm not bad,' vamps Jessica, 'I'm just drawn that way.') Zemeckis' technically painstaking blend of live action and animation (by Richard Williams) typifies his affectionately parodic approach to traditional Hollywood genres, his fascination with state-of-the-art special effects (made, unusually, an integral dramatic element of his stories), and his interest in hypothetical, half-fantasy worlds: here, the Toons are a real minority with their own neighbourhood – a ghetto as sinister as Polanski's *Chinatown* and as grotesquely surreal and violently anarchic as anything depicted by

Avery or Jones – in an otherwise iconographically familiar, *noir*-tinted LA. Zemeckis' best films (this, the *Back to the Future* trilogy and *Death Becomes Her*) are flights of imagination into the impossible, revelling in complex narrative conundrums (can *Back to the Future*'s hero, having travelled back in time, fend off his own mother's advances and unite her with his father so that he himself will be born?) and frantic, slapsticky action; in the later *Forrest Gump* and *Contact*, his special effects remained impressive, but the strenuous pretensions to political/philosophical significance were melodramatic and contrived. His virtues are those of a comic-strip artist: vivid characterisation, pacy action, and a forthright, faintly lurid, relentlessly inventive visual style that manages to merge conventional movie 'reality' and feverish fantasy.

Robert Zemeckis b. 1951 USA. **Who Framed Roger Rabbit** USA 1988/ w Bob Hoskins, Christopher Lloyd, Joanna Cassidy, Stubby Kaye, Alan Tilvern. **Films include** *Used Cars* 1980; *Romancing the Stone*, 1984; *Back to the Future*, 1985; *Back to the Future II*, 1989; *Back to the Future III*, 1990; *Death Becomes Her*, 1992; *Forrest Gump*, 1992; *Contact*, 1997. **See also** AVERY, CAMERON, DANTE, JONES, LUCAS, SPIELBERG

A sedan chair, taking a girl to an arranged marriage to an elderly leper, crosses a barren landscape that fore-shadows a bleak future. Soon, however, in a chair-bearer who drives off a bandit, she finds a worthy, virile lover who kills her husband and helps build up her newly inherited sorghum-wine distillery. The red in this opening scene rhymes both with the life-enhancing wine and, more importantly, with blood, spilt first during the couple's illicit tryst in a sorghum field, later in the leper's murder and the carnage wrought by invading Japanese. Former cameraman Zhang's directing debut uses natural symbols and heightened, coded colours to transform history into full-blown folk myth, while the fluid, swooping camera matches the vitality of the peasantry the film celebrates. A visually eloquent, adventurous film-maker, Zhang is occasionally uncertain with narrative structure and not averse to softening characterisations of authority figures to prevent censorship by China's bureaucracy. He is, however, adept at conveying passion and turmoil through exhilarating, exact deployment of colour, lighting and movement (*Ju Dou*'s pacy, heady tale of adultery and revenge made delirious use of a dye workshop), and attuned to the claustrophobic connotations of architecture and liberating moods of open landscape. *Raise the Red Lantern* adopted a more restrained, symmetrical compositional style, while *The Story of Qiu Ju* ventured into gritty 'realism'; restlessly experimental, he recently seems to have lost his sense of direction, though his visul flair, ambition and intelligence still make him a director of considerable interest.

Zhang Yimou b. 1950 China. **Red Sorghum** China 1987/ w Gong Li, Jiang Wen, Teng Rujun, Liu Ji, Qian Ming, Ji Chunhua.
Films include *Ju Dou*, 1989; *Raise the Red Lantern*, 1992; *The Story of Qiu Ju*, 1993; *To Live!,* 1994; *Shanghai Triad*, 1995; *Keep Cool*, 1997.
See also CHEN, HOU, KUROSAWA, MIZOGUCHI, YANG

FRED ZINNEMANN

Preparing for the gunfight that will follow the arrival of a vengeful killer and his gang, marshal Gary Cooper, already deserted by the town's citizens, now faces pacificist disapproval from Quaker bride Grace Kelly. With screen time roughly equalling the story's 'real time', Zinnemann's cool, taut western – an allegory on the silent majority's reaction to the McCarthy witchhunts – repeatedly features shots of ticking clocks, typical of his meticulously decorative preference for portentous 'realism'. For all its mounting tension, *High Noon* seems almost disdainful of the western's mythic potential, heroic simplicity and feeling for wild landscape; the tidy compositions, picturesque use of sunlight and shadow and emphasis on moral dilemmas make it clearly a movie with a 'message' (though its liberalism is somewhat undermined when Kelly finally lends Cooper her support). Zinnemann repeatedly treated serious themes – from the plight of children in ravaged postwar Berlin in *The Search* and the disillusionment of paraplegic war veterans in *The Men* to the challenges to religious faith in *The Nun's Story* and *A Man for All Seasons* – often depending on authentic locations and literary sources for prestige. While he was adept with actors (his casting could be surprisingly adventurous), his attempts at realism could be swamped by cautious tastefulness, so that, for example, *From Here to Eternity*, notwithstanding Burt Lancaster's adulterous roll in the surf with Deborah Kerr, was tame compared to James Jones' novel. Later, his films seemed increasingly out of touch with the world, his visuals grander and glossier, highlighting his trademark fastidiousness.

Fred Zinnemann b. 1907 Austria, d. 1997 England. **High Noon** USA 1952/ w Gary Cooper, Grace Kelly, Lloyd Bridges, Katy Jurado, Thomas Mitchell, Otto Kruger. **Films include** *Act of Violence, The Search*, 1948; *The Men*, 1950; *Member of the Wedding, From Here to Eternity*, 1953; *Oklahoma!,* 1955; *The Nun's Story*, 1959; *A Man for All Seasons*, 1967; *Day of the Jackal*, 1973; *Julia*, 1977; *Five Days One Summer*, 1983. **See also** IVORY, LEAN, PREMINGER, VISCONTI, WYLER

PICTURE ACKNOWLEDGEMENTS

page 1 United Artists (courtesy of The Ronald Grant Archive); **2** Orion; **3** El Desea-Lauren (courtesy of The Kobal Collection); **4** United Artists/Lions Gate (courtesy of The Kobal Collection); **5** Rank (courtesy of The Kobal Collection); **6** Theo Angelopoulos Productions, Artificial Eye; **7** Kenneth Anger (courtesy of BFI Stills); **8** MGM (courtesy of The Kobal Collection); **9** Universal (courtesy of The Ronald Grant Archive); **10** RKO (courtesy of BFI Stills); **11** ©1949 Turner Entertainment Co.; **12** Galatea/Jolly (courtesy of The Kobal Collection); **13** Speva (courtesy of The Ronald Grant Archive); **14** Svensk Filmindustri (courtesy of The Ronald Grant Archive); **15** Warner Bros. (courtesy of The Ronald Grant Archive); **16** United Artists/Prod Europée Asso (courtesy of The Kobal Collection); **17** Gaumont/Tiger (courtesy of The Kobal Collection); **18** Lightstorm Entertainment (courtesy of The Kobal Collection); **19** CAPAC/UPF/SN; **20** Columbia (courtesy The Joel Finler Archives); **21** MGM (courtesy of The Kobal Collection); **22** Contemporary Films (courtesy The Joel Finler Archives); **23** 20th Century Fox (courtesy The Joel Finler Archives); **24** Artificial Eye (courtesy of The Ronald Grant Archive); **25** Parc/Svenska Filminstitutet (courtesy of The Ronald Grant Archive); **26** 20th Century Fox (courtesy of The Kobal Collection); **27** MGM (courtesy of The Ronald Grant Archive); **28** Nacional (courtesy of The Kobal Collection); **29** 20th Century Fox (courtesy of The Kobal Collection); **30** 20th Century Fox (courtesy of The Kobal Collection); **31** Entertainment/ CIBY (courtesy of The Ronald Grant Archive); **32** Columbia (courtesy of The Ronald Grant Archive); **33** Gaumont/Artificial Eye; **34** Cine Alliance/Pathe (courtesy of The Kobal Collection); **35** Rank/Avco Embassy (courtesy of The Kobal Collection); **36** Maurice McEndree (courtesy of BFI Stills); **37** AYJM (courtesy of BFI Stills); **38** MK2 (courtesy of the ICA); **39** Charles Chaplin (courtesy of The Ronald Grant Archive); **40** Thompson Films/China Film/Beijing (courtesy of The Kobal Collection); **41** Universal/EMI; **42** Les Films Cissé; **43** Tobis (courtesy of The Kobal Collection); **44** Filmsonor/CICC/Vera (courtesy of The Kobal Collection); **45** Andre Paulvé/Films du Palais Royal (courtesy of The Kobal Collection); **46** Universal/Working Title; **47** Paramount (courtesy of The Kobal Collection); **48** Alta Vista (courtesy of The Ronald Grant Archive); **49** Polygram/Universal (courtesy of The Kobal Collection); **50** Universal (courtesy of The Kobal Collection); **51** MGM (courtesy of The Kobal Collection); **52** Warner Bros. (courtesy of The Kobal Collection); **53** Warner Bros. (courtesy of The Kobal Collection); **54** Universal (courtesy of The Kobal Collection); **55** BFI/Channel 4 (courtesy of The Kobal Collection); **56** Paramount (courtesy of The Ronald Grant Archive); **57** Universal (courtesy of The Kobal Collection); **58** Parc/Madeleine/Beta (courtesy of BFI Stills); **59** Universal (courtesy of The Ronald Grant Archive); **60** Produzione de Sica (courtesy of The Kobal Collection); **61** Warner Bros. (courtesy of The Kobal Collection); **62** ©1937 Walt Disney (courtesy of Photofest); **63** MGM (courtesy of The Kobal Collection); **64** VUFKU (courtesy of The Joel Finler Archive); **65** Palladium (courtesy of The Kobal Collection); **66** United Artists (courtesy of The Kobal Collection); **67** Malpaso, Warner Bros.; **68** Goskino (courtesy of The Ronald Grant Archive); **69** Artificial Eye (courtesy of The Ronald Grant Archive); **70** Tango (courtesy of The Kobal Collection); **71** Cineriz (courtesy of BFI Stills); **72** Gaumont (courtesy of BFI Stills); **73** Hammer (courtesy of The Kobal Collection); **74** Revillon Frères (courtesy of The Ronald Grant Archive); **75** Turner Entertainment, Paramount; **76** Warner Bros. (courtesy of The Ronald Grant Archive); **77** United Artists/Fantasy Films (courtesy of The Ronald Grant Archive); **78** Champs Elysées/Lux; **79** United Artists/MC (courtesy of The Kobal Collection); **80** Allied Artists; **81** top: Kevin Brownlow Collection (Photoplay), bottom: Societe Generale de Films (courtesy of The Joel Finler Archive); **82** Republic (courtesy of The Ronald Grant Archive); **83** Chaumiane/Filmstudio; **84** Palace; **85** United Artists (courtesy of The Kobal Collection); **86** Cactus (courtesy of The Joel Finler Archive); **87** Ealing Studios; **88** Haneke, WEGA film; **89** MGM (courtesy of The Joel Finler Archive); **90** Palace; **91** Columbia (courtesy of BFI Stills); **92** Film Four/Zenith/Killer/Single Cell; **93** Hessicher Rundfunk (courtesy of The Joel Finler Archive); **94** United Artists; (courtesy of The Ronald Grant Archive); **95** Warner Bros. (courtesy of The Joel Finler Archive); **96** Columbia; **97** ICA Projects; **98** International Film; **99** Warner Bros. (courtesy of The Kobal Collection); **100** Im Kwon-Taek; **101** Merchant Ivory; **102** Mafilm/Mosfilm (courtesy of The Joel Finler Archive); **103** Megalovision (courtesy of The Joel Finler Archive); **104** MTI/Orion (courtesy of The Kobal Collection); **105** Entertainment; **106** ©1951 Warner Bros.; **107** Sputnik Oy, Metro/Tartan; **108** Warner Bros. (courtesy of BFI Stills); **109** Metro (courtesy of The Kobal Collection); **110** MK2, Artificial Eye; **111** Artificial Eye; **112** Office Kitano, ICA; **113** Mosfilm (courtesy of The Joel Finler Archive); **114** Warner Bros.; **115** Toho (courtesy of The Kobal Collection); **116** Enterprise; **117** Nero Film (courtesy of The Ronald Grant Archive); **118** United Artists (courtesy of The Kobal Collection); **119** Columbia; **120** Universal (courtesy of The Kobal Collection); **121** Film Four; **122** Paramount (courtesy of The Ronald Grant Archive); **123** Paramount (courtesy of The Ronald Grant Archive); **124** Woodfall/Lopert (courtesy of The Kobal Collection); **125** United Artists (courtesy of The Kobal Collection); **126** King Brothers/Universal-International (courtesy of The Ronald Grant Archive); **127** Woodfall/Kestrel (courtesy of The Kobal Collection); **128** Elstree/Springbok (courtesy of The Ronald Grant Archive); **129** Paramount (courtesy of The Ronald Grant Archive); **130** Lucasfilm/20th Century Fox (courtesy of The Kobal Collection); **131** 20th Century Fox/Bazmark; **132** United Artists/Orion-Nova (courtesy of The Ronald Grant Archive); **133** courtesy of BFI Stills; **134** Filmakers (courtesy of The Kobal Collection); **135** courtesy of Joel Finler Archive; **136** De Laurentiis (courtesy of The Kobal Collection); **137** Ealing Studios (courtesy of The Ronald Grant Archive);

138 Avala (courtesy of The Joel Finler Archive); **139** MK2/ICA Projects; **140** Paramount (courtesy of The Kobal Collection); **141** Paramount (courtesy of The Kobal Collection); **142** Paramount (courtesy of The Ronald Grant Archive); **143** 20th Century Fox (courtesy of The Ronald Grant Archive); **144** MGM (courtesy of The Ronald Grant Archive); **145** De Laurentiis Group (courtesy of The Kobal Collection); **146** Argos films; **147** courtesy of BFI Stills; **148** National Film Board of Canada (courtesy of BFI Stills); **149** courtesy of The Joel Finler Archive; **150** Artificial Eye/Les Productions Montaigne (courtesy of The Joel Finler Archive); **151** RM Films International (courtesy of The Joel Finler Archive); **152** Warner/A-Team (courtesy of The Ronald Grant Archive); **153** MGM (courtesy of The Kobal Collection); **154** Shin Toho (courtesy of The Joel Finler Archive); **155** Sacher Film/Artificial Eye; **156** BFI (courtesy of BFI Stills); **157** 20th Century Fox (courtesy of The Ronald Grant Archive); **158** Sacha Gordine (courtesy of The Ronald Grant Archive); **159** Academy (courtesy of The Joel Finler Archive); **160** Films de L'Avenir (courtesy of The Kobal Collection); **161** Shochiku (courtesy of The Joel Finler Archive); **162** Nero Film (courtesy of BFI Stills); **163** Paramount (courtesy of The Kobal Collection); **164** Armenfilm (courtesy of The Joel Finler Archive); **165** Aardman (courtesy of BFI Stills); **166** Orion (courtesy of The Kobal Collection); **167** Arco/Lux (courtesy of The Kobal Collection); **168** Warner/Seven Arts (courtesy of The Joel Finler Archive); **169** Warner/Seven Arts (courtesy of The Joel Finler Archive); **170** Pennebaker (courtesy of The Joel Finler Archive); **171** Gaumont (courtesy of The Kobal Collection); **172** ZRF Kamera (courtesy of The Ronald Grant Archive); **173** Casbah/Igor (courtesy of The Kobal Collection); **174** Edison (courtesy of BFI Stills); **175** Anglo Amalgamated (courtesy of The Joel Finler Archive); **176** Columbia (courtesy of The Kobal Collection); **177** Koninck; **178** Warner Bros. (courtesy of The Kobal Collection); **179** The Government of West Bengal (courtesy of The Joel Finler Archive); **180** British Lion (courtesy of The Ronald Grant Archive); **181** Nouvelle Edition Francaise (courtesy of The Kobal Collection); **182** Terra/Tamara/Cormoran (courtesy of The Kobal Collection); **183** Leni Riefenstahl (courtesy of The Ronald Grant Archive); **184** Les Films de Losange (courtesy of The Joel Finler Archive); **185** BL (courtesy of The Kobal Collection); **186** Les Films de Losange (courtesy of The Joel Finler Archive); **187** Image Ten (courtesy of The Ronald Grant Archive); **188** Lux/Vides/Galatea (courtesy of The Joel Finler Archive); **189** Titanus/Sveva/Junior/Italiafilm (courtesy of The Kobal Collection); **190** Rank (courtesy of The Ronald Grant Archive); **191** BFI Films (courtesy of The Joel Finler Archive); **192** United Artists (courtesy of The Ronald Grant Archive); **193** Buena Vista; **194** Emiliana Piedra Productions (courtesy of The Kobal Collection); **195** Atchafalaya (courtesy of The Ronald Grant Archive); **196** RKO (courtesy of The Ronald Grant Archive); **197** Paramount (courtesy of BFI Stills); **198** Columbia (courtesy of The Kobal Collection); **199** Warner Bros. (courtesy of The Ronald Grant Archive); **200** Filmi Domireew (courtesy of The Kobal Collection); **201** Keystone (courtesy of The Kobal Collection); **202** Universal (courtesy of The Joel Finler Archive); **203** Universal (courtesy of The Kobal Collection); **204** Universal (courtesy of The Joel Finler Archive); **205** MGM (courtesy of The Ronald Grant Archive); **206** Entertainment; **207** Columbia (courtesy of The Ronald Grant Archive); **208** courtesy of BFI Stills; **209** Warner Bros; **210** Warner Bros. (courtesy of The Kobal Collection); **211** IDI/Rai/Seitz (courtesy of The Kobal Collection); **212** Paramount (courtesy of The Ronald Grant Archive); **213** Nikkatsu (courtesy of BFI Stills); **214** Koninck/Kratky Film Praha/Jiri Trnka Studio; **215** Mega/Cinetel (courtesy of The Joel Finler Archive); **216** Rank (courtesy of The Kobal Collection); **217** Mosfilm Unit 2 (courtesy of The Kobal Collection); **218** 20th Century Fox (courtesy of The Joel Finler Archive); **219** Cady/Discina (courtesy of The Kobal Collection); **220** Filmtre (courtesy of The Kobal Collection); **221** RKO (courtesy of The Ronald Grant Archive); **222** Films du Carrosse (courtesy of The Ronald Grant Archive); **223** ICA/Kaiju Theatre (courtesy of The Kobal Collection); **224** Producers' Releasing Corporation (courtesy of The Kobal Collection); **225** VUFKU (courtesy of BFI Stills); **226** MGM (courtesy of The Kobal Collection); **227** Gaumont (courtesy of The Ronald Grant Archive); **228** 20th Century Fox (courtesy of The Ronald Grant Archive); **229** Paramount (courtesy of The Ronald Grant Archive); **230** Metro-Goldwyn (courtesy of The Kobal Collection); **231** Zentropa (courtesy of The Kobal Collection); **232** Film Polski (courtesy of The Ronald Grant Archive); **233** Warner Bros. (courtesy of The Kobal Collection); **234** Vaughan/Factory Films; **235** Dreamland Productions (courtesy of The Kobal Collection); **236** Warner Bros./ Spring Creek (courtesy of The Ronald Grant Archive); **237** RKO (courtesy of The Kobal Collection); **238** David O. Selznick (courtesy of The Joel Finler Archive); **239** Wim Wenders Productions (courtesy of The Ronald Grant Archive); **240** Universal (courtesy of The Ronald Grant Archive); **241** Decla-Bioscop (courtesy of The Ronald Grant Archive); **242** Paramount (courtesy of The Ronald Grant Archive); **243** ICA/Jet Tone (courtesy of The Kobal Collection); **244** Palace (courtesy of The Ronald Grant Archive); **245** Edward D Wood Jnr (courtesy of The Kobal Collection); **246** Samuel Goldwyn (courtesy of The Ronald Grant Archive); **247** ICA/Yang and his Gang; **248** Touchstone/Amblin (courtesy of The Kobal Collection); **249** Palace/Xi'an Film Studio (courtesy of The Ronald Grant Archive); **250** Stanley Kramer (courtesy of The Ronald Grant Archive).